THE GOLDEN THREADS

New England's
Mill Girls and
Magnates

The Golden Threads

NEW ENGLAND'S

MILL GIRLS AND

MAGNATES

By

Hannah Josephson

NEW YORK / RUSSELL & RUSSELL

To Matty

Acknowledgments

THE subject of this study was first suggested to me by Slater Brown, who many years ago urged me to look into the story of the Lowell mill girls, and the period in which they flourished. My interest was quickened when I discovered that Van Wyck Brooks assigned these "literary" factory operatives a significant if modest role in the cultural history of New England. As the work progressed, many scholars gave me good counsel, beginning with William Miller, who directed my early researches into the part played by the Boston Associates in the development of Lowell. I had a stroke of extraordinary good luck when, through Arthur Schlesinger, Jr., I was able to get in touch with Robert L. Edwards, who had assembled a large amount of unpublished material on Abbott Lawrence in preparation for writing a biography. With unexampled generosity Mr. Edwards permitted me to study and quote freely from his notes.

I also received fruitful suggestions from Ferris Greenslet, the historian of the Lowell family, John Coolidge, authority on the architecture of the mill town, Frederick W. Coburn, chronicler of Lowell, Massachusetts, and Miss Frances X. Gregory, who is writing her doctor's dissertation on Nathan Appleton. C. S. Brigham of the Worcester Antiquarian Society and Joseph Reilly of the Massachusetts Historical Society were of great aid in directing me to material for my purpose.

Special thanks are due my friend Thomas Cochran of New York University for his constant encouragement and provocative criticism, as well as for reading part of the manuscript. From first to last I was fortunate in having the advice and assistance of my husband.

To all of these I wish to express my gratitude, while warning the reader that the responsibility for any mistakes in fact or interpretation rests only with me.

Contents

THE GOLDEN THREADS

New England's
Mill Girls and
Magnates

Chapter 1

A PORTENT AND A SYMBOL

IF ANY motives of business or pleasure had brought you as a tourist to the United States of America in the second quarter of the nineteenth century, your journey would have had a certain pattern already prescribed by custom. Despite the tedium and inconvenience of traveling, you would have covered what were then immense distances to see Boston, New York, and Washington, Niagara Falls and Cincinnati, the rising center of the new West, a Southern plantation with live slaves, a school, a prison, an insane asylum, an Indian encampment, and Lowell, Massachusetts. New York even then promised to be a commercial metropolis; Boston was a thriving port with pretensions to old world culture; but Lowell, the seat of the new American cotton textile industry, was a portent and a symbol. As such it was seen by young Michel Chevalier, who was sent to the United States by the French government in 1834 to study problems of transport and public works.

A very different type of person from the engaging aristocrat De Tocqueville, whose mission to America had been completed two years earlier, Chevalier was the son of a Limoges shopkeeper. Thanks to the French Revolution, he had been educated at the Ecole Polytechnique and the Ecole de Mines, and had received a post as civil engineer to the Département du Nord. By 1830, however, he had grown interested in the socialistic theories of

3

Saint-Simon, and abandoned his career as an engineer to become editor of *Le Globe*, the organ of the Saint-Simonians, and of that particular sect of Saint-Simonians who advocated free love. The French are no more inclined to grant countenance to such evil practices than any other people, and young Chevalier, arrested on a charge of outraging public morality, was condemned to prison for a term of one year. Released through the influence of Thiers after six months, he gladly accepted the minister's commission to go to America, and from that time forward eschewed all his radical beliefs, becoming known thereafter as an advocate not of free love, but of the more respectable heresy of free trade.

Chevalier's trip to America proved to be no exile, but an opportunity to redeem himself, of which he took prompt advantage by sending back reports of his travels to the *Journal des Débats*. These notes were afterward published in book form, and translated under the title of *Society, Manners and Politics in the United States*. As an interpreter of the American scene Chevalier holds little interest for us today, but as a reporter he was first-rate. His eye was keen and impressionable, his ear sensitive, and, besides, his frame of reference was so different from that of a new, raw country that he could not fail to recognize its particularities. His description of Lowell, Massachusetts, in the 1830's is therefore one of the most graphic accounts we possess of the then leading manufacturing town in the country.

Many years later, when a Lowell resident called on him in Paris, Chevalier recalled his delight on seeing Lowell for the first time. "It was new and fresh, like a setting at the opera," he said. To a traveler from the ancient cities of Europe, Lowell must in truth have given the impression of a painted stage set, having been settled only ten years before on the site of what had been a sleepy farm community. Here, at the confluence of the Merrimack and the Concord Rivers, where a few modest farmhouses had formerly stood, Chevalier saw in 1834:

A pile of huge factories, each five, six, or seven stories high, and capped with a little white belfry, which strongly contrasts with the red masonry of the building, and is distinctly projected on the dark hills in the horizon. By the side of these larger structures rise numerous little wooden houses, painted white, with green blinds, very neat, very snug, very nicely carpeted, and with a few small trees around them, or brick houses in the English style, that is to say, simple, but tasteful without and comfortable within; on one side, fancy-goods shops and milliners' rooms without number . . . and vast hotels in the American style, very much like barracks . . . on another, canals, water wheels, waterfalls, bridges, banks, schools and libraries. . . . All around are churches and meeting houses of every sect, Episcopalian, Baptist, Congregationalist, Methodist, Universalist, Unitarian, etc., and there is also a Roman Catholic chapel.

Not only the sights, but also the sounds of this mushroom town seemed memorable to Chevalier: the clap of hammers as new buildings rose from the ground, the buzzing of the spindles in the mills, the ringing of bells that called the operatives to their work or marked the end of the day, the uproar about the inns when the stages drew up or departed with a load of passengers, the repeated explosions as rocks were blown to make a new road or a millrace. To Chevalier all this turmoil was like music, "the peaceful hum of an industrious population, whose movements are regulated like clockwork."

The operatives no less than the town itself and the industry that had spawned it excited his wonder. As he observed the girls —at that time a little under five thousand of them, mostly between the ages of seventeen and twenty-four, were employed in the mills—walking through the streets at morning and evening, and at the dinner hour in the middle of the day, he was astonished to find that many were well favored, while all were neatly, or rather smartly, dressed, with scarves and shawls and green silk hoods to shelter them from the sun and dust. English manufacturing towns could boast of nothing like this, he wrote. Neither was it possible for him to conceive of a situation in France in which such comely young girls could be trusted to live separated from their families by a distance of fifty to one hundred miles, without older friends or gimlet-eyed duennas to watch over their conduct. That it could happen in America without casting a stain on the character of the young women working in Lowell was due, he thought, to the Protestant training, which "draws around each individual a line over which it is difficult to step." Chevalier was informed by one of the factory directors that up to that time only three cases of illicit connections had been discovered among all the thousands of girls who had passed through the town, and since in "all three instances the parties were married immediately, several months before the birth of the child . . . we have had no case of actual bastardy." And, as if personal beauty and sterling character were not enough, the girls were thrifty, Chevalier learned. Out of their wages of two dollars, a great many of these girls saved a dollar or a dollar and a half a week. "After spending four years in the factories, they may have a little fortune of 250 or 300 dollars, when they often quit work and marry."

How had this teeming little industrial paradise come into being?

Unlike the cities of Europe [wrote Chevalier in a burst of historical reference], which were built by some demigod, son of Jupiter, or by some hero of the siege of Troy, or by an inspiration of the genius of a Caesar or an Alexander, or by the assistance of some holy monk, attracting crowds by his miracles, or by the caprice of some great king, like Louis XIV or Frederick, or by an edict of Peter the Great, it is neither a pious foundation, a refuge of the proscribed, nor a military post. *It is a speculation of the merchants of Boston.*

And, summing up his impressions of the town, he added:

Lowell, with its steeple-crowned factories, resembles a Spanish town with its convents; but with this difference, that in Lowell you meet no rags or Madonnas . . . Lowell is not an entertaining place, but it is neat, orderly, quiet, and prudent.

Chevalier was only one of innumerable visitors, both from abroad and at home, who viewed the thriving young town on the Merrimack as an industrial Utopia. The hope, the enthusiasm, the excitement engendered by this experiment in the making of cotton cloth are almost incredible today. It seemed miraculous to those who were aware of the filth and gloom and despair of similar towns in England and on the Continent. Here, even more than in other fields, the United States seemed to be making a new departure, lending dignity and a certain beauty to a common, onerous task, clothing it with a spirit of high-hearted adventure and idealism.

Praise for the Lowell enterprise seemed to be divided almost equally between the merchants of Boston, who had made such a great success of their "speculation," and the fair maidens, so respectable and self-respecting, so bent on improving their financial situation and educational opportunities. If men could provide the world with a much-needed staple, at low prices, line their own pockets, and yet offer rich satisfactions to working people, all at the same time, the millennium was certainly at hand.

Modern industry, save for a few corporation heads and labor leaders, is anonymous. Lowell was self-conscious and articulate; the eyes of the world were upon it, the scrutiny so intense that every event in its history was recorded, reviewed, extolled, or deplored in greater detail than the history of any town of comparable size in the United States. The Appletons, the Lawrences, and the Lowells who had a share in its establishment became national figures in finance, politics, education, and philanthropy. To many of their contemporaries these men were heroes; from Maine to Kansas towns were named for them; at the christening of innumerable little boys the magic words were pronounced by hopeful parents; even Louisa May Alcott, in searching for a name for one of her nobler characters, could think of none better to convey her sense of his worthiness than Lawrence.

The achievements of the Lowell capitalists were in fact considerable, even though modern research has cut them down to size. In developing the textile industry they showed a breadth of imagination and a spirit of enterprise that are the finest traits of American businessmen. They set a pattern for the future by combining all the processes of manufacture, from raw material to finished product, in one establishment—the first example of complete rationalization of industry in the world. Anticipating the tycoons of today by almost a hundred years, they set up corporations in which they retained absolute managerial control despite widely dispersed stock ownership. And, at the beginning at least, they established living and working standards for the workers in their mills so far in advance of their time that they had few imitators until modern times.

The girls who worked in the mills at Lowell were of equal importance in making the town world-famous. They had, moreover, precisely the same background as did many of the men who launched the textile industry in this country. Their fathers' farms had been equally stony and unprofitable, their parents equally pious, their early instruction in thrift and self-denial, their longing for education and "culture" the same. A certain distinction still clings to the names of some of them: Lucy Larcom, the poet, Harriet Farley, the editor, Harriet Hanson Robinson, the suffragist, Sarah Bagley, the labor leader, Margaret Foley, the sculptor; but it is rather as a group than as individuals that the mill girls stood out. Besides the distinguished foreign visitors, such as Dickens and Harriet Martineau, three presidents of the United States, a constant succession of senators and congressmen, and innumerable others of high and low estate came to observe them at work. The newspapers of the time were full of references to the "ladies of Lowell," tributes were paid to their virtue and beauty in comic valentines, poems, and novels, and their own literary productions were read and discussed in all the capitals of the Western world. Their admirable qualities stirred a man as reserved as Hawthorne to write in *Mosses from an Old Manse:* "These factory girls from Lowell shall mate themselves with the pride of drawing-rooms and literary circles, the bluebells in fashion's nosegay, the Sapphos, and Montagues and Nortons of the Age."

Not only were the founders of Lowell and their operatives remarkable, but the town thus created had a charm noticeable to all who visited it in its early days. Since the mill workers all came from a distance to settle in Lowell, homes, a place of worship, facilities for recreation, study, and the care of the sick were furnished by the corporations. This provision of basic social services led to the creation of a planned town, with the mills as a focal point, and dwellings for the operatives nearby, not crowding on one another, but with open spaces, vistas of water and green hills, lawns and flower gardens, a town planned for living and working with no loss of human dignity. This was Lowell as Chevalier saw it.

On his return to France, the young Saint-Simonian mended his ways. Abandoning his radical beliefs and associates, he rose steadily to a position of importance and influence, until in 1851 he greeted the seizure of power by Napoleon III as the dawn of a new era. Napoleon showed his gratitude by naming Chevalier councilor of state, and in 1867 put him in charge of the Universal Exposition at Paris. Over thirty years had passed since the aging courtier had visited Lowell, but he still remembered the neat, orderly, quiet mill town, the pretty girls who were not "notoriously dissolute or dishonest or intemperate," who attended divine service regularly and never flew in the faces of their employers. The Councilor of State sat down and wrote a letter to his old friend Charles Sumner, then Senator from Massachusetts, asking to have a group of Lowell girls sent to Paris, with their looms, so that visitors to the exposition might see them at work as they were to be seen at Lowell.

But in the thirty years that had passed, many changes had taken place in the textile city on the Merrimack. The accomplished New England operatives who had helped to make the town famous were gone; even in 1861, when Prince Jerome Bonaparte and his consort, the Princess Clotilde, visited the place, they had found a motley crowd, consisting of a few native Americans, some English, Scottish, Dutch and French Canadians, all of them outnumbered by immigrant Irish girls. To Charles Cowley, the historian of Lowell, these newcomers "were hardly likely to arouse that exquisite poetic sentiment which Chevalier felt for the factory girls of 1834."

No delegation of Lowell girls went to France with their looms in 1867. A group of operatives from the Pacific Mills of Lawrence, the "model" mill in that otherwise blighted offshoot of Lowell, made the trip instead, winning all sorts of special awards for their enlightened employers. But on April 1, the day the exposition was formally opened by the Emperor in Paris, the spinners of Lowell, acting in concert with the spinners of other textile cities, went out on strike for a reduction in their working hours.

What had happened to the idyl, what serpent had entered the industrial paradise that Lowell seemed to be in 1834? Chevalier had seen a busy, forward-looking town, surrounded by laughing rivers and pleasant hills, still visible beyond the white cupolas of the factory buildings. It was a town with a homogeneous population, whose movements were regulated, as he said, by clockwork. The clock moved, however, at a pace within the limits of endurance of healthy, independent, ambitious young women. In the next decade, fundamental changes were already perceptible; the smiling landscape was blocked out as the mills grew taller and stretched along the river bank in a solid mass. Even the clocks played tricks, for by slowing down toward closing time they enabled the overseers to get as much as half an hour of extra work out of the operatives. When President Jackson visited Lowell in 1833, a parade of young women employed in the mills was arranged in his honor, but when President Tyler came ten years later to view this paragon of American industrial cities, he was greeted by a parade of schoolboys!

Chapter II

ANTECEDENTS

THE man responsible for almost everything that was good in the town of Lowell, the man in whose honor it was named, never heard of the place. But although Francis Cabot Lowell died before the foundations of the future textile center were laid, it was in a sense his creation as much as if he himself had drawn the blueprints. As Nathan Appleton wrote later, Lowell's was the "informing mind" of the new industry that was to change the face of New England and, in the long run, all America. Probably the only man of genius in a family that produced many second-rate talents in various fields, Francis Cabot Lowell was the archetype of the creative, daring capitalist who was to exploit American resources so energetically during the nineteenth century.

At a moment when the industrial revolution had scarcely begun in this country, he established the manufacture of textiles in a mature form that was the model for modern American industrial development. By-passing the intervening stages through which other manufactures were to progress, he plotted the whole pattern of rationalization that ended a hundred years later in the belt line and mass production. Financier, administrator, technician, inventor, he planned every detail of the infant industry, saw around every obstacle that threatened its advance. It was notable also that his large views embraced an attitude of social responsibility toward those who were to tend his spindles and looms, as well as a keen awareness of the role that government could play in aid of enterprise.

In attempting these bold schemes, Lowell met no little opposition, not only from prudent friends and relatives, but also in the inertia of the country itself, which, during his lifetime, was a dominantly agricultural society. Except for the inhabitants of a few cities on the coast, thriving ports of international trade, the population of the United States at the beginning of the last century was engaged in tilling the soil. The ever-expanding West drained off so much of the national energy that it was difficult to see how any of it could be spared for other pursuits. The British consul in Philadelphia, for example, reported to his government in 1789:

In a country . . . so extensive as this continent, with a seaboard frontery of 1500 miles in length and a Western limit hitherto undefined, at present inhabited by scarcely more than 3,000,000 of people possessing a strong natural disposition to husbandry . . . a series of centuries must elapse before this country will be peopled to such a degree as to make the encouragement of manufactures an object of necessary recourse; Agriculture will long continue the source from whence the mass of people will draw their subsistence.

Since England was enormously interested in seeing to it that the United States developed no manufacturing interests to compete with her own profitable exportations, the Philadelphia consul told his superiors only what they wished most to be assured of. But the British were not alone in desiring the United States to continue as a producer of raw materials. Political thinkers in this country, such as Jefferson, pleaded for agriculture as a way of life, and powerful mercantile interests backed him up on the theory that the more thriving the rural regions, the more certain the profits of the carrying trade. In his famous report of 1791 on manufactures, Hamilton had noted that industrialization was looked on with great mistrust in most quarters. Nevertheless, he argued that enough experiments in domestic industry had been successful to warrant further essays in that direction, and that the development of manufactures was essential to national independence and security. And by 1815, after eight years of interrupted commerce from abroad had pointed up the inconveniences of relying only upon agriculture to supply the nation's wants, even Jefferson had come around to Hamilton's view. "To be independent of others for the comforts of life," he wrote, "we must manufacture ourselves. . . . Experience has taught me that manufactures are as necessary to our independence as to our comfort."

To men who looked on the development of manufactures as both desirable and necessary, the making of cotton cloth seemed to offer the greatest possibilities. It was an article of common use, low in price but capable of large volume sales, the raw material for which was produced in our own country. The only obstacle was the absence of proved machinery for the business, such machinery as had been used in England with fantastic success. England, however, not only had a head-start over all other nations in the development of machinery and the factory system; she protected her monopoly of the new processes with laws, strictly enforced, prohibiting the export of textile machinery, plans, or models of these machines, as well as the emigration of skilled workers who had tended them.

If manufacture, especially textile manufacture, were to succeed in this country, the first object of American enterprise was to crack this monopoly. Early attempts to set up textile mills with machinery of American design had met with discouraging failure. Of these the first to attract notice was the Beverly Cotton Manufactory, incorporated in 1789 by Alexander Hamilton's friend, the Salem merchant George Cabot, with whom were associated other members of the Cabot family, Israel Thorndike and Henry Higginson, two prominent merchants of the time, and several others. By 1791 they were employing forty hands to operate nine horse-driven spinning jennies and sixteen fly-shuttle looms. On the invitation of George Cabot, President Washington visited this factory in the course of his journey through New England in 1791, but in spite of the great man's blessing the venture did not prosper. The owners found that the cost of production was about equal to the selling price of their goods, and their investment of $10,000 was a total loss, as well as $4,000 worth of grants in land and lottery privileges offered them as a subsidy by the Massachusetts Legislature. The mill shut down before 1807, the owners candidly admitting that their failure was due to lack of skill in constructing and operating the machinery, "added to our want of a general knowledge of the business we had undertaken."

All other experiments with machines of American make failed similarly, while another, that of Slater and Brown in Pawtucket, patterned after the British model, had an immediate success, on a small scale. Samuel Slater had grown up in the textile industry in England, rising to be superintendent in one of the Arkwright spinning mills. Attracted by the offer of a bounty for the encouragement of textile manufacture in Pennsylvania, he managed to dodge the vigilance of the British authorities and emigrated to America in 1789. He could not, of course, bring any models or plans with him, but he was familiar enough with the Arkwright water frame for spinning cotton thread to make a workable copy. The next year he formed a partnership with Moses Brown, a Providence merchant who had already been dabbling in the textile field without great results, agreeing to build replicas of the Arkwright frame for half the profits of the manufacture.

Their first mill at Pawtucket contained only 72 spindles as against 636 spindles at the Beverly plant, but the machinery was so far superior to any other in the country that the Slater-Brown venture prospered from the start, earning profits of $8,000 a year between 1793 and 1803. After the Pawtucket mill proved successful, Slater put up mills at Rehoboth, Massachusetts, and at Slatersville, Rhode Island. These were, however, mills for the manufacture of cotton thread, it must be remembered, the cloth being let out to be woven elsewhere. As late as 1815, when William Gilmore, another British immigrant who had been trained in the Lancashire textile mills, offered to build a power loom for Slater, his proposal was turned down. Slater had the caution and limitations of a mechanic with but one skill. His lack of enterprise cost him the leadership of the industry, for in the very year that he refused Gilmore's offer, Francis Cabot Lowell's mill at Waltham went into production, spinning thread and weaving cloth under one roof.

Although it was late in his life that Lowell interested himself in the manufacture of cotton cloth, the subject must have been familiar to him from his early years, for he was the son of Susanna Cabot, whose brother had been the guiding spirit of the Beverly experiment. Born in 1775, he was fourteen years old when that ill-starred venture was launched. His father, John Lowell, besides being attorney for many New England merchants, had allied himself in marriage with three wealthy and prominent merchant families, the Higginsons, the Cabots, and the Russells. Even without his own natural aptitudes, these connections would have been sufficient to assure young Francis of a successful mercantile career.

At the early age of fourteen Francis was entered at Harvard, where he distinguished himself principally as a founder of Porcellian, the most exclusive society at the college. In his last year he was rusticated for lighting a bonfire in the Yard, a commonplace prank for fashionable undergraduates, who completed their studies under a tutor before standing for a degree. The tutor of Francis Lowell, the Reverend Zedekiah Sawyer of Bridgewater, reported on his pupil to the Old Judge in prophetic terms: "He has a happy genius for mathematics. I presume few if any of his class equal him in mathematics and astronomical attainments. He is very accurate in calculating and projecting eclipses."

Of the two or three careers open to talent at that time, the church, the law, or trade, Francis chose the one in which his mother's family had long been successfully engaged. On his graduation from college in 1793 he went into business with his uncle, William Cabot, gaining experience first as a supercargo, as scions of wealthy merchant families were wont to do. In 1795 he sailed for France to superintend the sale of cargoes of rice and flour in a vessel that was twice boarded by British cruisers on the lookout for blockade runners. The captain of one of the warships questioned the officers and the young supercargo very closely, "but not finding any evidence of our going to France," Lowell wrote to his father, "he dismissed us." Thus early did he develop those arts of dissimulation in business affairs that proved so useful later on. Or perhaps he saved his cargo by keeping his mouth shut in the manner said to be characteristic of the Cabots from whom he was descended.

On arriving at Bordeaux, he wrote his father a letter indicating clearly his tendency to judge things from his own personal observation, instead of on the basis of hearsay or prejudice:

The ideas you have of France in America are quite erroneous. There is full as much safety here as in America. We walk about the streets without being troubled and a pickpocket or thief has not been heard of this long time. It is true no man here regards his life at all and other peoples very little. . . . People here have as much religion as ever. None but the public officers mind the new style and the churches on Sunday are well filled.

Back in Boston the following year, he settled down as a partner of William Cabot at the Long Wharf. In 1798 he married Hannah Jackson, the daughter of his father's oldest friend, Jonathan Jackson, merchant, of Newbury, and sister to Patrick Tracy Jackson, who was later associated with him in the establishment of the cotton industry.

In Boston, city of hard-headed businessmen, Francis Lowell could hold his own with anybody. At his father's death in 1802, the largest single item of the Old Judge's estate was found to be $30,000 invested in "Adventures at Sea," on eight ships sent out by his son Francis. Although the Old Judge had earned as large fees as any lawyer in the United States up to that time, he had been far from skillful in the handling of his funds, and it was Francis, according to his brother John, who restored their father's "dilapidated fortunes." But his mercantile interests were only a part of Francis Lowell's business activity. He bought and managed a distillery, engaged in banking and foreign exchange, speculated in Maine lands, and launched several real estate projects in Boston, notably the building of India Wharf in 1808.

It was fortunate for Lowell that he had more than one iron in the fire, for by 1810 merchant shipping had virtually come to a standstill in the ports of New England. As neutrals furnishing goods to the two warring coalitions in Europe, the merchants of Boston and Salem had done a land-office business until 1807, when British Orders in Council and French decrees of blockade aroused Jefferson to such fears of war that he induced Congress to pass the Embargo Act. At this a howl of rage went up from the counting houses of Massachusetts, where everyone knew that for every cargo taken by either the British or the French, the value of one that slipped through increased tenfold. The failure of the Embargo Act led to the passage of the Non-Intercourse Act that lifted the embargo on all countries except Britain and France and, in 1810, the Macon Act, which offered resumption of trade with whichever one of these two countries repealed its blockade decrees. Despite these palliative measures, the shipping business did not revive.

The decline of business gave Francis Lowell time to pay some attention to his health, which since 1804 had given serious concern to his family, and in 1810 he decided to go abroad for a rest and cure. Accompanied by his wife and children, and fortified with a plentiful supply of Spanish gold doubloons, he sailed for England late in the year, making Edinburgh his headquarters. But, like most American businessmen on a holiday then and ever since, he was unable to free his fertile mind for total relaxation. He visited relatives, he called on old Boston Tories now regretfully dragging out their lives in England, he saw the sights and the theatres of London, but his real interests lay elsewhere. From Edinburgh he wrote home in some excitement that he had just met a large iron manufacturer, who invited him out to visit his plant. Lowell described these iron works as the most extensive in all Scotland. Eighty men are employed in making nails only. They have several furnaces for the manufacture of steel of various kinds. They make an immense number of shovels, axel-trees and cast iron of various kinds. It is astonishing to see large bars of iron roll out easier than you would paste, and cut up as wished, as easily as scissors can cut paper.

Machines of such power, manufacturing on such a scale, were totally unknown in America, and to the mind of Francis Lowell, now living in unaccustomed idleness, the sight was enormously stimulating. The production of steel, however, offered too many difficulties to be introduced in a large way into the United States, while the manufacture of cotton cloth, which kept Americans fearfully dependent on Britain, could perhaps be imitated more successfully.

Sometime during the winter of 1811, Mr. Nathan Appleton, another Boston merchant who was traveling abroad during the lull in business, called on his compatriot in Edinburgh, and learned that Francis Lowell was about to visit Manchester to look into the cotton manufacture. The Lancashire visit proved to be no mere tourist's brief glimpse, but an extended sojourn of several weeks, during which Lowell watched the machines at work for hours on end, and plied both operatives and owners with innumerable questions. As an American merchant, living abroad for reasons of health, a past and probably future buyer of their goods, Lowell was made welcome by these Lancashire mill owners, who, if they had known him for a potential competitor, might have been less affable.

Up to that time, the British had been fairly successful in keeping their monopoly of the new textile processes intact. Slater was one of the few to slip through their embargo. The inventions and patents that had given England command of the textile markets of the world had been born as a result of certain special industrial conditions, a series of happy accidents, and a wholesale stealing of processes and devices among the various producers. Having stolen the new inventions from one another to build up their industry, the British manufacturers were exceedingly loath to share their skills with other countries, even at a price. Hence Francis Lowell felt fully justified in appropriating machine designs which under other circumstances he might presumably have been willing to pay for.

In piracy of this kind, so monumental that it takes on the character of a patriotic act, there was needed not only the power to dissimulate, but also a gift for observation, a grasp of mechanical principles, and training in mathematics. Francis Lowell had all these, and an excellent memory besides. When he left Lancashire, his mind was stored with all the information he required to set up a cotton mill in the United States.

No letters from him concerning his visit to cotton mills in Britain have come down to us, hence it is impossible to name any specific establishments that influenced his thinking. There was, however, one important spinning mill in Scotland at that time that was more accessible to him than any of those in England. Moreover, this mill was being operated by a man acknowledged as the foremost cotton spinner in the British Isles. After years of experience at Manchester, Robert Owen had in 1800 settled down as manager and part owner of a mill at New Lanark, in Scotland, only about thirty miles from Edinburgh, where Lowell was staying with his family. Although Owen's experiment at New Lanark was not known to the general public in 1811, in fact, not until his *New View of Society* appeared in 1813, Owen himself was famous in the industry as having been the first to use cotton from the American Southern states in the manufacture of thread, and as having produced the finest grade of thread in the United Kingdom.

It is fairly probable that Lowell visited New Lanark. Manchester, to be sure, afforded him a view of weaving as well as spinning processes, but was of no assistance to him at all in its labor patterns. How to obtain skilled workers was a most vexing problem in the infancy of American manufactures. British poorhouses supplied the factory population of Lancashire, a labor force for which there was no counterpart in the United

States. New Lanark, on the other hand, was a very small village, and had to obtain its mill labor from afar, just as Francis Lowell would be obliged to do. Since there was great reluctance among the country folk in that part of Scotland to go into the factories —just as in the United States—Owen was obliged to make the working and living conditions at his mill extremely attractive to overcome their prejudices. The factory village at New Lanark was proof that high wages, fair employment practices, and clean, decent housing could pay dividends in an industry where the opposite was the general rule. When Francis Lowell was in England, such notions were not in the air, they were not yet universally discussed. They were the exclusive conception of Robert Owen, and unless Lowell saw New Lanark with his own eyes, it is difficult to understand how he was to parallel it so closely.

On his return to America in 1812, just before the start of the war, Lowell set to work immediately on his new scheme. His first plans called for a power loom only, but when he learned that it would cost him less to manufacture his own thread than to buy it, he extended his labors to include a water frame for spinning. For all his brilliant mathematical attainments and exact visual memory, he lacked the mechanical training to build the necessary models. He therefore employed the services of a well-known practical mechanic of Amesbury, Paul Moody, who had been an associate of Jacob Perkins, the inventor of a machine for making nails. Lowell hired a workroom in Boston, where he and Moody "planned and tried, altered and rearranged" each part of the machinery. It was in reality a process of "re-invention," as it has been called, for difficulties sprang up in the course of which they made some improvements on English techniques, while other problems were solved rather clumsily by English standards.

When their machine models were completed, Lowell and Moody had designed not only a cotton-spinning frame and a power loom, but a labor-saving dressing frame superior to those in use in England, for treating the yarn so that the machinery need not stop every time a thread was broken, and a double-speeder for winding the loose roving evenly on a spool.* Machinery of such efficiency was very uncommon in the United States, and was not universally employed even in England. Who has not dreamt of someday being under the compulsion to replace all the machines produced in thousands of years of human ingenuity which have been destroyed in some holocaust? Francis Lowell and Paul Moody realized this dream to such an extent that with the slightest clue they could find the answer to a specific difficulty.

Although most of Lowell's machinery was modeled after the English pattern, there were enough experiments going on at home to provide his photographic mind with fruitful suggestions. There is a hint of this in a letter of February 14, 1815, from Patrick Tracy Jackson to Lowell, who was then traveling in the South: "See if Stimpson has got a patent for his loom. As you return, go to Paterson, New Jersey. If Stowell is there, he can show you all worth seeing. See the looms in Baltimore if you can."

Anyone who showed Lowell or Moody his textile machinery was naive. Sometime after the first power loom was set up, the two men called on a Mr. Shepherd of Taunton to buy rights to his winding machine, which was somewhat superior to their own. Since he meant to use the machine on a large scale, Lowell asked for a reduction in the price named, but Shepherd refused, saying, "You must have them; you cannot do without them, as you know." As Moody and Lowell were looking over the model, which embodied a small, though important modification of a machine with which they were familiar, Moody said reflectively, "I am just thinking that I can spin the cops direct upon the bobbin."

Shepherd saw which way the wind was blowing.

* Nathaniel Bowditch, the renowned navigator and mathematician, later testified at a suit for patent infringement in connection with the double-speeder that its invention required mathematical calculations so advanced that he was surprised to discover that anyone but himself in America was capable of making them.

"You be hanged," he said, and turning to the other man, "Well, Mr. Lowell, I accept your offer."

"No," said Lowell, "it is too late." And Lowell and Moody departed to devise a machine incorporating Shepherd's contribution and their own improvement on it.

But it was not only in technical procedure that Lowell planned to outstrip his contemporaries. None of the other cotton manufacturers in America had the large, comprehensive views that made him such a great innovator in American industry. As a relative of the Cabots, Lowell knew that their experiment at Beverly had failed because of the lack of good machinery, adequate capital, and a dependable labor force. Once his machinery proved practicable, Lowell went into the equally important problems of what type of goods was to be produced, who were to operate the machines, and how the capital for the new establishment was to be raised.

Since he was a tyro in the industry, the goods to be produced had to be material of the simplest and coarsest variety, not the finer fabrics for which long experience in manufacturing was necessary. The fact that he was obliged to rely on unskilled operatives also led him in the same direction. His product, then, was to be a heavy, unbleached cotton sheeting. And as long as the United States was dominantly an agricultural community, much of it still in the pioneering stage, this coarse material, he felt, should find a ready market, and moreover permit of considerable economies in production.

The question of how to obtain a dependable labor force had not been satisfactorily solved by any other textile manufacturer in America. The supply of skilled labor was extremely limited, whatever trained hand operatives there were having congregated largely around Philadelphia, then the center for fine and fancy goods such as could not be made here with the existing machinery. Slater in his Rhode Island mills had tried to rely on apprentices, and when this failed resorted to the family system, whereby little children as well as adults and old folks could be put to work.

Nevertheless, Slater had great trouble keeping his help, despite his philanthropic schemes and Sunday schools. Children from five to ten years old, who worked in the mills fourteen hours a day six days a week, were strangely inappreciative of the boon of Sunday school on the seventh day.

Moreover, much of the resistance to manufacturing came from those who feared that agriculture would thereby be depressed, and the ease with which men could take possession of their own farms made factory life less appealing to the masculine part of the population. On the other hand, the work of spinning and weaving was not unfamiliar to women; indeed, before the introduction of factories all the spinning and a large part of the weaving done in America had been the work of women in the home. It was a common assumption that girls and young women who were not incessantly occupied were subject to temptation and vicious habits, as well as being a financial drain on their parents and a burden to society. Many thoughtful and prominent men held this view of the other sex. By offering employment to this "useless" class of the population, Lowell saw that he would not only have docile and tractable workers, but he would overcome much of the opposition to his schemes that might be expected from the agricultural interests.

Having decided on the employment of young women, Lowell realized that he must provide living quarters for them, for the little town where his mill was to be erected could supply neither enough operatives for his purposes nor dwellings to house them. Like Owen, he had to draw his help from a distance. The girls to tend his looms and spindles were to be farmers' daughters from the rural districts of New England and, in order to overcome the scruples of their parents, certain moral and physical standards would have to be met. New England farmers of Puritan traditions were not so indifferent as to permit their daughters to live away from home without the proper safeguards. Fully aware of this, Francis Cabot Lowell built neat boarding houses where the girls could eat and sleep, under the supervision of respectable women who played the role of a "house mother" in a college dormitory today.

Like Owen, too, Lowell planned to pay his help at higher rates than women were able to earn at any other occupation at that time. A satisfied and willing labor force was an important part of his scheme, not for Utopian but for practical reasons. His friends and followers in the industry, imbued with the religious cant of the nineteenth century, tried to lend him moral and patriotic impulses that were not so much foreign to him as beside the point. Thus his nephew, John Amory Lowell, later a well-known textile manufacturer in his own right, describes his uncle's motives: "Then Mr. Lowell had another idea in his mind, which was one of the greatest importance, and that was the moral and religious instruction of the operatives. He was going to introduce this business for American girls." It is true that churches were built in the neighborhood of the mills, not because Francis Lowell wished to elevate his operatives by religious instruction, but because they were New England girls to whom life without religious observance was unimaginable.

With machinery and labor problems settled, Lowell turned to the question of financial backing for his new venture. The merchant shipping of New England, crippled first by Jefferson's policy and then by the war beginning in 1812, was in a state of acute depression. Some merchants managed to survive by privateering, but more turned a dishonest dollar by sailing under British licenses to Lisbon with goods for the army in Spain, or by bringing goods down from Canada. Francis Lowell was among those engaged in this traffic. In general, however, the profits from legitimate commerce over the first twenty years of the century averaged no more than six percent, a piddling return for merchants who had formerly realized as much as five hundred percent on ventures at sea. With the prospects so dark, the more forward-looking among the New England merchants were keen to discover new areas of profitable investment. They had the capital for new projects, the training in the minutiae of business, and the experience in handling large affairs that were indispensable for Lowell's ambitious project.

One day in 1813 Lowell and Patrick Tracy Jackson approached Appleton on the Boston Exchange, and informed him that their plans to establish a cotton factory were well advanced —they had already purchased a water-power site in Waltham, and had obtained a charter of incorporation from the Legislature in the name of the Boston Manufacturing Company. The corporation form was at that time a comparatively recent device for industrial activities. Slater and Brown, and most of the great English mills, were owned and operated as partnerships. However, the new methods of production introduced by the great revolution in industry called for a complex structure that was more easily handled by the corporation, under charter from the state. Just as in the past special privileges had been conferred on the great trading companies for the purpose of developing new trade in foreign countries, so a monopoly of a certain area or service was granted to the new industrial corporations in return for exploring the new sources of wealth in large-scale factory production. There were other incidental benefits in the corporate organization: the delegation of authority to selected agents and personnel, a more advanced system of bookkeeping, with controlled budget, cost accounting, and auditing, and the assembling of large amounts of capital, which permitted certain economies in manufacturing.

The capital authorized for the new company was $300,000, a huge sum for that period, but only $100,000 was raised at first. The incorporators agreed that no more than two-thirds of the capital was to be invested in machinery, fixtures, and real estate, the rest being left liquid for carrying on the business. Patrick Tracy Jackson was the largest subscriber, taking $20,000 of the stock, his brothers $15,000, and Lowell the same amount, while the rest was distributed among the Thorndikes, father and son, Nathan Appleton, Uriah Cotting, James Lloyd, Benjamin Gorham, and Warren Dutton. Lowell offered Appleton $10,000 of stock in the new project, but Appleton, wary of investing a large sum in so "hazardous an enterprise," would risk only $5,000.

The Boston Manufacturing Company was almost exclusively a family affair. Gorham, Dutton, the Jackson brothers, and Nathan Appleton were all related either by blood or marriage to Mr. Lowell, while the Thorndikes had been close business associates of the Cabots in the earlier venture at Beverly, and Uriah Cotting was a partner of Lowell in his Boston real estate ventures. But, although Lowell was persuasive enough to carry this small group with him, many of his other relatives and friends, as Colonel Henry Lee wrote, "used all their influence to dissuade him from the pursuit of what they deemed a dangerous and visionary scheme. They too were among those who knew, or thought they knew, the full strength of his mind, the accuracy of his calculations, his industry, patience and perseverance." Not all the Boston merchants had that spirit of enterprise which every American is supposed to imbibe at his mother's breast. There was an important element of risk in Lowell's scheme, to be sure, that made his more conservative associates reluctant to take the plunge. It was up to him to show that there was real gold in his glittering visions.

Our gifted "madman," however, ignored the gloomy prophets and pushed forward with his plans, once the necessary capital was raised. As a member of a committee to select a site for the factory, he fixed on Boies's paper mill in Waltham, only a few miles outside of Boston. As soon as the water-power rights on the Charles River were purchased, Lowell set to work to design buildings for the project, the first of which was to be the machine shop where all the necessary carding, spinning, and weaving machinery could be manufactured. The next building projected was the mill itself, and when that was finished dwellings for the operatives were set up.

There was so much more to be done than one man could conceivably accomplish that it was necessary for Lowell to delegate some of the authority to others. Paul Moody could be depended upon to superintend the installation of the machinery, but someone else was needed to take charge of all the operations after Lowell's plans. This function was entrusted to Patrick Tracy Jackson, the largest investor in the new project, and, like Lowell, a merchant, new to the business of manufacturing textiles. After the mill got into production Jackson was named agent at a salary of $3,000 a year, a post that involved supervision of all production details.

Meanwhile, unforeseen difficulties, as in every new operation, caused provoking delays. The power loom, for example, took far longer to make and install than anyone had expected, and over a year passed before the Boston Manufacturing Company was ready to turn out cloth in February, 1815. The first sale of goods, however, was not made until September of that year. Stockholders like Nathan Appleton were extremely vexed by the delay. The interruption of commerce with Britain because of the war, he reasoned, could not be expected to continue forever. It behooved the new producers, therefore, to establish themselves and their product before the end of the war should bring a flood of foreign goods to swamp the market. Uneasiness on this score was justified by the failure of innumerable small mills at the beginning of the next year, after the coming of peace. Thus in a letter of February 14, 1815, Patrick Tracy Jackson wrote Francis Lowell about the closing of a nearby mill. As a sign of the times it might be considered portentous, but Jackson saw no cause for worry in their case. "I do not imagine," his letter said, "the Waltham Company suffered any loss in the affair, and they certainly gain by having this take place before their new establishment gets under way."

Appleton's fears proved groundless. Although the war ended eight months before the first sale of goods was made, the Boston Manufacturing Company showed that it was able to hold its own against the most formidable competition. In the growing settlements west of the Alleghenies there was a terrible hunger for the stout sheeting turned out by the mill, and the Boston Manufacturing Company was able to sell every yard it could produce of its ever-increasing volume. The way in which the goods were to be sold, however, was the only aspect of the enterprise that had not been planned in advance by Francis Lowell. He had designed machinery and a factory that could take in raw cotton at one end and turn out finished goods at the other, the first of its kind in the country and probably in the world, but he had made no arrangements in advance for the sale of his merchandise.

When the Waltham mill began to operate, the only person in Boston who sold domestic goods was Mrs. Isaac Bowers in Cornhill Street. Some of the Waltham sheeting was placed in her hands, but the prejudice against domestic cloth was so great that when Lowell and Appleton called to check up on sales, she told them that no one seemed to want it though everyone praised their product. In preparation for the end of the war, Appleton had set up a commission house under the name of B. C. Ward and Company, to import English cotton goods. When Mrs. Bowers reported the indifference of her customers to the Waltham sheeting, Appleton had a lot sent over to B. C. Ward and Company, who, according to the practice of the time, placed it in the hands of an auctioneer. To everyone's surprise, the goods fetched over thirty cents a yard, which was five cents a yard more than Lowell himself considered enough for a reasonable profit. Indeed, Lowell was more astonished than anyone at the success of his brain-child. Nathan Appleton reports on how far the results exceeded Lowell's expectations: "He used to say, that the only circumstance which made him distrust his own calculations was, that he could bring them to no other result but one which was too favorable to be credible."

In consequence of the first sale of their goods, B. C. Ward and Company became the exclusive selling agents of the Waltham mills at one percent commission, which was later raised to one and a quarter percent, a rate extremely profitable as the output of the mill increased to "thirty miles of cloth per day." For once the company got into full production, the profits were large and steady, with dividends averaging 18¾ percent from 1817 to 1826. The original band of hardy investors could now at long last congratulate themselves on their perspicuity.

By the following year, when "the success of the power loom at Waltham was no longer a matter of speculation or opinion," but "a settled fact," as Nathan Appleton wrote, he visited the mills of Rhode Island with Francis Lowell. The effects of peace on this textile center were ruinous. "We proceeded to Pawtucket," wrote Appleton. "There was not a spindle running . . . except a few in Slater's old mill, making yarns. . . . We saw several manufacturers; they were all sad and despairing."

Francis Lowell pointed out to the Rhode Island manufacturers that if they were to meet British competition they would do well to mechanize their plants further by buying power looms, which he was prepared to sell them, but many years passed before they acted on his suggestion. They were inclined to seek relief from British dumping not in greater mechanization or improved methods but in a subsidy from the government in the form of a high protective tariff. From all the available evidence, Lowell was the only textile manufacturer in the country who had no need for protection, since the coarse cottons from India that competed with his product were vastly inferior, and soon disappeared from the American market. Nevertheless, if any gravy were to be handed out he was not the man to forego it.

When a tariff measure came up for discussion in Washington in the spring of 1816, Francis Cabot Lowell was on hand with a memorial urging its passage. Like all New England Federalists, he had been strongly opposed to "Mr. Madison's War," but, unlike most of them, he was extremely reserved about expressing his political opinions publicly. Hence he had no difficulty in making himself agreeable to two of the most prominent leaders of the war party, Calhoun and Lowndes. At that time there was unanimity among Northerners and Southerners (always excepting the New England merchants) for the protective policy; the only question was the degree of protection that should be imposed. Calhoun and Lowndes were deeply impressed by the fact that the sale of raw cotton to Northern mills had reached the high figure of 27,000,000 pounds in 1815. Distress among Northern manufacturers might be reflected in Southern plantations. In his memorial to Congress, Lowell played on this regional interest:

The articles, whose prohibition we pray for, are made of very inferior materials, and are manufactured in a manner calculated to deceive rather than to serve the consumer. No part of the produce of the United States enters into their composition. They are the work of foreign hands on a foreign material. Yet are they thrown into this country in such abundance as to threaten the exclusion of its more useful and substantial manufactures.

And then, to overcome any possible prejudice against high tariffs on the part of these same Southerners, he asked for only a modest duty on cotton cloth, provided that a minimum valuation of 25 cents a yard was set on all imports. The low duty of 25 percent, as Congress fixed it, on a minimum of 25 cents per yard amounted to 83½ percent on the only imported goods that competed with the Waltham product, the coarse cottons from India. The Rhode Island manufacturers by this arrangement were left out in the cold, for the calicoes they made in competition with England cost far more than 25 cents per yard; they could be undersold at small sacrifice even with the tariff.

When Lowell's proposal was made public, his rivals in the textile industry raised loud cries, which were echoed by their champions in Washington. Thomas R. Gold, a congressman from New York who was also interested in cotton manufacturing, wrote Nathan Appleton on April 5, 1816: "Now that Mr. Lowell has left us some of the opposers of Manufactures quote him as having said that little if any protection was wanted as to cottons. Can this be so? . . . These things have embarrassed us much, and may in the Senate, unless *promptly* corrected. . . ." In the course of the debate on the floor of the House, Daniel Webster also made a veiled reference to Lowell, as supporting low duties. To this Mr. Hulbert of Massachusetts replied with indignation that the gentleman to whom Webster referred, "although intelligent and honorable, was a manufacturer of large capital," and could more readily stand up under low duties than others "whose means were limited and who had not got well established."

Lowell's sweet reasonableness prevailed against the exaggerated demands of the "little fellows," however, the bill being passed substantially in the form that he desired. He had helped to establish the principle of protection for industry, but he had played his cards so well that his own products were fully protected, while those of his American competitors, which stood in far greater need of assistance, were not. The importation of fine British textiles still constituted a large part of the New England shipping business, to which Lowell was also closely tied by family and fortune. While the tariff of 1816 further strengthened the position of the Waltham mill, it did no great harm to the mercantile interests whence capital for expansion of the textile industry in the hands of Lowell's friends might be expected to flow.

As a result of his visit to Washington, Francis Lowell was to leave the young textile industry another legacy of far-reaching consequences: a great voice to plead for it. "In the session of 1815 and 1816," wrote Daniel Webster in his autobiographical memoir, "I also made the acquaintance of Mr. Francis C. Lowell. . . . I found him full of exact, practical knowledge, on many subjects." Hitherto the young representative of the shipping magnates of New Hampshire had stoutly opposed all notion of protective tariffs; after meeting Lowell, his ardor for free trade cooled rapidly. Possibly at Lowell's suggestion, and armed with introductions from his new acquaintance, Webster moved his law office from Portsmouth to Boston, where Lowell's friends helped him build up one of the largest practices in the country in return for his most selfish devotion to their interests.

Francis Cabot Lowell lived only one year longer. His health had always been poor, and the vast labors in which he had engaged since his youth finally overtaxed his frail constitution. He was only forty-two when he died in 1817, but the record of his accomplishment is prodigious. Not only did he establish the textile industry in New England, but he set the pattern of industrialization that the whole country was to follow in every field: the large plant, including every process of manufacture from raw material to finished product, the corporation of huge capitalization and efficient management, the production of cheap goods in quantity, and the protection of infant industries by a tariff that amounted in reality to a subsidy for successful enter-- prise. He did not *invent* any of these devices, not even the ma- chinery for his mills, but he used—he applied—them in a way that showed true creative genius.

Having been provided with the ingredients of success, the friends and associates of Lowell after his death proceeded to set up new mills and new textile centers according to his recipe. The first of these modeled on the Waltham experiment was the city on the Merrimack bearing his name, which twenty years later had become a mighty symbol of American business ingenu- ity and a monument to the high standards of American labor.

Chapter III

LOWELL BEGINNINGS

THE success of the Waltham experiment in the manufacture of cotton cloth was a delightful surprise to everyone involved but Francis Cabot Lowell. Some of his associates had been a trifle phlegmatic at the start, others felt that they were indulging an erratic friend, and still others betrayed some concern for their investment. But when the plump dividends began rolling in these astute New England traders took heart. It was as if they had dreamt that they were risking great sums on the turn of a wheel, only to awake in their familiar counting houses, reckoning up the steady and massive profits from their habitual affairs. That this success was no accident was further proved by the fact that the prosperity of Waltham did not come to an end when Francis Cabot Lowell died; indeed the directors soon felt that the business was flourishing enough to warrant further expansion. In 1818 they built another mill on the site of an old cotton and wool factory which had ceased operations several years earlier, and in 1820 they further extended their plant with the erection of a third mill and a bleachery.

Hard-headed businessmen though they were, the directors of the Boston Manufacturing Company did not assume that because they were contributing to the economic development of the town they had license to defile it, as manufacturers did later on in the century. On the contrary, while new mills and boarding houses were going up, the corporation laid out new streets, improved and widened others, and lined them with several thousand shade trees. Since Patrick Tracy Jackson was the only corporation officer to reside in Waltham, the shade trees were really for the benefit and enjoyment of the operatives, an investment, one might say, in good employer-employee relations. Another such investment by the corporation was the building in 1827 of a combination library and lecture hall, the Rumford Institute, for the use of the mill workers.

Visitors from afar came to see this strange Yankee phenomenon, this mill that took your bale of cotton in at one end and gave out yards of cloth at the other, after goodness knew what digestive processes. John C. Calhoun came in 1818 and was taken on a tour of the plant by Nathan Appleton, who observed later that his guest seemed to take pride in having contributed to the success of the establishment by helping to obtain passage of the tariff of 1816. It is possible, however, that Calhoun even then had in mind a plan to manufacture cotton blankets on his own plantation with slave labor, a scheme that somehow missed fire.

Waltham continued to interest visitors long after Lowell had surpassed it in importance. In 1834, when that most delightful of English tourists, Miss Harriet Martineau, arrived in America with her ear-trumpet and her boundless curiosity, she made it a point to include the older textile town in her itinerary. The quiet streets, one of which was lined with houses built with the earnings of the operatives, "some with piazzas, and green venetian blinds, all neat and sufficiently spacious," won her highest encomium. She noted with approval the church built by the factory people, standing conspicuously on the green, the lyceum presented to the townspeople by the corporation, the private libraries "of some merit and value," and "the well-dressed young ladies." The only asperity she permitted herself was in regard to the health of the operatives, which, she remarked, was "good, or rather (as this is too much to be said about health anywhere in the United States) it is no worse than elsewhere."

And yet by 1834 Waltham had become a kind of backwater.

In that year only five hundred operatives were working there, while Lowell, the rising queen of the textile industry, had about five thousand. The industry had outgrown Waltham on the Charles, whose sluggish water power had been exhausted when the third mill was put up in 1820. Profits were so steady, however, even during the panic and depression years of 1819–20, that the original investors could see no limit to the possible expansion of the business, save the restrictions of mechanical power. If they could find a site where a great many mill units could be accommodated by the available water power, what was to prevent them from duplicating or multiplying their triumphs at Waltham?

Two of the men who had collaborated with Francis Cabot Lowell since the very beginning, Nathan Appleton and Patrick Tracy Jackson, were the first to see the opportunity. Appleton had increased his original investment in the Waltham Company to $26,000 when the capitalization reached $400,000 before 1821, but he had, in addition, a larger stake in its profits through the selling agency, B. C. Ward and Company. As a successful merchant and banker he also knew from what sources capital for a new project could be raised. Jackson, after seven years as resident agent of the Waltham mill, was thoroughly familiar with all the problems of production and, although his duties at the original mill took up most of his time, he could be depended upon to give any new enterprise the benefit of his experience.

Appleton and Jackson therefore took it upon themselves to find a suitable mill site, but, aware of their want of technical knowledge, called in Paul Moody, the mechanic who had helped Francis Lowell build the Waltham textile machinery, to help them. Since there were innumerable sources of water power in the tumbling rivers of New England, the choice was fairly wide. Several sites were considered and rejected for various reasons, and chance played an important part in the final selection. One day in the fall of 1821 Jackson agreed to meet Moody and look over a water privilege near the present city of Lawrence, but a violent rainstorm prevented him from keeping the appointment. When Jackson failed to appear, Moody went on to Amesbury, where a former partner of his, Ezra Worthen, lived and had his business.

"I hear Messrs. Jackson and Appleton are looking out for water power," said Worthen. "Why don't they buy up the Pawtucket Canal? That would give them the whole power of the Merrimack, with a fall of over thirty feet." Moody was so impressed with this description that on his return to Waltham he made a detour by way of the Pawtucket Canal, and was able to give Jackson a very favorable report of its possibilities.

In November, Appleton, Jackson, and a few other interested persons visited the spot, which was at the northeast end of the village of Chelmsford. A light fall of snow covered the ground. "We perambulated the grounds and scanned the capabilities of the place," wrote Appleton later, in his stilted prose. It did not take them long to make up their minds. The Merrimack River at that point, just before its confluence with the Concord, fell in a series of rapids, around which the Pawtucket Canal had been dug in 1793 to facilitate the running of lumber. Besides this small canal, there was a larger one, the Middlesex, that connected the area directly with the port of Boston, a feature of no mean importance. The banks of the river were covered with farms, less than a dozen houses comprising the whole settlement, which caused one of the visitors to remark jocularly that they might live to see as many as 20,000 inhabitants in the area.

The East Chelmsford site seemed in every way suitable for the ambitious designs of Appleton and Jackson, which they proceeded to execute without delay. To possess themselves of the land and the water-power rights without having the price jump sky-high, "it was necessary to confine all knowledge of the project to our own three bosoms," wrote Nathan Appleton, referring presumably to his own, Jackson's, and Moody's. More likely there were over twenty-five persons in the secret. A man named Thomas M. Clark was employed to buy up the necessary land and as many shares of the Pawtucket Canal Company as were available in the neighborhood, while another man was commissioned to purchase the remaining shares of the Canal Company held in Boston. At one period during the negotiations there seems to have been some hitch that made Appleton and Jackson consider another site for their new mills. But the transactions at East Chelmsford were at length completed, the new owners paying $70,000 in all for the farms along the Merrimack and the Canal Company stock.

At this point Appleton and Jackson could make their scheme for a new textile development known to the public, since in order to float the corporation that they intended to set up, large amounts of capital would be needed. It was no longer so difficult to finance such a venture as it had been in 1813, when the Waltham Company was chartered, for the success of that project had made textile manufacturing a very desirable investment. Waltham shares were so highly regarded, in fact, that some of the original investors had been able to sell some of their stock holdings at an advance of thirty to sixty percent. Such profits were in part the basis of the capitalization of the new establishment at East Chelmsford.

The financial structure of the new company was probably designed by Nathan Appleton, who first sketched out a rough outline: the corporation to be capitalized at $600,000, each share to cost $1,000, Appleton himself taking 180 shares, Jackson the same amount, Paul Moody 60 shares, and Kirk Boott and his brother John 90 shares each. This was merely tentative, of course, until the charter of incorporation could be obtained, and it is doubtful that any of these men actually put up all the money at this time. Once title to the lands at East Chelmsford was secured, however, it was possible to broaden the base of stock ownership. On December 7, 1821, therefore, it was voted at a stockholders' meeting to permit certain other investors to subscribe to some of the shares held by the original five. Prominent in this list were Eben Appleton (Nathan's brother), William Appleton (his cousin), Benjamin Gorham and Warren Dutton (large stockholders in the Waltham Company), Nathaniel Bowditch, and Daniel Webster.

As a stock salesman Nathan Appleton showed talent of a very high order. On December 15, 1821, for example, he wrote a letter to Timothy Wiggin, outlining the prospects of the new company:

In addition to the accompanying *official* letter, I have thought it might be satisfactory to you to know a few additional particulars. Mr. Kirk Boott will reside at Chelmsford, and devote himself entirely to the business. We have full confidence in his being well qualified for the business. He with his brother John W. and Co.[?] will hold all the stock belonging to them. Mr. Jackson is the agent of the Waltham company and with his connections will hold all his stocks. . . . I am desirous of retaining nearly all the stock belonging to me. I am already offered a considerable advance if I will part with any. We are endeavoring to get our machinery made at Waltham, and shall probably make a bargain with the company . . . we are mostly interested in that company and have of course experimental knowledge of what can be done in manufacturing cloth. You are no doubt aware of the success of this establishment.

Then he described two samples of cloth which he had enclosed, and their cost of production:

You can judge if they can be made in England cheaper. We think not. But the capital required to carry on the business here is no doubt greater than in England. The capital at Waltham is $600,000. They drive about 8,000 spindles and manufacture about 1,800,000 yards of cloth per annum. This you will perceive must give them a very handsome profit.

Timothy Wiggin was sufficiently impressed with this picture to purchase twelve shares of stock. Before two years had passed the number of stockholders increased to over sixty, as shown by the early stock books. This did not mean, however, that *anyone* could buy a share who had the money to pay for it. You had to have the proper credentials, be a relative of Nathan Appleton or Patrick Tracy Jackson, a Lowell, a Lyman, a Thorndike, or a Cabot, a maiden aunt, a widowed mother, or a minor child allied to one of the great New England merchant families, to be allowed to join this select company. Naturally, these excellent people, knowing nothing at all about the management of a textile mill, were content to leave this to those who did, namely to Appleton and Jackson, the two largest investors.

On February 6, 1822, the whole scheme gained legal status when the Massachusetts Legislature granted a charter of incorporation to the Merrimack Manufacturing Company. Appleton and Jackson were now ready to begin work on the canals and factories. But, clever as they were in floating securities or directing a going concern, neither one had the technical skill needed to design a mill or lay out a town. Francis Cabot Lowell had possessed these qualifications in addition to his other talents, but men of such versatility were no longer common. The age of specialization was beginning.

It was almost by accident that the Boston merchants made their choice of an engineer for their new enterprise. One day in the summer of 1821, before the project had begun to assume definite shape, a young man named Kirk Boott came to call on Patrick Tracy Jackson at his country home in Nahant. Hearing Jackson murmur that he needed "a brief respite from numerous and pressing cares," Boott answered that he would like nothing better than to relieve his host of some of his burdens. The young man seemed ambitious, he had been trained as an engineer, and, what was more, he and his family had capital to invest. After consulting with Appleton, Jackson invited Boott to become a stockholder in the Merrimack Company, with the understanding that he was to be the resident agent and take charge of all the building operations at East Chelmsford. These were begun in April, 1822, and were destined to go on, almost without interruption, for another twenty years, until all the mill sites at this point were taken up and the water power could be expanded no further. As the representative of the corporation at Chelmsford, Boott was to be its town planner, its architect, its engineer, its agent in charge of production, and the leading citizen of the new community. The manner of man he was, therefore, had a great deal to do with the physical and moral aspects of the place.

Kirk Boott was born in Boston in 1790, the son of an Englishman who had come to America only a few years previously to establish a successful mercantile house. The father's loyalties belonged naturally enough to England, and young Kirk never considered himself wholly American. He went to Rugby for his early schooling, and then attended Harvard College for two years. In 1808 his father purchased him a commission in the British Army, where he served for five years, taking part in the Peninsular campaign under Wellington. The outbreak of war between Britain and the United States filled him with indignation, and all his life he was to harbor resentment against Henry Clay for having led this country into war. Nevertheless, when his unit was ordered to the Western Hemisphere to serve against the United States, he resigned his commission and enrolled at Woolwich, the British military academy, where he studied engineering and surveying. After his father died, he returned home in 1817 and entered into business with his brothers, with very indifferent results, owing to a severe post-war depression following the Peace of Ghent.

Boott was thirty-one when he entered the employment of the Merrimack Company. He was an energetic man, but so imperious that he endeared himself to few of his subordinates. A martinet, he insisted on immediate obedience, and was known to have whipped refractory boys with his riding crop. His willfulness became a subject of legend, the townsfolk laughing over the tale that when his workmen once found it impossible to make a current of water flow in the channel they had dug for it, someone suggested that Boott's hat and walking stick be brought and laid on the bank, on the principle that even water must react to their commanding influence. But, if Boott was arrogant, he was thorough. He rapped out his orders in low, clipped tones, then climbed the ladders himself to see that they were carried out properly, "his arms at full length, never bending the elbow, holding himself in such a position that he could see the end from the beginning."

Despite his haughty airs to his inferiors, Boott could evidently be courteous and deferent enough to the corporation bigwigs, for Nathan Appleton referred to him as a "high-toned gentleman," whatever that might be. For, in spite of his family's investment in the enterprise, Boott considered himself and was treated by the directors merely as the top employee of the Merrimack Manufacturing Company. This arrangement set the pattern for the hierarchical system that was to operate in all the textile factories launched by Appleton and his friends. At the head stood the stockholders and their directors in Boston; directly beneath them, and responsible only to them, was the resident manager or agent of the mill, with the superintendents and overseers next in importance, and the mechanics and operatives at the bottom of the heap. From the point of view of operating efficiency this order was not unnatural, but there was some danger in the tendency toward a rigid social stratification along these lines, especially as the directors and officers of the companies, who held the final authority, did not reside in the town.

The general pattern of the new textile settlement had been drawn by Francis Cabot Lowell, whose procedures were accepted as standard, since they had paid off so handsomely. But in many respects Kirk Boott had to rely on his own judgment at Chelmsford, for, besides building mills, he enlarged and extended the canal and laid out a town where there had been nothing before. East Chelmsford was a site of great natural beauty, situated at the junction of the Concord and the Merrimack, with gentle hills rising on all sides. The stormy rapids of the Merrimack lent the place a sort of wild charm, which was curiously enhanced by the man-made dam and canal. A waterway always offers an opportunity for striking effects in the planning of a town, and there are indications that Boott was not unaware of these. The topography of the area and the great bend in the river above the confluence presented problems he was to meet, on the basis of the foreseeable future development of the town, with some dignity and grace, for, in addition to his engineering training, Boott had an ordered mind and a sense of design.

To take full advantage of the drop in the water level he placed the mills by the river's side, but not in such serried ranks as to cut off all view of the stream. The original design of the Merrimack plant, with three large mills parallel to the river, the central building topped by a cupola, and three others at right angles to these, the space between adorned with trees and shrubs, offered a dignified and inviting prospect, not unlike the groupings at Harvard or Union College.*

Boott planned the boarding houses for the girl operatives to be set up in close proximity to the mills, for obvious reasons, and to be of simple, traditional design, far above the standards of working-class dwellings anywhere in America or in England. Some were of wood and some of brick, but originally all were semi-detached, or double houses, with a strip of lawn between each, which allowed three exposures for each building. The houses of the superintendents nearby were only slightly more pretentious single dwellings on the same model, with a modest amount of decoration to distinguish them from the others. Apartments for the male mechanics and their families were provided in long blocks of brick buildings or tenements. For himself Kirk Boott designed a Georgian mansion with an Ionic portico imposing enough to set off his home from the employees' dwellings by the whole breadth of the hierarchy.†

You could then, only a few years after the foundations of the first building had been laid, look down Dutton Street from Merrimack Street and see a broad tree-lined thoroughfare divided by a canal, with a pleasing and varied line of boarding houses and tenements leading the eye directly to the red-brick

* See John Coolidge, *Mill and Mansion,* for a brilliant analysis of Lowell architecture.

† The members of the corporation had every reason to congratulate themselves on their appointment of Boott, for in their interests he practically worked himself to death before he reached the age of fifty. It was he who drew up the plans of the company's land holdings, including every parcel disposed of in his time, he who made the ground plans and elevations of all the buildings, wrote all the deeds, and kept all the records of company transactions. He also made at least two trips to England on company business, entertained all visiting celebrities and directors, was usually chosen moderator of town meeting, and served repeatedly as representative in the General Court.

mill with its white cupola in the background. New and fresh as it all was from the hands of the carpenter and the bricklayer, the whole scene had a look of permanence and solidity that well became the intentions of its designer.

This air of stability was also perceptible in the factories themselves. The main mill buildings along the river were five stories high, with the great water wheels in the basement, the carding machines on the second floor, the spinning machines on the third, and the weaving and dressing rooms on the fourth and in the attic. Smaller buildings in the mill yard were used for picking cotton and for storage purposes. Power was communicated from the water wheels in the basement by belts whose multiple webs stretched from story to story. The thick double floors were supported by wooden pillars, painted a bright green like the wooden framework of the machines, which gave the interior a certain gaiety.

It had been intended originally, as Appleton's letter to Wiggin indicated, to have the machinery for the new mills made at Waltham, but when it became clear that the enormous water power at Chelmsford could supply many new companies, a machine shop on the ground seemed more practical. Since the stockholders and directors of both companies were largely the same, there was no difficulty in making the arrangement. Nathan Appleton described the negotiations clearly:

A contract was made with the Boston Manufacturing Company, or Waltham Company, for machinery for two mills. As it was all-important to the Merrimack Company to have the use of the patents of the Waltham Company, and especially to secure the services of Mr. Moody, it was finally arranged to equalize the interest of all the stockholders in both companies, by mutual transfers, at rates agreed upon, so that there was no clashing of interest in any case. This could only be done by a strong feeling of mutual interest in favor of the measure, and a liberal spirit of compromise in carrying it out. Under this arrangement, it was agreed, in August 1823, to pay the Waltham Company $75,000 for all their patterns and patent rights, and to release Mr. Moody from his contract in their service.

J. P. Morgan himself could not have stated the principle of "community of interest" between so-called business rivals any more succinctly.

This community of interest was so strongly felt that there was never any intention on the part of the Merrimack Company founders to enter into competition with the Waltham Company. The market for standard cotton sheeting and shirting was left to the original factory, while the new mills at Chelmsford were to attempt the manufacture of printed calicoes. For the weaving of the cloth they had sufficient experience, but the printing was another matter, requiring great skill and long training. Their first experiments in this field were failures. Since they could not obtain the services of anyone at home to manage this department, the directors asked Timothy Wiggin, then in business in London, to get J. D. Prince, a well-known English calico printer, to come to Chelmsford. Prince was willing to make the change, but stipulated that he receive $5,000 a year in salary, a fantastic sum for those days. "Why, $5,000 a year is more than the Governor of the State of Massachusetts earns," he was told. "Can the Governor of Massachusetts print cloth?" asked Prince. He got the job at his own figure. With the employment of Prince all the technical arrangements were completed.

On September 4, 1823, Kirk Boott made a solemn entry in his diary:

After breakfast, went to factory, and found the wheel moving round his course, majestically and with comparative silence. Moody declared that it was "the best wheel in the world." Appleton became quite enthusiastic. In the afternoon, he spent an hour looking at the wheel, after which he returned home by Andover.

On October 9, Boott's diary reads:

Set a few cards after dinner, and tried a double-speeder. It did not twist very well, the cards being too rough. Both Moody and Borden said they "never saw machinery start better." The latter thought it would take us a month before we should commence weaving.

On October 29, one picker was in operation, on November 11, six looms were started, and on January 3, 1824, Boott's diary describes a trip he made from Boston to Chelmsford:

> Hired a hack from Holmes and set off at 10 o'clock, the roads very rough, arrived at home by 3:30. Met the Waltham teams with some goods. The Waltham teams had taken down 16 bales of goods, the first sent away.

Thus a little over two years after the Boston merchants had first seen the snow-covered farms on the banks of the Merrimack, the mill at Chelmsford was turning out cotton cloth. They were off!

Once the mill got into production, enough people were assembled at Chelmsford—operatives, boarding-house keepers, mechanics, and day laborers, not to speak of the shopkeepers and purveyors of various sorts—to develop characteristic community needs. The town selectmen at Chelmsford center, which was several miles away from the new settlement, seemed glad to surrender their governmental functions to the corporation, which had the funds as well as the will to perform them. The first of these was the establishment of a school, which the Merrimack Company put up on their own property, defraying all the expenses for a year. While this would seem an act of disinterested benevolence, it is more likely another instance of good employer-employee relations, for the heads of families who had come to the town would have demanded schooling for their children wherever they went. The textile corporations were not interested in education *per se*, and were determined to transfer the expense and the responsibility to the town as soon as possible. In the following year Kirk Boott wrote to the selectmen at Chelmsford that, because of the increase in the population, the children could no longer be accommodated at the original schoolhouse:

> The Merrimack Manufacturing Company [he went on] have in consequence erected a School House for the convenience of all chil-

dren residing on their premises. Therefore we the undersigned request that an article may be inserted in the warrant for the next Town Meeting . . . to ascertain if the Inhabitants will appropriate the money paid by the Merrimack Manufacturing Company and persons in their employ for supporting the School established by them.

The necessity for fire protection in a mill handling such inflammable material as raw cotton was so great that even before the first cloth began rolling out of the looms the company bought a fire engine and asked the town selectmen to appoint engine men. Thanks to this fire company, and to certain precautions taken in the building of the mills, no serious fire broke out until 1829. Another public project undertaken by the corporation was the establishment of the Middlesex Mechanics Association in 1825 for the benefit of their male employees and the appropriation of $500 to provide a library and reading room for their use.

But by far the most conspicuous of all the Merrimack Company's philanthropies was the building of a church and its presentation to the religious community. For the operatives and mechanics who had come to Chelmsford from their New England homes a place to worship was of prime importance, hardly second to a school. The proprietors of the Merrimack Company being of the same opinion, Kirk Boott and William Appleton invited a newly ordained Episcopal minister, the Reverend Theodore Edson, to preach in Chelmsford on March 7, 1824. His bearing and conduct pleased the agent of the company, but to the rest of the worshipers, the first service of Dr. Edson was somewhat of a mystery; no one present but Kirk Boott knew how to assume the office of clerk, and very few knew the responses. Among the mill population gathered to hear him, there were Congregationalists, Baptists, Universalists, and members of almost every denomination save the Episcopalian. Nevertheless, William Appleton and Kirk Boott, who were communicants of that church, had their way; the corporation appropriated $5,000 for the building of an Episcopal church and engaged Dr. Edson to be its rector. Regardless of their own religious persuasion, the operatives at the mill were taxed 37½ cents quarterly for the support of Saint Anne's and, until they formed their own congregations, were obliged to attend divine worship there.

As the population increased, new congregations began springing up all over the town. Even before Saint Anne's was completed, one Jonathan Morrill began holding prayer meetings at his home for Baptists who resented being assessed for a "foreign" church. When Kirk Boott heard of this he sent word to Morrill that he must quit or leave his house, which was the property of the Merrimack Company. Soon after, Morrill was appointed postmaster of the town, and betook himself and his family and his prayer meetings to an apartment over the post office. Another young man named Greenwood who was discovered to be collecting funds in the Number One mill for the erection of a Universalist church, was forthwith dismissed. The Universalists were religious radicals of the time, holding the unorthodox view that it was God's purpose to save every human being through divine grace; in other words, they believed in a complete democracy in the next world. Young Mr. Greenwood was also considered a subversive agent by Kirk Boott because he openly espoused the principles of the Workingmen's Party. Democracy in the next world was bad enough, but if it were to be extended to this world as well what would become of the authority of agents and mill-owners?

But though he was cold and unfriendly to the many Calvinist churches that kept springing up in spite of all he could do, Boott went out of his way to offer the help of the corporation to the Catholics. Large numbers of workingmen of Irish stock had come to the town to put up the buildings and work on the dams and roads; these were in reality the first settlers of the town. Since the corporation made no provision for their living quarters, they huddled together in a crowded, squalid settlement variously known as "Paddy Camp Lands," "New Dublin," and "the Acre." Certain acts of vandalism were attributed to the Irish, and fights between them and the rest of the population were frequent and bloody. In the hope that the discipline of the church would put an end to these disorders, Boott invited the bishop of the diocese to dine, offered him the old schoolhouse building as a temporary chapel for the holding of mass, and soon presented the Catholics with a lot on which to build their church. Thus although most of the mill operatives, like most of the mill owners, were traditionally dissenters, the only two churches that had the financial backing and official recognition of the corporations were authoritarian.

Meanwhile, the town and the corporations were growing as if by magic. By 1826 three mills and two print works were turning out calicoes for the Merrimack Company, without using more than a fraction of the available water power. The first Merrimack mill had not got into production before its directors busied themselves with plans for a new field of exploitation. On December 23, 1823, Nathan Appleton wrote to Samuel Batchelder, who was then running a small but successful cotton mill in New Ipswich, New Hampshire: "There seems to be a pretty strong disposition to get up a new company at Chelmsford, provided we can conclude a satisfactory agreement as to water power and making the machinery."

In the following year, William Appleton and Patrick Tracy Jackson were named a committee by the Boston Manufacturing Company, which at that time might be described as the "parent company," to offer subscriptions for their newest venture, that was to be called the Hamilton Company. These subscriptions were not offered to the public, but to the shareholders in the parent company, and consequently the new list of stockholders bore a startling resemblance to those of the Boston and the Merrimack corporations: the names of Appleton, Lowell, Thorndike, Dutton, Gorham, Jackson and Boott being prominent among them. Samuel Batchelder also took some shares, but he was considered an outsider by the larger investors, taken in probably only because of his technical knowledge of the manufacture of twills, which the new company was set up to produce.

A charter of incorporation for the Hamilton Company was granted by the Legislature on February 27, 1825, with one provision that was later to cause the directors some embarrassment. The third section of the charter stated that "Every stockholder should be liable in his private capacity, after his membership shall have ceased, for all debts contracted during the time that he was a member of the corporation." At the time the investors did not resent this unlimited liability clause; they may even have desired it, for it made certain that none but men of large capital would take the risk involved in such an undertaking, that is, it excluded the "riffraff" who might be inclined to take a flyer in something that looked good. While unlimited liability suited the purposes of the textile magnates for a while, a business crisis late in the twenties gave them such a fright that they changed their views and persuaded the Legislature to pass a general limited-liability law.

Before any new projects could be carried out, however, it was necessary to devise a scheme whereby the water power could be leased by the Hamilton Company on favorable terms. The Merrimack Company, having purchased all the shares of the Pawtucket Canal Company, took over all the water rights and permitted the Canal Company to lapse. When it was seen that not only the Hamilton Company but other companies also would probably want to make use of the water power, the Canal Company was revived under the name of the Locks and Canals Company, to which the Merrimack Company returned all the property it had acquired. It then bought back its own mill sites, leased the water power necessary to run them, and left the Locks and Canals Company to sell the remaining land, dig the necessary canals, and lease such water power as might be desired by other corporations. Since the directors and main stockholders of all these companies were largely the same, the transfer was merely one of convenience.

Thanks to this device, progress was unimpeded. The Merrimack and Hamilton Companies brought such a tidy return on the invested capital that further ventures were being launched constantly. In 1828 the Lowell Manufacturing Company and the Appleton Company were set up, the second a large establishment whose prime movers were again Nathan Appleton and Patrick Tracy Jackson. But, while many of the Boston and Merrimack stockholders were involved in this latest enterprise, two new names among the investors were of special interest: Thomas Handasyd Perkins and Ebenezer Francis. These were the wealthiest and most powerful East India merchants in Boston, who had long held out against this upstart industry as a threat to their shipping business. With the adhesion of Perkins and Francis to the textile industry, the cleavage between merchants and manufacturers in New England was practically at an end. A few diehards like some of the Lee family resisted the trend a little while longer, but within ten years all the merchant capitalists of Boston, including two comparative newcomers to the merchant ranks, Amos and Abbott Lawrence, had a stake in the manufacture of textiles, not only in Lowell, but in many other textile centers that were springing up at the same time all over northern New England.

So closely were the boards of directors of these various corporations integrated that they were beyond any vulgar competition for markets, each factory being designed for the production of another type of goods. Even when the Appleton Company seemed to be competing with the Boston Manufacturing Company at Waltham in the manufacture of heavy sheetings and shirtings, for example, there was no reason for their common stockholders to feel any alarm, for the broadening of the market gave scope to the products of each. Besides, the Waltham Company by this time had branched out into other types of fabrics, which reduced the rivalry considerably.

High dividends in those early years bore witness to the sagacity of the entrepreneurs at Chelmsford, and stimulated further expansion. The Locks and Canals Company averaged over thirteen percent, the Merrimack over twelve percent, and the Hamilton and Appleton Companies were not far behind with ten percent. And still the limit of the water power had not been reached. During the thirties, therefore, the building of new mills and the floating of new companies went on until at last the saturation point was reached.

The population of the town kept pace with these extraordinary developments. An area that had supported five families in 1821 included 2,500 persons in 1826, 18,000 ten years later. Up to 1826 the local administration, although nominally in the hands of the selectmen of Chelmsford, was in reality conducted by Kirk Boott, acting for the corporations. Not only was Chelmsford Center four miles away from the new settlement, but the interests of the rest of the township were still dominantly agricultural, and therefore at odds with the fast-growing mill population. The directors of the Merrimack Company had considered the problem of setting East Chelmsford up as a separate township as early as 1824, but legislative approval of this was not granted until 1826. If Kirk Boott had had his way, the town would have been called Derby, after the place where his parents were born, but Nathan Appleton firmly opposed this proposal, insisting that no name would be more appropriate than that of the founder of the industry.

In 1827 the town of Lowell was already a busy little hive of activity, apart from its humming mills, as can be seen from Captain Basil Hall's description:

> Several school-houses were pointed out to me, and no less than three churches; besides innumerable boarding-houses, taverns, newspaper offices, watch-makers, book-shops, hatters, comb-makers, and all the family of Stores, every one of them as fresh and new as if the bricks had been in the mold but yesterday. I was much pleased to see a great brewery starting up like a Leviathan, amongst all the small fry of buildings.

This was really an extraordinary achievement in five years, even though Captain Hall was erroneously informed that five years before only "painted savages" had walked where he now saw crowds of "merry damsels."

But with the coming of self-government, differences between

the town and the corporations presently began to crop up. On the one hand, the mill owners were glad to shift the administrative responsibility to the town officials, but on the other they did not want those officials to be heedless and forget whose money had made the town what it was. It was very well to have the corporations' fire department supplanted by a town agency in 1830, to have the burden of the school system borne by the whole population, to have the paving and repair of streets turned over to the Lowell town government. And, when Lowell acquired a city charter in 1836, more ambitious schemes still were projected: a market house and courtroom, a jail, parks, sewers, and a hospital.

But all these schemes cost money, money that could be raised only by taxation on the land in the town, three-fourths of which was owned by the corporations. In the interests of public economy and their stockholders, a cry with which we are now painfully familiar, the corporations fought stoutly to keep taxes down, throwing all the weight of their influence against any extravagant notions of the citizenry. In one famous case they withdrew their patronage from the Reverend Dr. Edson, who, they felt, owed his position to their good offices, and yet flew in the face of their expressed wishes. This was during the school crisis of 1832, when a town meeting was called to pass on a proposal for two large new schoolhouses, at a cost of $20,000. The rector of Saint Anne's not only spoke in favor of the measure at this first meeting, but continued to do so most eloquently at a later meeting, although opposed by the most distinguished corporation satraps then residing in Lowell, Kirk Boott, Eben Appleton, and Luther Lawrence. When the motion was passed by an overwhelming majority of the townspeople, Kirk Boott significantly absented himself from church.

But this gesture was evidently considered too subtle to show the displeasure of the corporations, who thereafter carried on a mean vendetta with the public-spirited Dr. Edson. William Appleton was particularly vindictive; after the lease of the Locks and Canals Company on the church expired, he headed a group of directors who demanded that the religious society of Saint

Anne's pay a sum considerably in advance of the original cost for the church property, which had been so widely advertised as a free gift to the congregation. And, because he had presumed to bite the hand that fed him, Dr. Edson was evicted from his parsonage until 1866, when he was at length able to raise the $16,000 demanded by the corporation in payment.

The school issue was symptomatic, to be sure, but it was an unusual case. Most of the citizens humbly acknowledged their indebtedness to the corporations, even though on political grounds they might disagree with the textile magnates. An editorial of April 24, 1830 in the Lowell *Mercury*, a Democratic newspaper, stated this position:

The growth and prosperity of this town depends altogether upon the success of the manufacturing establishments, which have literally made it what it now is. There should be a unity of views and feelings (as there certainly is of interest) on all important questions of a local character. . . . Let the machinery in the factories cease to move and all kinds of business must come to a dead stand. . . . To oppose the manufacturing interests would be nothing less than suicidal.

But despite a general acquiescence in this point of view, other divisions between the townspeople and the corporations gradually made themselves felt as time went on. The speech of Dr. Elisha Bartlett on his inauguration as first mayor of Lowell in 1837, reflected a certain sense of insecurity that was widely felt:

The graves of our fathers [he said] are not here. The haunts of our childhood are not here. . . . The large and gradually accumulated fortunes of nearly all our older towns are not to be found here. The great mass of wealth which is centered here, and which has made our city what it is, is owned abroad. Its proprietors do not reside among us. Its profits are not expended among us.

This criticism did not die down but tended rather to grow sharper with the passage of years, for in 1876, speaking at the semicentennial exercises of the founding of the town, Ben Butler brought up the same old grievance:

Our city has been a hive of industry, and as a rule the honey has been gathered by others. . . . Indeed the great drawback upon the prosperity and growth of our city . . . has been that the owners of our mill property here did not live here and give our city the advantage of their expenditure, their public spirit and the investment and re-investment of the money earned by our citizens under their own eye, in the place where it was earned.

The fundamental indifference of the corporations to the welfare of the populace was indicated in the unbalanced development of Lowell apart from the mill buildings and workers' housing. They had allowed a certain amount of room for business and residential growth, but the area allotted to this purpose was too cramped to permit any planning or order. The tradesmen and shopkeepers crowded into a narrow space, and put up shacks and shanties for the display of finery with which they hoped to separate the operatives from as much of their earnings as possible. These shanties were at length replaced with more permanent shops and stores of no particular distinction, while the residential quarters developed along the hit-or-miss lines of most American towns of the time.

Since the corporations had decided not to establish any business offices in Lowell, none of the directors or junior executives except those connected with the actual process of manufacture resided in Lowell. There were hence no social relations between the leading figures of the town and the bigwigs in the textile industry. Only one person with a large financial interest in cotton manufacture ever attempted to live in Lowell during the period we are discussing, and he remained only a short time. This was John Lowell, son of Francis Cabot Lowell, who planned to build a chateau like Lafayette's at Lagrange in the environs of the town. But John Lowell's wife and two children died, his own health failed, and when he too died on his trip around the world he left his great fortune not for the benefit of the citizens of Lowell but to set up the institute for public education which bears his name, in Boston.

Throughout its triumphal progress, Lowell was enormously self-conscious; every detail of its history was recorded, annotated, compared. Certain apocryphal tales about the origins of the place became current and were commemorated in verse and song, such as the one about Kirk Boott having gulled the farmers:

> *There came a young man from the old countree,*
> *The Merrimack River he happened to see.*
> *What a capital place for mills, quoth he.*
> *Ri-toot, ri-toot, ri-toot, ri-toot, rumpty ri-tooten-a.* . . .
>
> *And then these farmers so cute,*
> *They gave all their lands and timber to Boott.*
> *Ri-toot, etc.*

This type of error was sternly corrected by Nathan Appleton in various papers and letters: Kirk Boott had had nothing to do with the purchase of the land for the Merrimack Company, and besides the company had paid what were then fair prices for the farms they had bought. Another mythology, however, based on the infallibility of industrial capitalism, was permitted to flourish unchecked.

In the making of the legend, the corporations appropriated unto themselves the credit for all that was good in the town, whether these benefits had come about as a result or in spite of their efforts. Thus for several years after the great school fight of 1832, none of the corporation executives would have anything to do with "the schools thus erected contrary to their sovereign will and pleasure," wrote Charles Cowley, the historian of Lowell. "It was only when Henry Clay came to Lowell that their High Mightinesses were graciously pleased to let the light of their countenances shine for a moment on the benighted

little Hottentots that filled the North and South Grammar
Schools." If the schools of Lowell were good—and for many
years they were known as a model of public education in Massachusetts—Mr. Clay must be made to understand that this was
attributable to the disinterested benevolence of the Boston merchants who had conceived and built the town.

Most of the inhabitants of Lowell accepted the myth without
question, in the characteristic American boom-town tradition.
"Look at us! See what we have done!" they crowed. "Behold
the results of Yankee thrift and Yankee ingenuity! And note how
respectable and virtuous and moral we are while we're making
so much money!" For twenty years almost no one questioned
the truth of this myth because for twenty years the boom went
on without interruption, regardless of panic and depression in
other parts of the country.

Taking a middle point in this period, we can see what progress
had been made only ten years after the completion of the first
mill. By 1833 nineteen five-story mills were in operation, with
a capital investment of over $6,000,000, and containing 84,000
spindles and 3,000 looms. The population had grown to over
12,000, of whom 5,000 were operatives in the mills, 3,800 of these
girls and women. New inventions, such as Danforth's cap-spinner
in 1829, had made it possible to step up production to a point
where 27,000,000 yards of cotton cloth were turned out in 1833.
The town boasted of ten churches, to prove its piety, several
banks to prove its thrifty ways, and, as a symbol of continued
progress, could point with pride to the Boston and Lowell Railroad, one of the earliest in the entire country, then under construction, although it was not opened for traffic until 1835.

All these laudable achievements advertised Lowell, advertised
its product, proclaimed the farseeing intelligence and worthy
character of the Boston merchants who had conceived the original plan. Lowell was their showplace, even though, meanwhile,
the Appletons, Lawrences, Lowells, and Jacksons had extended
their textile interests to many other towns in four New England
states. The greatest publicity value Lowell had for the superficial

observer, however, was something else again. It was, to everyone's surprise, certainly their own, the 3,800 young women who had come from the farms and villages of New England to tend those looms and spindles, to fill those churches, deposit their money in those banks, and make the name of Lowell a byword in two hemispheres.

Chapter IV

THE LOWELL GIRLS

AT LOWELL's greatest moment, the girls who operated the looms and spindles in her mills occupied the center of the stage. In 1833, ten years after the completion of the first mill, the town had become so renowned that it was honored by the visit of a President of the United States. He was not such a President as the principal stockholders of the textile mills enjoyed paying homage to; in fact, earlier in this very tour, when General Jackson had passed through Boston, he had received a marked snub from the ruling caste of that city. As he rode his charger through the streets where the great merchant families lived, no one saluted him but one small child; all the windows were closed and the curtains drawn tight.

The ruling caste of Boston was made up largely of investors in the cotton mills, and hence their representatives in Lowell held the same views about the triumphant leader of the "rabble." Kirk Boott only a year before had made a campaign speech in which he uttered those grim warnings with which political conservatives are accustomed to terrify the timorous voter: "Elect General Jackson," he cried, "and the grass will grow in your streets, owls will build their nests in the mills, and foxes burrow in your highways." In fact, hatred of the President went so far that when the directors of the Boston and Lowell Railroad wished to name its first train after Patrick Tracy Jackson, they found the connotations so odious that they called it the "Patrick" instead!

But the man was President of the United States, however much right-thinking people might hold him to be a blackguard, and the opportunity for nation-wide publicity was too good to be ignored. The town boosters, on hearing of the President's intention to visit Lowell, immediately held meetings to plan how he should be received. A few of the proposals seemed so lavish that some citizens shrank from the expense, but Kirk Boott, speaking for the corporations, allayed their fears. "Gentlemen," he said, "give yourselves no uneasiness about a deficit. We will take care of that." Amos Lawrence grew almost lyrical in his anxiety to make the President's visit a memorable occasion. "We will feed him on gold dust, if he will eat it!" he said, and his son actually overcame his political scruples to the point of accompanying the presidential cavalcade.

For several days before Jackson was due to arrive, torrents of rain had fallen in the neighborhood, to the dismay of the reception committee and the townsfolk. On the morning of June 27, 1833, the weather was still threatening, but before noon the skies cleared and the sun came out bright and warm. Thousands of people from the surrounding towns and villages began flocking into Lowell for the festivities; martial music hung on the air as fife and drum corps practiced their part in the show; horsemen flew about the streets on important errands; rifles cracked and guns roared. In their ignorance of firearms, two young men had their arms blown off while rehearsing the presidential salute, but even this could not dampen the general enthusiasm.

At last the tidings echoed all over the town: "He's come! He's come!" and Jackson drove up from the Andover road in an open barouche, with "Machiavelli" Van Buren sitting beside him. At the junction of Church and Central Streets, near what was then the end of the town, the carriage rolled between two fine hickory trees, specially transplanted for the occasion, and all along its passage there were arches of welcome, bunting, and decorations, including signs referring to the capture of New Orleans in 1815 and Jackson's stand on nullification. After a brief speech of welcome by one of the selectmen, and an even shorter reply by Jackson, amid the booming of artillery and the wild cheers of the crowd the President stepped from his carriage and was led up to the balcony of the Merrimack House, the leading hotel of the town, to review the procession got up in his honor.

For the veteran of so many campaigns, the parade of the poorly trained militia must have been tedious. Nor could the thin line composed of the town selectmen, the judges of the police court, the school committee, and other town officers be expected to quicken the beat of any heart. By way of novelty, therefore, the chief attraction of the procession consisted of the girls who worked in the cotton mills, 2,500 of them, each in a white muslin dress with a blue sash carrying a parasol over her bare head. It had been intended to have all the parasols green, but some blue ones were discernible in the hands of the paraders. The costumers of the pageant apologized profusely to the President for this jarring note in the color scheme. "They had done their best, they said," wrote Josiah Quincy, Jr., who was one of the young men in the President's cavalcade.

Boston had been ransacked in vain, and New York was in those days far too distant to be drawn upon. But when these same parasols were waved in graceful salute, as the bearers passed before their chief magistrate, Jackson's enthusiasm mounted high, and he was pleased to say that this distressing variation in color did not mar his satisfaction with the scene.

Marching two abreast, with the line stretching out for two miles, the 2,500 girls took half an hour to pass the President's balcony. "Very pretty women, by the Eternal!" said the gallant old soldier when their fresh young faces swung past in review, and he bowed to each couple as they came abreast of him until fatigue forced him to stop. But the textile magnates did not intend to let Jackson off merely with a view of good-looking women, to whom he was notoriously susceptible. Lest he miss the point of the whole fête, it was spelled out for him in so many words. In fact, the parade was arranged with this object in view. Operatives from the oldest established corporation headed the line of march, followed by girls from the other mills according to the date at which they were incorporated. Within each corporation group all the girls who worked in one room marched together, with their overseers in front, carrying batons to signify their authority. And at the head of each corporation division a silk banner was displayed, white on one side and green on the other, bearing the name of the company and a scroll held in an eagle's beak, with the inscription, *"Protection to American Industry,"* in bold letters across it.

"After passing the President," wrote an observer of the occasion, "the young women marched to their respective corporations, and partook of collations, which were in readiness for them." Late in the afternoon the President made his appearance at the No. 2 mill of the Merrimack Corporation, where the girls, still in their "holiday attire," stood at their machines and performed their tasks for the visiting party. Jackson then went on to see the Print Works, and passed out of the mill yard under an arch of water operated by the force pumps from the canal.

Throughout the day the spotlight had been focused on the operatives. It was their looks and their deportment that were supposed to catch the President's eye, and through them the industry they adorned. In their holiday clothes they made a pretty picture, parading or tending their machines, but was it a true picture? The reality was quite different, not quite so pretty, perhaps, but charming and exciting in a way that could with difficulty be translated into a pageant. The girls had not come to Lowell to posture before distinguished visitors; they had come to the mills to earn money. Intelligent, ambitious, energetic, they were conscious, moreover, of participating in a novel experiment that presaged great changes in the world they knew. Like all of America at that time they had a sense of making history, of being in at the start of something untried and remarkable. And with this awareness went the knowledge that whatever interest they held for their contemporaries derived from the work they did.

De Tocqueville, visiting America at this very period, had observed that labor was not dishonorable in the democracy of the West. "In America no one is degraded because he works, for everyone about him works also . . . every honest calling is honorable." And in another connection he remarked that nowhere else in the world were young women "surrendered so early or so completely to their own guidance." American girls, he said, were full of reliance on their own strength, and that reliance was shared by all about them. Charles Murray, an Englishman visiting in America a year or so later, also commented on the "innocent fearlessness" of young women here, a trait very flattering to a European man of the world.

It was this belief that an American woman was safe in doing whatever she wished, since all men, anywhere, were supposed to come to her rescue whenever she needed protection, that made it possible for girls of respectable parentage to enter the mills at Lowell without loss of status, whereas in England and on the continent of Europe factory operatives not only came from the lowest social strata but were also supposed to be fair game for any seducer. If the country had possessed a large subservient lower order, there is no doubt that it would have been drawn upon for a docile labor supply for the textile mills in their early days. Lacking such a resource, Francis Cabot Lowell had tried New England farmers' daughters with signal success at Waltham. In the establishments at Lowell the same procedure was followed in this as in so many other respects.

Far from belonging to a downtrodden class, the operatives who worked in Lowell and the other mill towns from 1814 to 1850 came from precisely the same stock, with the same traditions, as the overseers, agents, and even the Boston investors themselves. Like the men who employed them, the girls were descendants of early settlers, the children of Revolutionary

patriots, God-fearing and church-going, hard-working and passionately eager for education. Their spirit, moreover, was equally
venturesome, for to go to a new town and a new occupation,
although it involved no moral dangers, involved a rupture of
old ties and an absence of familiar things that must have cost
many of them moments of anguish.

It grew habitual with the mill owners at Lowell to claim credit
for the high moral character of their operatives. Repeatedly they
stated that one of their prime purposes in launching the textile
industry was to give employment to respectable women, to save
them from poverty and idleness. But the New England tradition, in which the mill girls had been steeped since infancy, had
always considered labor virtuous and idleness a fertile field for
the devil's works. In their own farm homes these girls had been
far from slothful. After the age of twelve, to be sure, it was uncommon for them to be employed in any of the outdoor labor
required on a farm, but spinning and weaving were familiar to
them, as well as the wide range of household tasks, of domestic
manufacture, really, in which they assisted their mothers. The
girls might have resisted the temptation to look for work elsewhere, to be sure, had the farms been large and profitable, but
the inheritance laws kept them small by requiring the equal
distribution of property to the heirs, while the opening up of
rich Western farm land offered competition that the stony soil
of New England could not meet. Nevertheless, the farm population of New England was at its peak in the thirties, and for the
two decades before and after that period there was a steady flow
of country girls into the textile industry.

There were two other avenues of paying employment then
open to these girls: domestic labor and teaching. Domestic service
paid almost as well as factory work, but the small tyrannies of
a mistress, the submissive role required of a servant were not to
the taste of these high-spirited young women. Lucy Larcom,
the most famous of all the Lowell mill girls, described their attitude toward this type of work:

We used to see it claimed, in public prints, that it would be better for all of us mill girls to be working in families, at domestic service, than to be where we were. Perhaps the difficulties of modern house-keepers did begin with the opening of the Lowell factories. Country girls were naturally independent, and the feeling that at this new work the few hours they had of every-day leisure were entirely their own was a satisfaction to them. They preferred it to going out as "hired help." It was like a young man's pleasure in entering upon business for himself.

Teaching was more to their liking, and many of them kept school in intervals of factory work, either for the change and rest, or in a spirit of dedication, for until many years later factory work brought six to seven times as much money as teaching.

Hearing of the high pay and pleasant working conditions, the girls came trooping into Lowell from the towns and villages of Massachusetts, Vermont, New Hampshire, and Maine. Massa-chusetts provided only one-eighth of the operatives in 1840, a much larger proportion coming from New Hampshire, whose girls were noted for their earnestness and capability, their readi-ness to try anything that seemed "worth doing." An idea of the distance many of them traveled to reach Lowell may be gathered from the record of one of the mills, where the average girl in 1838 came from eighty-four miles away.

Not all were farm girls; some, like Lucy Larcom, were the daughters of sea captains who had died leaving their widows and children without a competence, others of poor clergymen or teachers, or of unsuccessful tradesmen. Middle-class girls who had known better times would leave home, officially "on a visit" to friends, go to the mills, and send back what they earned to help their families keep up appearances. A few seemed to have come in flight from some shadow; these were very secretive, and had strange callers. Girls came for every reason and for no reason, as one of them wrote in the *Lowell Offering:*

I will speak to you of my acquaintances in the family here. One, who sits at my right hand at table, is in the factory because she hates her mother-in-law. . . . The one next her has a wealthy father, but like many of our country farmers, he is very penurious, and he wishes his daughters to maintain themselves. . . . The next has a "well-off" mother, but she is a very pious woman, and will not buy her daughter so many pretty gowns and collars and ribbons . . . as she likes. . . . The next is here because her parents and family are wicked infidels, and she cannot be allowed to enjoy the privileges of religion at home. The next is here because she must labor somewhere, and she has been ill-treated in so many families that she has a horror of domestic service. The next has left a good home because her lover, who has gone on a whaling voyage, wishes to be married when he returns, and she would like more money than her father will give her. The next is here because her home is in a lonesome country village, and she cannot bear to remain where it is so dull. The next is here because her parents are poor, and she wishes to acquire means to educate herself. The next is here because her "beau" came, and she did not like to trust him alone among so many pretty girls.

Others still came for the avowed purpose of paying off the mortgage on the family farm, or of sending a brother to college.

What drew them primarily, of course, was the high wages, and they flocked eagerly to the mills and boarding houses, not only of Lowell, but of all the cotton textile centers where the same conditions obtained. None were turned away for lack of a place in the factories. By stagecoaches, by canal boat, by railroad, or by a combination of all three, they converged on the town in a constant stream. It was never necessary for the mills to advertise in the newspapers for help, as Samuel Slater had been obliged to do, for a Lowell mill girl on returning home for a brief vacation was a walking advertisement of the advantages of factory work, with her new clothes and citified manners and speech. The corporations also sent agents up north to recruit labor whenever there was a shortage of operatives, paying them a dollar a head for each girl they brought back in the thirties and forties, and as much as three dollars a head just before the Civil War. By 1845 the labor agent had taken on the role of the villain in a melodrama to critics of the factory system, appearing in small country villages with a long, low black wagon, like a hearse, and luring the girls to the mills with tales that "the work is so very neat, and the wages such, that they can dress in silks and spend half their time in reading." It was such fanciful accounts of the comforts of mill work that brought Margaret Foley, who afterward achieved some small fame as a sculptor, from her home in Canada to Lowell in the late eighteen-thirties. She had been led to hope that she could study art while working, but in a short time discovered that she must choose one or the other.

At the end of their journey to Lowell, the newcomers were met with either the patronizing or compassionate glances of those who were already used to the ways of the town. Harriet Hanson Robinson wrote that the country girls presented a very curious sight "when the large, covered wagon arrived in front of a 'block' on the corporation. . . . Dressed in various and outlandish fashions . . . with hair done up in . . . almost impossible ways, and with their arms full of bandboxes . . . of all sizes, many of them being large enough to hold quite a wardrobe." Some of the bandboxes, obviously home-made, were covered with calf-skin, hair and all, to which a card was attached with the name of the owner, generally an old-fashioned New England name that made the townsfolk smile: Samantha, Trifeny, Elgardy, Florilla. Not all of the girls were confident at first; some were frightened and homesick, some were exhausted and weak from days of traveling. A couple of young girls who came down from Canada had had their transportation paid by the agent, but, not having been informed that the trip would take several days, had not provided themselves with money for food. The word "homesick" was always to remind Mrs. Robinson of the "picture of a young girl with a sorrowful face and a big tear in each eye, clambering down the steps at the rear of a great covered wagon, holding fast to a cloth-covered bandbox, drawn up at the top with a string, on which was sewed a paper bearing the name of Plumy Clay." Their speech was said to be almost unintelligible, with a nasal Yankee twang superimposed on the English and Scotch spoken by their forbears.

Once they had reached Lowell the girls discovered quickly
that although they had been "important personages" in their own
home circle, they were "nobodies" in Lowell, as one operative
wrote in an article of advice to candidates for mill work. Another girl wrote that on first entering a factory boarding house,
she found the rooms strange and comfortless, the women cold
and unsympathetic. But many came directly to the boarding
house of a neighbor from home, and the first shock of strange-
ness was cushioned by a friend who knew the ropes and understood how homesick a new hand could be.

After a period of adjustment, the new girl found living and
working conditions at Lowell quite tolerable, at least in the early
stages of its development, the mills being distinctly superior to
those in other industries, and the boarding houses comparing
very favorably with the standards of lower and middle-class
homes. In the minds of European observers who were not familiar
with Owen's experiment at New Lanark, they were of course
exemplary, and it is not to be wondered at that foreigners saw the
boarding houses in a picture-postcard view. Although Americans
were more inclined to notice the less agreeable aspects of the
scene, there were rhapsodists among them also who described
the mill girls as being surrounded by creature comforts. In a
novel called *The Factory Girl, or Gardez la Coeur*, by Dr. Ariel
Ivers Cummings, published in 1847, the interior of a boarding
house is portrayed with all the trappings of wealth and culture:

It was a small apartment, neatly furnished. In the center was a small
table, covered with various books and periodicals, embracing in the
variety some of the gems of literature. On one side of the room was
a small secretary, and a library of well-selected and choice volumes,
indicating that the mind of those humble operatives was not forgotten.
The floor was covered with an elegant carpet, and a polished grate
contained a few coals only, as it was but the beginning of autumn.
Writing materials were at hand, and indeed every part indicated more
the *sanctum* of the poet, or the *studio* of the artist, than the residence
of the operative. An air of neatness prevailed, and in possession of such

a home, and an agreeable companion, who would be unhappy or discontented?

The new girl found no sanctum of the poet or studio of the artist in her boarding house, but she found something that served better the purposes for which she had come to the mills. The boarding houses were a woman's world. At most periods there were almost three times as many women as men employed in Lowell, and in the cotton mills the proportion was almost five to one. The corporations provided dwellings where they could eat and sleep, from fifteen to thirty girls occupying houses of different sizes. These were leased to respectable widows—often well-bred and somewhat cultivated—who in return for low rental terms agreed to keep the property clean and see to it that the girls obeyed the company's rules. The frame buildings were painted every spring at the company's expense, an operation that evoked many admiring comments. It was not for philanthropic reasons that this was done, but as a measure of simple upkeep, to maintain property values.

The design of the boarding houses was what we are accustomed to call "colonial," of which so many examples line the greens of New England villages. They were dignified, barnlike structures, two and a half stories high, with a chimney at either end. The first room as you entered on one side or the other of the double house, was the dining room, so that the girls could slip in and out, to and from their meals, without loss of time. An English commentator, Patrick Shirreff, who visited Lowell in 1833, was impressed to find that the diet called for fresh meat at least twice a week, and that the girls were not obliged to eat salmon more than once a week. But whether fresh or cured, meat was part of every meal in America at that time, breakfast, dinner, and supper providing approximately the same menu. Some girls complained that they were forced to gulp down their meals in the utmost haste in order to get back to the mills in time, but every foreigner observed that such were the eating habits of almost all the citizens of the United States, so this condition could hardly have been peculiar to Lowell.

The dining room of the boarding house served as the only common or sitting room where the operatives could congregate of an evening or entertain their friends. Here the presence of quantities of chairs needed at mealtimes could hardly have made circulation easy. The girls also murmured about the

peddlers, candy and newspaper boys, shoe-dealers, book-sellers, etc., breaking in upon the only hours of leisure we can call our own, and proffering their articles with a pertinacity which will admit of no denial. That these evening salesmen are always unwelcome, we will not assert, but they are too often inclined to remain where they know they are considered a nuisance.

Phrenologists and charlatans of all kinds came, too, offering their services at bargain prices or trying to sell tickets to lectures on every conceivable subject.

While there were too many chairs in the dining room for comfort, there were too few in the bedrooms for normal requirements. As a rule each bedroom contained three beds, with accommodations for six girls. Considering that these rooms held not only six "chattering females," sometimes as many as eight, but their bandboxes and trunks, their dresses and shawls and aprons and pelerines, their books and papers and writing materials, not to speak of nuts, cake, and fruit for late snacks, it is not surprising that they were looked upon as crowded and stuffy. Harriet Martineau found the lack of privacy very disturbing.

In America, where space is of far less consequence [than in England], where the houses are large, where the factory girls can build churches, and buy libraries, and educate brothers for learned professions, these same girls have no private apartments, and sometimes sleep six or eight in a room, and even three in a bed. This is very bad. It shows a want of inclination for solitude, an absence of that need of it which every healthy mind must feel, in a greater or less degree.

It is doubtful that the girls themselves were as distressed by this as Miss Martineau, with her comfortable English middle-class background. Certainly the New England farmhouse bedroom was scarcely better ventilated or less cramped than those at Lowell. Harriet Hanson Robinson, for example, speaks of having slept in one bed with her mother and three brothers when she was seven years old, sometime before her family moved to Lowell.

Crowded though the boarding houses may have been, they were far from being slum dwellings. The sense of responsibility that the corporations felt for their employees was reflected in other ways; for example, all the operatives were vaccinated against the smallpox at the companies' expense. Each boarding-house keeper, by the terms of her lease, was required to set aside one bedroom as an infirmary, and in 1841 the former house of Kirk Boott was converted into a hospital for the use of the operatives. Running water was installed in the tenements and in the mills, each of which boasted of sinks for washing, "a most healthy, as well as cleanly operation," said an English visitor, "which is punctually attended to before every meal, soap being supplied for this purpose by the proprietors." The price of board also included laundry charges, but that this meant anything more than bed linen and towels is neither clear nor probable. Essential services were provided, but anyone who suspects that there was any mollycoddling of the operatives misreads the character of the New England textile magnates.

In order to maintain the living and working standards set up by the corporations, regulations were drawn up for the instruction of operatives and boarding-house keepers. Since it was the responsibility of the local agents, superintendents, and overseers to see that the rules were observed, varying interpretations were evolved by different personalities. In the course of time some were imperceptibly relaxed, while a whole new body of conventions grew up, having the same or more force than the printed regulations.

The printed regulations were considered "a part of the contract with the persons entering into the employment" of the various manufacturing companies, and were virtually the same all over New England in the boarding-house mills. An agent touring the countryside for mill hands would be most likely to have a copy of these rules with him in order to reassure the parents of prospective operatives that their daughters would be housed in clean quarters under the supervision of respectable matrons, that they would be paid regularly, that they would be protected from association with depraved persons, and that they would be able to attend church on Sunday. While the girls looked forward to being independent, neither they nor their relatives would have considered the change favorably had they not ascertained that all possible safeguards existed to preserve their good repute. After the first quarter of the nineteenth century the stern Puritanism of earlier days had been somewhat relaxed, perhaps by this very trend of young women to leave home to earn a living, but still it was not possible then, any more than it is today, to leave large groups of girls to their own devices without any superintendence. As far as obligatory church attendance was concerned, it would have been just as difficult to deny those New England operatives access to Sunday worship as it would be to deny their descendants access to the movies. The rules governing the conduct of the operatives were merely the standards of behavior of young women all over New England at this time. The corporations, that is to say, were not offering ideal conditions but bowing to the *mores* of the period.

The regulations of the Lowell Manufacturing Company, which we may take as typical, stated the duties of overseers and boarding-house keepers as well as of the operatives. The overseers, in command of their respective rooms in the mills, were to see to it that everyone was at work on time, and to grant leave of absence if they saw fit. The boarding-house keepers were to "be answerable for any improper conduct in their houses," and were "not to permit their Boarders to have company at unseasonable hours"; they were to keep their premises clean, to reserve a room in each house for the use of the sick, and not to expose the company property to the risk of fire. It was required of the operatives that they live in the boarding houses of the corporation, go to church regularly, be at home by ten o'clock in the evening. More significant rules, however, concerned the terms of employment, whereby the girls agreed to remain at the mills for twelve months, and to give two weeks' notice of their intention to leave. In return the company bound itself to only two conditions: to pay wages once a month, and to have the employees vaccinated against the smallpox at its own expense.

The regulations of the Lawrence Company went into greater detail about what was expected of the operatives.

All persons employed by the company [they stipulated] must devote themselves assiduously to their duty during working hours. They must be capable of doing the work which they undertake, or use all their efforts to this effect. They must on all occasions, both in their words and in their actions, show that they are penetrated by a laudable love of temperance and virtue, and animated by a sense of their moral and social obligations.

This moral poppycock might have been insulting to the self-respecting girls of New England, had they not been accustomed to hearing such pompous platitudes from their earliest years. "A laudable love of temperance and virtue," forsooth! "All persons must devote themselves assiduously to their duty," as if habits of industry had not been drilled into them by primers and parents and preachers!

But to be "animated by a sense of their moral and social obligations" is one of those ample generalities capable of many interpretations, depending on the point of view of the interested person. The Cocheco Company at Dover, New Hampshire, was more explicit about the "moral and social obligations" of its operatives, who were specifically enjoined against engaging "in any combination whereby the work may be impeded; if we do, we agree to forfeit to the use of the Company the amount of wages that may be due us at the time."

Gradually the corporations lost interest in some of their "moral police" schemes, as they were called. Regular church attendance by the operatives fell off toward the forties without any measures being taken to implement the rule. In an early issue of the *Lowell Offering*, Harriet Farley deplored this unfortunate situation:

> That there are many in Lowell who do not regularly attend any meeting . . . is . . . true. . . . There are many who come here for but a short time, and who are willing for a while to forego every usual privilege, that they may carry back to their homes the greatest possible sum they can save. . . . Pew rent, and the dress which custom has wrongly rendered essential, are expenses which they cannot afford.

Later Miss Farley suggested plaintively that the rule should be enforced or else dropped from the list of requirements.

The regulations about seemly behavior were equally difficult of enforcement. In the forties there was talk of a band of young bloods in the town called "The Old Line," store-clerks and the like who practiced the arts of seduction and brought about the downfall of many an innocent country maiden. The mischief was said to have its origin at balls, where men mingled freely with the girls in the dance—always of questionable propriety —after which the unsuspecting females were taken to "infamous places of resort," and not returned until daylight. But such incidents were rare, for although the corporations could not impose seemly behavior by fiat, other pressures in the same direction were more effective. The "moral police" powers supposed to have been exercised by the corporations were, in fact, assumed by the operatives themselves. One corporation apologist indicated this when he wrote that a girl merely "*suspected* of immoralities, or serious improprieties of conduct, at once loses caste." Her fellow boarders, he added, refused to live in the same house with her or work beside her.

Robert Owen had said of his experiment at New Lanark: "I can make manufacturing pay without reducing those whom I employ to misery and moral degradation." Nathan Appleton might well have made the same boast. Like the manufacturers at Lowell, Owen had created a complete industrial community on a humane basis, and by the same autocratic, paternalistic methods; as G. D. H. Cole says, he enjoyed ordering men about for their own good. But while these similarities are striking, there are even more arresting differences between Lowell and New Lanark. Owen raised the standards of his operatives, while the Lowell magnates simply met them. And, more important still, Owen's paternalism was progressive, directed toward a constant improvement of living and working conditions. He branched out into fields such as education, to which the American manufacturers were indifferent. The paternalism of Lowell was static; it not only refused to recognize changes in the times, but in the pursuit of higher output and profits it permitted a steady deterioration of the standards that had been Lowell's pride.

To effect greater output and maintain profits a whole new series of rules and regulations grew up and took on binding force even though they were not written down. Hours of labor were lengthened, the number of machines to be tended was increased, the piece rate was reduced, and the pace of the work was stepped up year by year. Since it was up to the overseers to see that the demands of their superiors for more and more cloth was met, they developed a code that governed every phase, every moment, of the operatives' activities from the time they entered the mill in the morning until the closing bell rang. In order to forestall any insubordination by the girls, the most important regulation of all was devised, sometimes written, sometimes implied, but more strictly enforced than any of the formulas for moral behavior: a definite prohibition against any attempt to improve wages, hours, and working conditions. A girl who betrayed any yearning for such changes was marked as a morally reprehensible character, lacking in the sterling qualities required of one who would work in the "philanthropic manufacturing college" of the Boston textile magnates.

Chapter V

WORK AND PLAY

AT NINE o'clock in the evening in Lowell the curfew rang; at ten, according to the corporation regulations, the keys were turned in the locks of the boarding houses, and the town was still save for the occasional ringing of the print-yard watchman's bells. A new girl might fall asleep to its faint music.

In the morning she was wakened by bells again, tolling now from the mill towers along the canal, and her day advanced to their command. To the middle-class townspeople they were "saucy bells," a charming accompaniment to one's daily tasks, but some of the operatives thought otherwise when all the belfries in all the various mill yards broke out in a wild clamor. "Up before day, at the clang of the bell—and out of the mill by the clang of the bell—into the mill, and at work, in obedience to that ding-dong of a bell—just as though we were so many living machines," wailed the character Ellen Collins, in a story written by one of the Lowell mill girls.

During the winter it was still dark as the girls followed the bells into the mills, tripping along smartly, for lateness was not tolerated without some very good excuse, and

> At the stroke of five
> All laggards saw the gates against them swing.

Once within the mill, a newcomer was often terrified by the moving belts and wheels, the whirling and twisting and clapping of machine parts, the trembling floor. The thunder was so great that you could see lips moving without hearing a word unless the head of the speaker almost met yours. Lucy Larcom, who went to work at the age of eleven, never overcame her dislike of machinery. "The buzzing and hissing and whizzing of pulleys and rollers and spindles and flyers around me often grew tiresome," she wrote many years later.

Despite the seeming confusion and the deafening clatter, however, the process performed by the machinery to make cloth was essentially the same as that carried on by many of these New England girls in their farm homes, using wool or flax, or sometimes even cotton. Here, however, the various stages of the manufacture were minutely divided, each being entrusted to different types of machinery in the care of different operatives. First the bales of upland cotton were opened, the various grades mixed and freed from dirt or seeds. This fluffy mass was then sent through a "lapper," which flattened the cotton into sheets and wound it round a cylinder. The "laps" then passed through the carding machine, which by means of teeth in sets of rollers drew the fibers in the cotton parallel and pulled out the knots. A drawing frame then brought the fibers together and twisted them into a loose "roving," which was again wound on cylinders and sent to the spinning room. There the cotton was drawn out in strands and twisted into thread of the required degree of fineness. This thread, being wound on spindles, was ready for the woof; the thread for the warp needed to be sized and brushed before it could be used in the weaving room.

Weaving, although mechanized, was more like the domestic process than spinning, which was subdivided into so many operations. Nevertheless, it required more skill and was better paid. To the newcomer it was equally confusing. "At first the sight of so many bands, and wheels, and springs in constant motion was very frightful," wrote one girl in a story recalling her first days at Lowell.

She felt afraid to touch the loom, and she was almost sure she could never learn to weave; the harness puzzled and the reed perplexed her; the shuttle flew out and made a new bump on her head; and the first time she tried to spring the lathe she broke out a quarter of the threads. It seemed as if the girls all stared at her, and the overseers watched every motion, and the day appeared as long as a month had at home. . . . At last it was night. . . . There was a dull pain in her head, and a sharp pain in her ankles; every bone was aching, and there was in her ears a strange noise, as of crickets, frogs and jews-harps, all mingling together.

This was a far cry from the "romantic sport" many beginners had expected to find in mill work. It was possible, however, to grow accustomed to it; the second day for the raw operative was a little less trying, the various parts of the machines less mystifying, and the clatter more easily ignored, until at length when the novelty wore off the only problem was one of monotony.

Most of the New England girls attained a high degree of skill, and it was soon established that the amount of education they possessed bore a direct relationship to their efficiency as workers, operatives who had been schoolteachers, for example, earning 17¾ percent more in wages than the average, and 40 percent more than the few illiterates. One agent found that he could speed up the machinery from 12 to 15 percent without damage to the product by using better-educated girls, while another was obliged to return to the production of a coarser type of material when illiterate immigrants replaced them. In Lowell's heyday, the Merrimack Mills alone boasted 124 girls who had formerly taught school, and 25 or 30 more who were planning to teach during the summer months. The other mills could have supplied 350 more schoolteachers.

The girls were encouraged to acquire skill quickly, for they were paid by the piece, and although the corporations paid $1.25 a week for their board; the beginners' rate of 55 cents a week above board and lodging offered little incentive to an ambitious young woman. The wages varied, according to speed and skill, some few operatives earning as much as $4 per week above board.

But as Seth Luther, a stern critic of the corporations, said: "If *one girl* earns, by extra exertion, $4 per week, it is blazed abroad, from Maine to Mexico, that the *girls* in that mill earn from $1 to $4 per week." The truth of the matter was that over a period of about forty years, regardless of increased production per worker, variations in the cost of living, smaller or larger returns on the investment, the average wage never fell much below nor rose much above $2 a week beyond board. In order to keep wages constant, it was necessary for the corporations to reduce the piece rates every time another notch was taken in the pace of the work. Whenever this was done, there was generally a temporary drop in the pay each girl received until she had adapted herself to the speed-up.

To the new girl, nevertheless, her first pay-day was the highlight of her experience. Unlike the Slater and other Rhode Island mills, which paid in scrip for goods bought at company stores, the Lowell mills paid in cash monthly. There was sometimes, to be sure, a delay of from a week to ten days in settling accounts, during which period girls who were leaving the mills for good found that some of their savings were consumed in living expenses, but this complaint was not general. The wages at the Lowell and other boarding-house mills were also somewhat higher than those paid in the smaller textile centers. In the early days, moreover, the fact that payment was in cash made earnings seem larger than they were, for in the farm homes from which the girls came actual money was a great rarity.

True to their New England training, the girls were thrifty souls. In one factory, with an annual payroll of about $60,000, Patrick Tracy Jackson wrote in 1832, the savings of the girls over a period of four years amounted to $26,400, or "eleven percent on the whole amount of wages paid." In the forties the sum deposited by the girls in the Lowell Savings Bank had risen to about $100,000, but the number of operatives who kept an account was only about 900. Harriet Farley, in an article in the *Offering*, said, however, that many more girls sent their savings back to their families or friends, or to banks near their own homes.

But if the wages at Lowell were higher than elsewhere, some of this advantage was lost through the temptation to spend money on female finery. Dozens of shops had sprouted in the shadow of the mills, almost before the mortar was dry, to tempt the girls into parting with their cash. As early as 1830 Isaac Minot advertised in the *Lowell Mercury* that he had on display: "Ladies Superior Work Boxes, Needle Books, Macassar Oil, Cologne Water, Rowland's Kalydor, for beautifying and preserving the complexion, Battledores, Dominoes, Fancy and Ring Top Inks and Sands," while George Flagg informed the public that he kept constantly on hand "every description of Silk Goods, Merino-Thibet, Raw Silk, Brocade, Crape and Valencia Shawls, Thread and Bobinet Laces and Lace Veils." Several other trades-men announced that they carried "Fancy Goods" of every kind, including tortoise-shell combs, jewelry, etc. It needed a strong-minded young woman to put aside all her money for the mort-gage on her father's farm when such alluring objects were dangled before her eyes. From the remark of Captain Basil Hall in 1827 that *all* the operatives wore high tortoise-shell combs at the back of their heads, one gathers that certain fashions of the town were considered imperative, even though they must have made quite a hole in the earnings of these country girls.

The comparatively high cost of board and the greater skill of older workers made the use of child labor unprofitable, and hence there were few children working in the Lowell mills, in contrast to the family mills run by Slater. In this respect the boarding-house mills resembled Robert Owen's factory at New Lanark, where the practice of working pauper children to death, long considered the cornerstone of the British textile industry, had been abandoned in favor of well-paid adult labor. Two of the most distinguished women who ever worked in the Lowell mills, however, Lucy Larcom and Harriet Hanson Robinson, began their factory experience before they had reached their teens. The mothers of both were boarding-house keepers, who, as widows with large families of their own to provide for, needed even the pittance earned by these youngsters to make ends meet.

The work assigned to them as "doffers" was not hard, consisting of changing the bobbins on the spinning frames every three-quarters of an hour. In the intervals the little bobbin girls frolicked around the great rooms "teasing and talking to the older girls, or entertaining ourselves with games and stories." On long winter afternoons the doffers would gather in a corner and while away the time by singing old ballads like "Barbara Allen," "Lord Lovell," "Captain Kidd," or "Hull's Victory."

The amount of freedom the children enjoyed and the kindliness with which they were treated depended of course on the overseer in the mill where they happened to be working. "When the overseer was kind," wrote Harriet Hanson Robinson, "they were allowed to read, knit, or go outside to play." She herself was often granted permission to go home during the day to help her mother with the housework at the boarding house. Tales of cruelty to child workers such as were commonly told of Slater's mills were not current in Lowell.

In the early years at the boarding-house mills the overseers were not required to drive any of the operatives at their work. One overseer who had formerly been a sea captain said to Harriet Hanson Robinson's mother, "I should like to rule my help as I used to rule my sailors, but so many of them are women I dare not do it." A domineering attitude was all the more difficult for most overseers to assume as the girls were well-bred and often better-educated than their superiors within the mill. Outside of working hours, at church, and elsewhere in the town, overseers and operatives frequently met on terms of equality. Throughout the thirties and forties, however, as orders for greater and greater output came from the Boston counting houses, the relations between overseers and operatives soured gradually, the overseers becoming more harsh and exacting, while the girls grew resentful and suspicious.

In the early years the work was not oppressive, and the long hours were mitigated by the opportunity to rest from time to time. A strong country girl tending only one loom for twelve hours a day might find the work wearisome but not exhausting.

But after 1830 not only were the hours lengthened to almost twelve and a half hours a day (longer in summer, when the work was done by daylight, and shorter during the winter months, when artificial illumination was necessary), but the number of machines assigned to each operative was increased steadily, with an accompanying nervous strain.*

Perplexing as the scene was to a girl newly arrived from the country, the appearance and ventilation of the interior of the mills at Lowell were strikingly superior to the general conception of a factory at that period. Except for the first process of cleaning and mixing the cotton, which was done in small detached buildings in the mill yard, most observers found the working rooms unusually clean and bright. The walls were whitewashed, and in some rooms there were potted flowers growing in the south windows. Captain Basil Hall in 1827 was deeply impressed by the ventilation within the mills, but by the forties even favorably inclined visitors acknowledged that the air was extremely stuffy. A certain amount of moisture was necessary to keep the threads from snapping, and this was obtained by spraying steam in the air. Even in the heat of summer most overseers kept the windows nailed shut to maintain the proper degree of humidity, while in the winter hundreds of oil lamps made the heat almost suffocating. In this atmosphere the operatives put in a day of over twelve hours, on the average, six days a week, twelve months in the year. The summer working time which amounted to as much as fourteen hours a day, spent for the most part on their feet, must have been especially trying to young women of rural extraction.

And yet up to the middle forties they remained in the mills an average of four and a half years,† after which they returned home permanently, either to be married, or to engage in other

---

* Nevertheless, it must be remembered that conditions worsened only by contrast with the easy gait of earlier times; compared with the speedup of today the mills would seem to have been run at a plodding pace even in the forties.

† Caroline Ware points out that this is a lower rate of turnover than exists in the textile industry in the present century. But while there are more replacements in the mills today, this is probably because of transfers from one mill to another, not because the operatives give up factory work altogether.

work. To one French visitor in the forties, Léon Faucher, this
pattern of recruiting temporary factory labor from the farm
regions seemed to offer an admirable solution of a basic industrial
problem, even though the analogy he drew might have seemed
odd to the Lowell girls:

In a citizens' army like that of the French, only the cadres have a
permanent character. The period of enrollment is limited . . . in
such a way that a large part of the population serves under the colors.
Why should it not be the same in manufacturing? When we have
made agricultural labor the permanent occupation and factory labor
the temporary occupation of simple workers, we shall have taken a
great step forward.

Freed from their labors and their enforced silence by the closing
bell, the girls exploded into shrill chatter and nervous laughter
as they swarmed into the street at the end of the day. The solemn
observance of the Sabbath was a welcome break in the succession of busy days, but aside from this there was little opportunity
for healthy renewal. There were only three holidays a year:
Fast Day, which came sometime in March or April, the Fourth
of July, and Thanksgiving. Starved for a sight of the country,
most of the operatives spent their days off wandering over the
surrounding hills, or took passage on the "square-sailed gunda-
low" described in Whittier's poem, for a day's sail down the
Merrimack to Newburyport or Salisbury. Every Fourth of July
the Sabbath School Union, to which many of the mill girls belonged, held a parade and marched to Chapel Hill, where the
only beautiful grove of trees within the town was to be found.
After a picnic lunch the participants listened to long speeches
by the ministers of the various congregations and drank lemon-
ade with abandon.

Aside from these three (unpaid) holidays, there were occasionally intervals of a couple of days when the mills were shut
down for repairs to the canals or the machinery, during which
time the corporations continued to pay the girls' board. In addi-

tion, many operatives returned home for a few weeks or months during the summer, some to teach school, some to take a vacation at their own expense. But this can hardly have been as common as it was supposed to be, since most mills obliged the girls to sign a contract for a full year's work. It was a happy circumstance for the corporations that most of the girls had homes in the country to resort to when they were worn out or ill, for during their period of recuperation they were not a charge upon the taxpayers, chief among whom were the mill owners. As one admirer of the Lowell system remarked:

Employing chiefly those who have no permanent residence in Lowell, but are only temporary boarders, upon any embarrassment they return to their country homes, and do not sink down here a helpless caste, clamoring for work, starving unless employed, and hence ready for a riot, for the destruction of property, and repeating here the scenes enacted in the manufacturing villages of England.

There were other festivities in the course of the year, which, although they involved no time off from work, must have been relished no less than the holidays, especially the "lighting up" and "blowing out" balls on March 21 and September 21, which celebrated the kindling and extinguishing of the lamps in the mills. But from the fact that these balls were held at the Stone House, an inn of no great size, it is safe to assume that only a small proportion of the operatives were able to attend. The Lowell Company, however, once gave a ball when its plant was enlarged, providing a picnic supper and music for 5,000 guests. One hundred sets of dancers were said to have appeared on the floor in a cotillion at once. A contemporary described the event in the fulsome terms of a society reporter:

The whole scene presented a *coup d'oeil*, which in extent and brilliancy could not be surpassed. Every one in this vast assemblage, clad with extreme neatness, and conducting themselves with good breeding and decorum, afforded but another proof of the superiority and refinement of the class of operatives in Lowell.

Too much dancing by the operatives, however, was frowned upon. In the thirties Miss Martineau saw a notice posted up in a Waltham mill warning that any young lady who attended dancing school would be discharged. If the girls spent all their evenings hopping about, the overseer explained, either their work or their health would suffer. He added, however, that he was about to organize fortnightly dances for the girls, under the supervision of his wife and himself.

Most of the operatives passed their evenings in less glamorous pursuits: in sewing, reading, studying, "going upon the street" (paying calls or going shopping, not a moral offense), fetching the mail—as always in such situations a mad crush—attending church meetings or lectures. The focal social center was naturally the boarding house. Through close association at home, and very often at work, the girls living in one house developed a strong feeling of solidarity. This grew up the more naturally as they were often either friends or relatives to begin with, or the friends of friends and relatives. They shared their advantages, helped one another with studies, exchanged books and papers, and when a girl was absent on account of illness or for some other urgent reason, several housemates combined to make up the work-time she had lost. If the boarding house happened to contain girls from different backgrounds, they counted it a piece of good luck to be able to learn something from one another that could not be gained without wide travel. In Harriet Hanson Robinson's house, for example, the fourteen occupants, of whom three were members of the family, represented nine different religious sects, including the Catholic and Mormon.

As was common all over the country at that period, religion was the main preoccupation of the young women of Lowell in their leisure hours. Their religious loyalties were only increased by sharp denominational differences in the community. After the foundation of Saint Anne's, Baptists, Congregationalists, Catholics, Universalists, Methodists, Unitarians, and offshoots of these established religious societies. Twenty-two churches were built before 1850.

There was such a passion for church building that some of it took on a highly speculative character. In 1837 one Elder Thurston, a Colonel Sellers type, induced some of the mill girls to withdraw their savings from the bank to help build the Freewill Baptist Church. When the money raised proved insufficient, Thurston drew again on the credulity of the operatives, who cheerfully supplied him with more funds without interest. Later the church building was attached for debt, and the smooth elder was convicted of fraud, although the verdict was afterward set aside by the Massachusetts Supreme Court.

Religious fervor in the operatives was not dampened by such incidents, which were, after all, comparatively rare. Most of the ministers were earnest, hard-working, poor in worldly goods, but with a high sense of their calling. To many girls living far from family and friends the church was the only substitute for home, and the minister the only person who could take the place of a parent. Outside of the crowded boarding houses social life was concentrated in church activities, which came to include many interests not narrowly religious. The ministers would entertain groups of girls at the various parsonages, join their picnics, visit them at work, or in their boarding houses, suggest books for them to read, advise them in their studies. It was in meetings for "self-improvement" in the vestry of the Universalist and First Congregational Churches that the idea of a mill girls' magazine was first conceived. One of the ministers helped several girls to have their books published.

Many of the girls found diversion enough in church activities, but large numbers had an insatiable thirst for knowledge that had to be gratified through other channels as well. "All over New England," as Van Wyck Brooks writes, "not only in the 'Literary Emporium,' as Boston was called . . . there was a passionate interest in self-culture." Young girls rose at five in the morning and started the day by reading two or three books of *Paradise Lost*. Not all the Lowell mill operatives yearned for culture, but certainly a larger proportion of them than any comparable group of young women even in New England. Ranging from sixteen to twenty-five years old, they were young enough to be susceptible to new ideas, and keen enough to take advantage of educational opportunities from which they had been cut off in their farm homes. In the remote villages whence they had come, seminaries for female education beyond the common school were almost nonexistent and, besides, whatever money their families could afford for such purposes was usually applied to the further schooling of their brothers. By working in the mills some of the operatives were able to assist in this worthy cause and, although none were so self-opinionated as to point out the obvious injustice, a young woman helping to support a brother at an academy or college was all the more greedy for the intellectual nourishment available at Lowell.

Like every town of some size in New England at the time, Lowell had its Lyceum and Institute for the Diffusion of Useful Knowledge, where capsules of information were dispensed at a low fee, a season ticket for a series of twenty-five lectures costing only fifty cents in the 1840's. People who frowned upon the theatre as an immoral pastime went freely to the lecture hall and surrendered themselves to the histrionics of the country's most gifted speakers, in the belief that they were being uplifted rather than diverted. For the country girls at Lowell, however, it must have been extraordinarily interesting to hear a talk by the former President of the United States, John Quincy Adams, to listen to the baroque periods of Edward Everett, or the golden voice of Ralph Waldo Emerson, uttering "his majestic intuitions of truth and justice." "The more original the speaker, and the more profound," wrote Theodore Parker, himself a lecturer of no mean ability, "the better he is relished."

Two-thirds of the lyceum audiences in Lowell in the thirties and forties were mill girls. Harriet Martineau, who was in Emerson's party when he lectured at the Mechanics' Institute on historical biography, declared that she saw no signs of weariness among them.

There they sat, row behind row, in their own Lyceum—a large hall, wainscoted with mahogany, the platform carpeted, well lighted, provided with a handsome table, desk, and seat, and adorned with portraits of a few worthies; and as they thus sat listening to their lecturer, all wakeful and interested, all well-dressed and ladylike, I could not but feel my heart swell at the thought of what such a sight would be with us.

One lyceum lecturer at Lowell described his audience as being made up almost entirely of factory girls, most of whom were reading books when he entered the hall. While he was giving his talk he observed that they all took notes very diligently, like so many earnest college students. Having paid for the lecture series, the girls were far too thrifty to sit passively by without making the most of their opportunity.

But more interesting by far than this ready-made culture were the girls' own efforts to educate themselves. They were not to be outdone by young ladies more fortunately situated who read two or three books of *Paradise Lost* before breakfast. They were otherwise engaged before breakfast, to be sure, since they put in an hour or two of work at the mill before they took the first meal of the day, but no sooner were their machines running smoothly than they surreptitiously drew forth their books to have a go at their studies. This had to be done with extreme circumspection, for reading on factory time was strictly against the rules and caused the discharge of many girls who refused to comply. Some operatives thought that the Bible might escape censure, but the factory regulations were no less severe in this case, and the overseers' desks were usually stacked high with confiscated copies of the Scriptures.

Some were determined nevertheless to have their way and hold their jobs too. Lucy Larcom as she grew older used to tear pages out of the Bible and smuggle them into the mill, or cut verses out of newspapers and paste them up over the sides of the window frame near which she worked. She and her sister Emmeline, working side by side, would recite poetry to each other by the hour. At length Lucy's frustrated desire for an education drove her to give up her work as a spinner and take a job in the cloth room of the mill, where she earned less money but was allowed to read as much as she liked.

For solid reading matter the girls drew on the lending libraries, which were said to be a very potent factor in drawing country girls to Lowell. The demand for books was so great, even though the cost of library membership was fairly high in relation to earnings—25 cents a month—that when local supplies proved insufficient, almost the whole circulating library of Dover, New Hampshire, was moved down to Lowell to meet the need. Serious girls like Lucy Larcom and her sister Emmeline read serious books: the works of Milton, Thomas à Kempis, and Bunyan, Locke on *Human Understanding*, Combe on phrenology, Abercrombie's *Metaphysics*, Carlyle's *Heroes and Hero Worship*, George Borrow's *Bible in Spain*, Frederika Bremer, and Macaulay. Few Lowell residents would have agreed with Sir Anthony in Sheridan's *The Rivals*, when he told Mrs. Malaprop that "a circulating library in a town is a tree of diabolical knowledge." And yet Harriet Hanson Robinson confessed that her reading was not always on an exalted plane. She had a girlish weakness for Gothic novels, and secretly devoured *The Mysteries of Udolpho*, *The Castle of Otranto*, and *Abellino, the Bravo of Venice*.

Current periodical literature also had a wide audience among the mill girls. In one of the smaller boarding houses, eleven different newspapers and magazines were taken regularly, while five others were borrowed as they appeared. Some of these were religious journals, or ladies' magazines, with poor literary fare, but the *Edinburgh Review*, the *North American*, *Blackwood's*, and *Graham's Magazine* were frequently purchased and passed from hand to hand. In this way the works of contemporary writers such as Dickens, Irving, Poe, Tennyson, and Whittier grew as familiar to the operatives as they were to the most educated class in America at that time.

This indiscriminate reading soon led the more thoughtful girls at Lowell to pursue a more organized course of study. It must be remembered that during this period the work-day averaged twelve and a half hours, and that meals and the time needed for walking back and forth between the mills and boarding houses took up perhaps another two hours. Allowing eight hours for sleep, there could hardly have been more than an hour and a half to two hours in the day free for all the various activities in which the operatives were engaged. It is therefore all the more remarkable that some of them should have set aside some of their few moments of leisure for evening classes. At least one group was formed, and a teacher procured, for a group of girls who wanted to study German. They met in a boarding-house parlor that contained a piano, and the lesson was often topped off with a concert. Lucy Larcom became proficient enough at German to translate Richter, Herder, and Jean Paul, and made a valiant attempt to render Goethe and Schiller into English verse. The minister of the First Congregational Church conducted a class in ethics, using Wayland's *Moral Science* as a textbook. Other girls took up the study of French, went to art classes, or formed botany clubs.

Perhaps all this was absurd, but certainly no more so than the kind of education then considered appropriate to women of much higher station than these mill girls. Harriet Martineau said that the formal education of all American women at that time was a harmless exercise, with its emphasis on religion and languages, for in reality they were intended to "consider marriage as the sole object in life, and to pretend that they do not think so." True as these charges were in general, they had less point in regard to the Lowell mill girls, who had to weigh every moment applied to studies against the repose and diversion they had earned by long hours of work. A few of them were so determined to acquire more learning that they spent only half the year at the mills and the other half at a local seminary for young women, anticipating by a hundred years the practices of the progressive colleges of today.

While many observers were awed by the spectacle of factory hands studying ethics and translating Goethe, there were a few supercilious critics who scoffed at these ambitious girls. Mrs. Trollope, with characteristic British middle-class snobbery, dismissed them as the *"précieuses ridicules* of industry." A distinguished French literary critic, Philarète Chasles, considered the Lowell mill girls interesting enough, as a phenomenon, to serve as the subject of one of his famous lectures, but charged them with "some little pedantry . . . as in Geneva and Glasgow. These moral factory girls are wrong in becoming *blues*," he declared roundly.

It is not evident from any of the writings of the mill girls, either when they were working at Lowell or later, that they considered themselves "blues." All of them were literate, and a large proportion of them were of the type nowadays to be found in colleges all over the country. Of these a certain number were studious, and among the studious it was inevitable that fifty or sixty should have a literary bent and seek some form of creative expression. Probably the ratio of literary girls to the whole group of operatives was not very different from the ratio of would-be writers to the entire student body of our colleges today.

The charge of pedantry arose from the fact that during the forties there appeared a little magazine containing poems, tales, and essays written exclusively by the mill girls at Lowell. Novel as this venture seemed to Europeans, it was almost a commonplace in New England, where hundreds of literary-religious journals flourished briefly in the first half of the nineteenth century, their pages filled with the outpourings of obscure "authoresses" in every country village. The operatives' magazine at Lowell was a more modest enterprise, developing naturally from the "self-improvement circles" in which the more contemplative girls had grouped themselves.

Several self-improvement circles had originally grown up under the direction of the ministers as part of church activities. Others had been formed in the various boarding houses, where some thoughtful older girl would organize classes to make up to the younger ones for their interrupted schooling. Gradually these circles broadened to include other boarding houses, met regularly, adopted a constitution, and, as they grew larger, became identified with the improvement circles attached to the churches. One such group was formed at the Lawrence Corporation as early as 1836, and in 1843 there were at least five distinct groups. Only two of them, however, became known as literary circles: the one attached to the Second Universalist Church and the other connected with the First Congregational Church. Around 1840 each group published an occasional issue of a magazine, but after a year or two both were merged under the name of the *Lowell Offering*, which appeared more or less regularly for several years, depending on its financial situation.

Busy as they were with work, with church activities, reading and study, the girls at Lowell were not insensitive to the currents of thought in the world outside, and held some independent views on the intellectual fashions of the day. Lectures on Fourierism and Brook Farm made some ardent converts, but the majority were repelled by the idea of phalansteries. Far from perceiving any Utopianism in Fourier's philosophy, they felt that it offered no improvement on a cotton mill, in that "an undue share of labor would naturally fall to those who had already contracted the working habit," as Harriet Hanson Robinson wrote. Phrenology and Mesmerism had their passing vogue in Lowell as in the rest of the country; there were girls who believed with Miller in the imminent end of the world, others who followed the vegetarian diet prescribed by Graham, some who took up the water cure, and a daring few who adopted the dress of Mrs. Bloomer. Large numbers gave money liberally to western missions, $1,500 having been raised in the mills in one day for this purpose. Many of the girls were ardent advocates of liberal causes such as the anti-slavery movement, or the defense of Kossuth and the Hungarian liberals.

For the majority of the operatives, however, the greatest personal change that came about as a result of their stay in Lowell was a change in manners and modes. After a short time in the bustling city, the unintelligible Yankee twang of the up-country girls became less harsh and grating to the ear. Experienced girls acted as mentors to the new arrivals, as when the painfully refined Harriet Farley entreated them to drop such unladylike phrases as "By the Lord Harry!," "I vow," and "Creation!" Eager to conform, the newcomers soon learned the "city way of speaking."

The girls would have been monstrously unfeminine had they held out against the "city way of dressing." Rustic maidens were struck with awe when they saw women wearing "velvets and furs and plumes and bugles and all" in the streets of Lowell. The city ladies wore rouge, too! Many country girls came to the mills for the express purpose of buying clothes, after seeing the smart attire worn by Lowell operatives on their visits home. In "Abby's Year at Lowell," a story that appeared in the *Offering*, Abby resolves to become an operative after two friends just returned from Lowell have been to see her; "ever since the visit of the Slater girls, with new silk dresses, and Navarino bonnets trimmed with flowers, and lace veils, and gauze handkerchiefs, her head had been filled with visions of fine clothes." In another story, "Evening before Pay-Day," the skinflints and old maids are teased unmercifully for not spending their money on finery.

"Pray, what shall you get that is new?" one girl asks of another as they reckon up the money due them.

"Oh, I shall get one of those beautiful new damask silk shawls which are now so fashionable. How splendid it will look!" answers her friend. Girls who now for the first time in their lives could dispose of a certain amount of cash for clothing were quick to discard the cambric bonnets, the calico or homespun woolen dresses that marked them as provincials.

And yet since most of the operatives were bent on saving a large part of their wages, even their new apparel tended to be simple and restrained; in the prevailing fashion, but not *le dernier cri*. Ruffles and elaborate ornament were not common, either because of the cost or because they constituted a cleaning problem.

A few wore gold watches or pencils for special occasions, but the early mill girl, said Harriet Hanson Robinson, was not "always suffering for a breast-pin." What made their costume distinctive was its excellent fit and trim cut. This unaffectedness probably gave the girls a look of greater chic than many of the bourgeois women of the time could boast, for of all periods of dress the middle nineteenth century was one of the worst. Josiah Quincy, who accompanied Jackson on his visit to Lowell in 1833, observed with satisfaction that the operatives wore no headgear on that occasion, "for the bonnet of the period was a hideous monstrosity, a proper companion for that masculine section of stovepipe."

The appearance of the girls in the street was the subject of much admiring comment.

They sally forth in the morning [wrote Miss Martineau] with their umbrellas in threatening weather, their calashes to keep their hair neat, gowns of print or gingham, with a perfect fit, worked collars or pelerines, and waistbands of ribbon. For Sundays and social evenings they had their silk gowns, and neat gloves and shoes.

Many of the girls had but one dress beside their working clothes, which they protected from too hard wear by a large apron. Putting a good face on the matter, like so many women before and since, Emmeline Larcom said it was "a great saving of trouble" to have so few clothes, "because she was not obliged to think what she should wear if she were invited out to spend an evening." Lizzie Turner, a contributor to the *Offering*, recalled in later years that she was one of a group of ten girls

who one summer had each a purple satin cape for street wear. These were trimmed with black lace, and this, with a small-figured, light Merrimac print, constituted our walking costume. We had nothing better for Sunday wear; and as we walked along, sometimes all together, I am sure that it never occurred to one of us that we were not as well-dressed as any lady we met.

And so with the acquisition of new clothes, new friends, and new interests, the operatives attained a dignity and poise that idle young ladies of fashion might have envied. Women who had always been dependent on their menfolks for a living became transformed after they began earning their own money. Confidence replaced the country girl's shyness; she held her head up and looked you straight in the eye; she sang at her work and walked with a springy step. The air of breeding about the Lowell girls amazed at least one visitor from abroad who wrote: "They commonly walked arm in arm without displaying levity. Their general appearance and deportment was such that few British gentlemen, in the middle ranks of life, need have been ashamed of leading any one of them to a tea-party."

Such airs and graces as these factory operatives possessed, however, probably seemed more remarkable to a foreigner than to a contemporary American. The daughters of yeomen farmers, they had never been members of "the lower classes," as factory workers in the Old World were and as factory workers were destined to become later on in the century even here. The aplomb that came to them after a few months in Lowell was due rather to a sense of financial independence and richer social intercourse than to any rise in station. They were not ashamed of working, as they stated repeatedly. "To be able to earn one's living by labouring with the hands, should be reckoned among female accomplishments," wrote one of them in the *Offering*. Since as a group they were continually being renewed from the country, where whatever class prejudices they might have had were middle-class prejudices, they resisted proletarianization to the end.

If when they first came to Lowell they had expected the work to be easy, they were soon disabused. To tend machines for twelve and a half hours a day was not strenuous, but it was tiresome work, and as the years passed its accelerating tempo made it more and more of a strain. Curiously enough, the more sorely they were pressed, the more eagerly they strove for knowledge and education, as if in resistance to the anaesthesia of purely mechanical labor. But there was a limit to how far they could go in this direction. A time came when the speed-up threatened to drain them of all energy for intellectual pursuits after working hours. They did not yield to this tamely, but fought a dignified campaign to regain their old standards. Once this was lost, they did not renew the struggle. They simply retired from the scene.

The same type of girls who went to work in the Lowell mills were to be found in the other boarding-house mills in New England during the second quarter of the nineteenth century: at Taunton, Chicopee, and Amesbury in Massachusetts; Manchester, Dover, and Nashua in New Hampshire; and at Biddeford and Saco in Maine. But Lowell was the exhibition town, the showcase; here the standards were higher, and the girls more articulate and prepossessing. The publicity value of such an unusual labor supply was exploited by the corporations to the fullest extent. Visitors from afar were invited to go to Lowell as guests of the textile magnates to see for themselves the superior young women whose intelligence and probity was supposed to be a direct consequence of superior working conditions. In return for various courtesies, no prominent visitor ever withheld his bread-and-butter letter in the form of a puff.

The fact that the girls were exceptional was used by the manufacturers to sell their wares, justify their profits, obtain higher tariffs, and, in a way, improve their own social position. If a Lucy Larcom read Milton and translated Schiller, after a long day in front of the machines, did it not follow that Nathan Appleton was a sage, a man of honor, and a public benefactor?

Chapter VI

THE BOSTON ASSOCIATES

> Chief among the civic virtues of
> this people is that steadfast cupid-
> ity that drives its citizens, under
> pain of moral turpitude, to ac-
> quire a "competence," and then
> unremittingly to augment any
> competence acquired.—VEBLEN

THE two most important families in the textile development of
New England sprang from precisely the same thrifty and laborious farm environment as did the operatives who tended their
machines. Like the Lowell girls, the Appletons and Lawrences
were avid for knowledge, God-fearing, and enterprising. Curiously enough, New England had been largely settled by religious
heretics who had formerly been cloth-makers in Britain, the
weavers and spinners of East Anglia. The racial and cultural
background of operatives and investors was hence indentical, and
whatever differences were to grow up between them were purely
economic.

As time went on economic differences created a gulf that could
not be bridged by cultural homogeneity. As is so often the case,
the acquisition of wealth did not give the magnates a sense of
security, but seemed to call for more and more accumulation,

which in turn only created greater anxieties. To lull their own unconscious fears, and give their power some moral sanction, the Appletons and Lawrences were in the habit of pretending that their money-making was merely incidental to nobler purposes. On the other hand, wages that provided little more than subsistence prevented the operatives from becoming unrealistic. However long the hours, the Lowell girls admitted frankly that they bore with them only because they needed the money. But, except for the forthright William Appleton, the investors preferred to pose as men dominated by unselfish, patriotic, or charitable impulses. In describing the character of Abbott Lawrence, for example, Nathan Appleton wrote: "Mr. Lawrence was always ready and foremost in supporting measures which promised benefit to the public. He was a large subscriber to the various railroads projected for the concentration of trade in Boston, and this from a feeling of patriotism rather than the expectation of profit." Since most of Lawrence's business projects were located in and around Boston, and might be expected to suffer if trade were deflected from the city, this distinction between "patriotism" and "expectation of profit" would seem fairly academic.

Robert Winthrop, in paying tribute to Nathan Appleton, wrote in a similar vein:

The very investment of so large a part of his property in domestic manufactures had many of the best elements of charity; and the satisfaction which he derived from the success by which he was himself enriched, was not a little enhanced by the consideration that he had been the means of affording employment to so great a number of operatives, of both sexes, who might otherwise have failed to obtain work and wages.

This pose of the lord of the manor distributing largesse to the deserving poor was ingrained in the ruling caste of Boston to which the Appletons and Lawrences were admitted. These two families were not born to the purple, but pushed their way into the charmed circle by dint of acquiring huge fortunes, embracing the proper views on public questions, and contracting suitable marriages. It was easier for them to do so than for others who followed them since this upper crust had only recently begun to solidify, and had not yet turned into the petrified tribal system it was soon to become. After the Revolution, "the most important people" in Boston, the old families of wealth and power, had followed the British Army back to England. Into the vacuum thus created in Boston society came the leading figures of other Massachusetts towns, such as the Lowells and Jacksons, Cabots and Higginsons, who had stood with the patriots against the mother country. There was no one to challenge the position they took at the head of affairs. The wealthiest men of New England, they had inherited or made their money out of merchant shipping to the far corners of the world, in ships they themselves either owned or chartered. The farther their ships sailed, the greater the profits and the prestige; hence the Northwest fur trade and the East India trade conferred glory not attainable by mere operators in the coastal traffic, or by shopkeepers, commission dealers, and auctioneers who also pretended to the name of merchant. As in England, where only the ownership of land tilled by others gave a man the right to call himself a gentleman, so in Boston only a shipping fortune permitted the assumption of authority in politics, business, or fashion.

In politics the Boston group were staunch Federalists, despite the Whig label they assumed in the thirties and forties. If, as someone has described it, Federalism was a state of mind, it was one that made few concessions to democratic nonsense. The Boston Federalists were Anglophile, aristocratic in temper; they believed in a strong centralized government, like Hamilton, with whom they were associated in the Essex Junto, but only if that centralized government were controlled by themselves or their friends. When the Embargo and the War of 1812 interfered with their shipping business they not only defied the law and traded with the enemy, but also plotted secession at the Hartford Convention. Twenty years later, these very separatists, now engaged in manufacturing, viewed South Carolina's nullification of the tariff with the utmost alarm. Love of their country and its institutions swelled in their breasts only when their influence in the administration was strong. On Lord Morpeth's visit to Boston in 1841, for example, he heard his hosts say frequently that the Constitution of the United States was a failure, particularly in the matter of electing fit men to the presidency.

Such were the standards of right-thinking in Boston among men of wealth and power, and no one could expect to penetrate into the upper levels of society unless he accepted those canons, and possessed a fortune suitable to them. Wealth and birth were not enough, for a man like David Henshaw, whose background and affluence were the equal of any member of the Boston élite, was excluded because of his opposition to the aristocratic principle. The upstart Appletons and Lawrences, however, had views so pleasing to the ruling caste that the doors of the citadel could not be kept closed to them, even though their first winnings had been garnered as mere shopkeepers and importers. By associating himself with Francis Cabot Lowell in the Waltham project, Appleton found an opening wedge, which he and the Lawrence brothers widened into a breach when they began investing their money in solid Boston banks. As a next step Nathan Appleton made himself extremely popular with the great Boston nabobs when he induced them to join him in financing the textile mills at Lowell, especially since manufacturing was to bring them rich profits just as the cream was being skimmed from merchant shipping. Thomas Handasyd Perkins, Harrison Gray Otis, Ebenezer Francis, the Dwights, the Eliots, the Lymans, and the Searses condescended to receive on equal terms this astute promoter. Only diehard free-traders among the merchants, those who had not been invited into the cotton manufacture, referred slightingly to the Appletons and Lawrences as "shopkeepers."

But with the admission of the Appletons and the Lawrences to their tight clique, the ruling caste of Boston closed up its ranks again to newcomers, and consolidated its leading position in the business affairs of Massachusetts and most of New England. The solidarity of this controlling group was maintained not only by their common economic interests, but also by a series of blood relationships and intermarriages bewildering even to the most impassioned genealogists in the clans themselves. Mrs. Ella Lyman, who was a daughter of John Amory Lowell, the most active member of that family in the textile business after the death of Francis Cabot Lowell, wrote in her journal that since her mother and father were third cousins, she was amused as a child to discover that she was fourth cousin not only to her brothers and sisters, but also to herself! John Amory Lowell's first wife, however, had been an even closer relation, his first cousin, which lends color to Percival Lowell's sardonic comparison between the Buddhists of Japan and the Brahmins of Boston, who, as he said, "make themselves objectionable by preferring their immediate relatives to all less connected companions, and cling to their cousins so closely that affection often culminates in matrimony, nature's remonstrances notwithstanding." *

Fortunately for his social credit, Nathan Appleton could claim a distant kinship with Francis Cabot Lowell, who, when he set up the Boston Manufacturing Company, invited his Cabot relatives, his wife's brothers, the Jacksons, and the husbands of his sisters to join in the venture. Lowell and Jackson said to Nathan Appleton "that they wished to confine the stock in as few hands as possible." No mere stranger was to be allowed to buy his way in. Dwights and Eliots, Lymans and Otises, Amorys and Searses, who made heavy investments in the textile mills, were all related by marriage. T. G. Cary, treasurer of the Hamilton Company, was the son-in-law of Thomas H. Perkins; T. Jefferson Coolidge, later treasurer of the Boott Mills, was the son-in-law of William Appleton. Abbott Lawrence helped to overcome his handicap as an outsider by marrying into one of the more prominent families in Boston society, politics, and finance.

This clannishness resulted in a further concentration of financial power through the control held by the Boston magnates over the estates of widows, minors, and spinsters who belonged to the leading families. Trust funds were set up for the survivors, and

* Quoted from Greenslet, *The Lowells and Their Seven Worlds*, p. 348.

investments made in their behalf, not only to assure them of a competence but also indirectly to give the executors of their estates continued voting rights in the various enterprises in which those executors were directors, very much the way voting rights are held by the philanthropic foundations set up in our time by the Rockefellers and the Mellons.

With the power over these funds held in comparatively few hands, the Boston Associates could make investments at pivotal points in the economy, or command enough capital for far-flung enterprises. Besides their practical monopoly of the merchant shipping of that area, these men dominated the textile industry in northern New England. Lowell was the most successful of their ventures in the manufacturing field, but it was only one of a host of others that dotted the New England landscape. In addition to their million-dollar corporations at Waltham, Chicopee, Holyoke and Lawrence in Massachusetts, Dover, Manchester and Nashua in New Hampshire, Biddeford and Saco in Maine, they held a majority interest in some smaller mills at Peterborough, Somersworth, and Salmon Falls in New Hampshire, and Taunton and Amesbury in Massachusetts. Outsiders might occasionally acquire stock in corporations that developed a town or set up a mill, but the associates of the Boston group exercised complete control over policy and finances.

Even though few critics of the time raised the cry of monopoly, it is possible to discern what can only be called monopoly practices by examining the lists of directors of the different corporations. The community of interest was perceptible in a most complicated series of interlocking directorates that assured most of the textile industry in New England of a uniform policy. For during the period we have under discussion it was never assumed that one of the mills financed by the Boston Associates should compete with any of their other enterprises. Each new factory set up at Lowell, as described earlier, was designed for the manufacture of a different type of material, unless the market was large enough to permit duplication of product.

Even when disagreements arose, either out of personal vanity or differences in technique, and new mills were projected, members of the old guard were sure to be down as principal stockholders in the proposed corporation. In 1830, for example, after Samuel Batchelder left the Hamilton Company in Lowell, of which he had been the agent and manager since its inception, he went upon 'Change in Boston the next day and was showered with offers to start a new company. The York Manufacturing Company of Saco, Maine, was immediately set up to take advantage of Batchelder's great technical skill; and whom do we find on the board of directors but one of the Lawrence brothers, a large investor in the Lowell mills, and Edmund Dwight, principal stockholder in the Chicopee and Taunton mills!

The community of interest between the various mills financed by the Boston Associates extended to the commission houses that held an exclusive franchise as sales agent for the product of one or more of the mills. The largest of these, the James W. Paige & Company, was formed in 1828 by the principal stockholders in the Waltham, Merrimack, Hamilton, and Appleton companies, and naturally handled the entire output of these companies. Amos and Abbott Lawrence had the exclusive selling agency of the Lawrence, Tremont, Suffolk, Boott and Massachusetts mills, while J. K. Mills held the exclusive selling agency for the Chicopee and Taunton factories. But the partners in the Paige Company, A. & A. Lawrence, and the J. K. Mills Company were at the same time large stockholders or directors in the textile corporations employing the "rival" commission houses, so that there was no reason to fear ruthless competition at this level either.

Because of a multiplicity of interests, as well as personal preference, the leading textile magnates lived in Boston, in the choice society of like-minded men and their intellectual satellites, far from the obnoxious sights and smells of a busy factory town. Lowell was their pride and their pet, but none of them could bring himself to settle there. Nevertheless, as noted earlier, someone had to be delegated to "see to things" on the spot in the interests of the stockholders. The chief executive officer of the corporations in charge of finances was generally the treasurer, who was often the senior partner of the selling agency, with headquarters in Boston. Just beneath him in rank was the agent, or manager, who lived at the site of the mills, and was in actual charge of production. The Boston magnates freely confessed that these agents were

gentlemen selected for their offices, not on account of any mechanical knowledge or experience in manufacturing, their training before their appointments having been wholly mercantile or professional, but for their executive ability, their knowledge of human nature, their ability to control large numbers of operatives and *their social standing*. [My italics.—H. J.]

In other words, they were chosen in accordance with the aristo-cratic principle, from Boston's leading merchant families. Since this practice needed to be rationalized, it was described as prefer-able to selecting the agent from among men with technical manufacturing knowledge (not related to the Boston families) because the very fact of long experience might lead to too great "conservatism" in methods! Patrick Tracy Jackson, therefore, became agent of the Boston Manufacturing Company at Wal-tham and, when other business interests called him away, he was succeeded by John Amory Lowell. Kirk Boott, son of another Boston merchant, was appointed agent of the Merrimack Com-pany at Lowell, and on his death was succeeded by George W. Lyman, a man with impeccable family antecedents. Samuel and William Lawrence were likewise agents for their brothers at the Middlesex Mills in Lowell. None of these agents, except possibly Kirk Boott, came to his post with any training in mechanical principles. Talent for machinery, wrote Abbott Lawrence to the General Agent of the Essex Company, "is a commodity that can be had, and is usually very cheap at what the world calls 'too high.'"

By 1850 the Boston capitalists controlled about one-fifth of all the cotton spindleage in the United States, but this figure does not do justice to their importance in the industry, since they formed a solid bloc with all their corporations, while their competitors were disunited and for the most part produced a different type of goods. Important though their textile interests were, however, they had many other profitable undertakings, more or less tied in with these, all of which were conducted along the same lines of comity and mutual helpfulness.

To men with capital to invest, golden opportunities in real estate, banking, railroads, and other subsidiary businesses were constantly presenting themselves at the beginning of the nineteenth century. It was in connection with a real estate venture that the term "Boston Associates" was first used, when fifty merchants formed a group to buy Boston property which was to be kept exclusively in their own hands. As the city grew in size and population, the rise in real estate values was therefore certain to benefit the right people. Later on, their property holdings in the towns where they purchased large tracts of land for factory development also brought handsome returns to members of the circle. The choicest plot for commercial development in Lowell, for instance, was sold to Patrick Tracy Jackson by the Locks and Canals Company at a figure so low he could hardly escape making a good deal of money on the transaction when he sold it.

Besides cotton mills and real estate the Associates controlled all the banks of Boston save one, the Commonwealth, Henshaw's institution, which failed after they refused credits to it during the crisis of 1837. The position of Boston bankers was very strong owing to the fact that during the War of 1812 a large part of the specie of the whole country had flowed there. In 1818 they formed the historic Suffolk Bank, which became a sort of clearing house for the issues of small country banks whose paper was highly uncertain and variable, anticipating by a hundred years some of the practices of the Federal Reserve System. This enterprise was profitable enough to pay an average dividend of 10 percent a year, and a stock dividend of 33⅓ percent in 1838, when most banks were tottering. Useful as the Suffolk System was, its self-assumed powers severely limited the business activity of other groups, who called it the "Holy Alliance," or the "Six-tailed Bashaw." One of the Boston Associates, William Appleton, as head of the Boston branch of the Bank of the United States, held a tight rein on the flow of credit from that source as well. Scarcely anyone, Henshaw moaned, received discounts from the Bank of the United States in Boston but "the millionists," as he called them, the Appletons, the Lawrences, and their friends.

As a corollary to the banks, insurance companies were also tightly held by the group of Boston merchant-textile magnates. One of their insurance companies, the American, paid out 187 percent of its capital in dividends in the ten years between 1815 and 1825, not a bad return in a very uncertain post-war period. The textile manufacturers were, however, so aware of the high cost of insurance premiums to other people that they insured themselves against fire in the early years at Lowell by funding a certain percentage of their profits to this account, and in 1835 formed the first mutual fire insurance company in the country. But their most impressive accomplishment in the insurance field was the Massachusetts Hospital Life Insurance Company, founded in 1818, which soon dropped the life insurance business and concentrated on the handling of trusts and annuities. The funds it controlled could therefore be used to supply capital to new undertakings planned by members of the group. Whether the Massachusetts Hospital Life controlled the textile corporations, as a critic charged later on in the century, or vice versa, is immaterial, for the founders and directors of both were identical.

The Boston Associates also extended their power over the railroad system of New England from its earliest infancy. One of the first railroads in the country, the Boston & Lowell, was financed by prominent textile mill investors, P. T. Jackson, John Lowell, George W. Lyman, and William Appleton; while others among the group did the same for the Boston & Providence, the Boston & Albany, the Boston & Maine, the Connecticut River, the Nashua & Lowell, the Taunton Branch, and the Western Railroad. Writing in 1856 to argue for an increase in rates, William Appleton described the stock ownership of the railroad companies in terms that might just as fairly have been applied to all the business interests of the Boston group:

By comparing, we find that the proprietors of the more than twenty millions of capital invested in the roads terminating in the Boston area are, to a very considerable extent, the same. We find that many of the stockholders have invested in all, or nearly all, the roads, which would show that any rivalry between companies was in all cases against the interest of the proprietors.

All this concentration of financial power in ships, mills, real estate, banks, insurance companies, and railroads required more than a casual attention to politics on the part of the group. Before the late forties, their wealth-given right to govern Massachusetts and the other New England states was rarely challenged. On the principle that government needed their firm hand in the direction of affairs, they cheerfully served in the General Court or the Congress at Washington, even at some sacrifice to their personal comfort. More often, however, the men who represented their districts were handpicked, reliable, experienced politicians who needed no briefing on the proper stand to be taken on issues concerning the interests of the Boston Associates. Edward Everett and Robert Winthrop served them faithfully in Congress; Daniel Webster was all to them that could be desired, even though his price came pretty high. When manhood suffrage was extended by the abolition of property qualifications, the Associates maintained their political hegemony in Massachusetts by coming to terms with the groups they most despised, using all the demagogic devices evolved by their opponents, and spending money liberally to gain their ends. The power of government to threaten or increase their profits was too great for them to allow it to fall into unfriendly hands without a struggle. In 1845 Theodore Parker described their tactics unequivocally:

This class is the controlling one in politics. It mainly enacts the laws of this state and the nation; makes them serve its turn. . . . It buys up legislators. . . . It can manufacture governors, senators, judges to suit its purposes, as easily as it can manufacture cotton cloth. . . . This class owns the machinery of society . . . ships, factories, shops, water privileges.

Leaders in finance, industry, and politics, the Boston magnates exercised no less autocratic control in the fields of religion, education, and moral values. "This class," thundered Theodore Parker, "is the controlling one in churches. . . . It buys up the clergymen . . . who will do its work." Most of the Boston nabobs were of the Unitarian persuasion, and resented deeply any idealistic fervor that challenged their comfortable and undemanding creed. Even among themselves too great outward piety marked a man off from his fellows. Thus William Appleton, a powerful lay figure in the Episcopal church, had to submit to no little teasing by his associates because he spent what seemed to them an exaggerated amount of time at religious services. It was therefore natural that they should be outraged by Theodore Parker's outspoken criticism of the merchant and manufacturing aristocracy. After Parker had with difficulty obtained his first parish in Boston, Thomas Gold Appleton said to one of his parishioners, "We will make Boston too hot for you." In the same spirit Amos Lawrence refused in 1842 to give any more money to the Harvard Divinity School because of the "bad influence" of Ralph Waldo Emerson, Theodore Parker, and Orestes Brownson in that institution. "Mr. Emerson is an amiable man," he wrote in answer to an appeal for funds, "but who . . . would choose him to instruct them in the ways of wisdom?"

The ways of wisdom were so clearly the prerogative of the Boston Associates that their advice and aid were sought constantly in matters pertaining to education, both public and endowed, in the lower and the higher branches. Though the Lawrences and Appletons who founded the family fortunes had not attended Harvard, they gave considerable sums of money to the college, a gesture which, although it was probably furthest from their minds in making the gift, conferred a certain social cachet on the donors, as well as earning them honorary degrees. Amos Lawrence also made generous bequests to Williams College, and all the Lawrences gave money to the academy in their native village. Colleges in the West also received help from the Boston merchants, although their benevolence was not wholly disinterested, for, as Edward Everett wrote when pleading for funds for a newly established college in Ohio, "They ask you to contribute, to give security to your own property by diffusing the means of light and truth." *

At the lower levels of education the Associates were not quite so generous. Their opposition to the improvement of the public schools of Lowell has already been discussed, and while Abbott Lawrence proclaimed his love of popular education in a widely publicized letter to W. C. Rives, his performance went no further than individual acts of charity to necessitous students or certain favored schools. It was in vain that Horace Mann pleaded with the Appletons and Lawrences for financial aid in his important work of raising standards of Massachusetts public education by setting up teacher training schools and improving school buildings. None of them would give him a cent. But Amos Lawrence did present "a marble image of himself" to the Mather School of Boston, whose needier pupils he had long patronized.

The character and moral standards of the Boston Associates were neither so high as they pretended nor so low as their enemies charged. That they worked long hours at their business, particularly in their youth, and often, out of habit, to their dying day, is beyond question. They were faithful husbands and doting fathers; they were kind to poor relations. Their scale of living was solidly comfortable, but neither ostentatious nor vulgar, far from the display of American millionaires of a later era. And yet a certain uneasiness is perceptible both in their professions

---

* Three-quarters of a century later Henry Lee Higginson put forth the same notion when asking a friend to give money to Harvard. "Educate," he wrote, "and save ourselves and our families and our money from mobs!"

of faith and in their actions; on the one hand, they took pride in their achievements and their wealth, and, on the other, they were aware of Heaven's reputed inhospitality to rich men. In his last year in college, Amos Lawrence's son admitted frankly that "to be rich would be my delight"; but four years later he noted in his diary that he was still worried about whether he would be rich enough and also good enough in religious matters. "I am constantly though not excessively anxious about something. . . . I am uncertain in case I should die whether I shall be happy." It was this gnawing uncertainty about the next world no doubt that led to the princely charitable bequests for which the Boston magnates became known, atoning perhaps, as Emerson said, for the manner of acquiring their fortunes by the manner of expending it. They knew that their conduct in life and business had been irreproachable, but did God know it?

Lest their contemporaries misunderstand the values by which they were animated, they formed a kind of mutual admiration society, every member of which glorified the deeds and character of his business associates and stressed the high standards of their occupation. In his memoir of Abbott Lawrence, Nathan Appleton describes the merchant's code in terms befitting a consecrated priesthood:

The merchant makes no claims to benevolence or patriotism as his ruling motive in trade; all he professes is absolute and undeviating justice. The morals of trade are of the strictest and purest character. It is not an uncommon opinion, that there is a laxity in the mercantile code, which looks with indulgence on what are called the tricks of the trade. It is not so. Whilst the direct object of all trade is gain, individual benefit, not the slightest prevarication or deviation from truth is allowable. There is no class of men with whom the Christian rule, of doing to others what we may expect or require in return, is more strictly demanded than amongst merchants. Mercantile honor is as delicate and fragile as that of a woman. It will not bear the slightest stain. . . . It is thus found, by experience, that integrity is almost uniformly the accompaniment of success, as it always is of character.

This passage was so "nobly self-revealing" that on Appleton's death a few years later his own eulogist, Robert C. Winthrop, was obliged to quote it in its entirety in praise of Mr. Appleton himself.

Against such sweeping claims it might seem irreverent to recall that Henry Lee, a reputable merchant of Boston, was not above suggesting to a correspondent that a worthless cargo of musty rice could be sold to the French army or navy. Nor did Lee shrink from the thought of bribing French customs officials to avoid paying a high duty on sugar. In a letter to his associates at Calcutta in 1810, Patrick Tracy Jackson advised that they spread false news of the international situation in order to obtain higher prices for his wares. On the other hand, the Lawrence letter-books over a period of years, while full of customers' complaints about short measure and imperfect goods, contain equally numerous promises by the Lawrences to make up for any losses suffered. Both brothers, however, showed uncanny skill at worming their way into enterprises and taking them over in times of economic distress. The mortgage was a powerful lever in their hands; the bankruptcy lists provided them with fascinating reading matter.

Such practices were common enough for Theodore Parker to have traced quite a different picture of the merchant from the one so lovingly drawn by Nathan Appleton:

> The bad merchant still lives. He cheats in his trade, sometimes against the law, commonly with it. . . . He over-reaches the ignorant; makes hard bargains with them in their trouble, for he knows that a falling man will catch at a red-hot iron. . . . No interest is illegal if he can get it. He cheats the nation with false invoices, and swears lies at the custom-house.

In considering the justice of Parker's charges, however, it must be remembered that he was not only a "radical," but also a man who was inclined to draw extremely nice moral distinctions. What Parker called cheating was the norm in a business society, in reality nothing but smart business practice, without which enterprising men could scarcely rise above their fellows.

If the New England merchant fortunes were not based on cheating, neither were they the result of thrift and Christian conduct. Fortunes are made by selling something at a slight or perhaps great increment over the cost, whether food, land, clothing, necessities or luxuries, it matters not, so long as the markup is high enough or the turnover great enough. "We have some ambitions," the Lawrence brothers wrote to a business connection in England, "to buy as cheap and sell as high as our neighbours."

Buying cheap and selling dear was, then, the key to success, and yet it must not be supposed that success could be won without considerable intelligence, experience, and practical knowledge. The Boston merchants were astute enough to learn the needs of the market, the various sources of goods, the price the traffic would bear, the prices demanded by their rivals. Their grasp of local, national, and world affairs enabled them to foretell and take advantage of broader trends, political and sociological, that might affect their business, while at the same time they paid strict attention to matters of detail and administration, even when that was delegated to others.

Business training such as this was invaluable when they embarked on textile manufacturing. They knew where raw cotton could be bought and at the most advantageous price through having handled it in quantity for export; they knew the demand for cotton cloth better than anyone in America through having imported it from England and India; they had the business experience to estimate manufacturing costs before a spadeful of earth was turned for a new mill.

Once they were well launched in the manufacturing of textiles, moreover, their financial inventiveness led to developments of great consequence. Until comparatively recent times the United States was a debtor country, with little capital of her own available for large enterprises. Up to the War of 1812 only the merchants of New England were farsighted enough to pool their resources in order to set up a huge industry with million-dollar corporations. And yet as that part of the industry under their control grew, more and more capital was needed, taxing the means of the most prosperous men in the group.

To speed up the flow of capital the Boston Associates resorted to several new expedients; first, they drew other merchants, such as Perkins and the Lawrences, into the manufacturing hierarchy; second, they took large cash dividends out of the longer-established corporations; third, when these dividends were insufficient, they issued huge stock dividends—in other words, watered the stock; and fourth, they gradually sold stock in the older corporations to the "public," or to as much of the public as could claim some connection with the merchant families. If a "desirable" investor did not wish to put down all the cash required for his shares, he could always get a loan on it from one of the Boston banks or insurance companies.

Commonplace as these devices may seem nowadays, and capable of so many abuses, they were quite new in the first half of the nineteenth century, and they served the very useful purpose of developing an important section of American industry, with American capital, at a time when no other means were available to that purpose. It was no idle boast on Abbott Lawrence's part, when, again and again, he spoke of his interest in developing the country's resources. The Boston Associates had a flair for large ventures and the technique for carrying them through.

Their contribution to American industrial and corporate processes had lasting effects on the economy of the nation. The large corporation, with millions in capital, held or dominated by a small group of financiers, with interlocking directorates that minimize competition in the industry, as first explored by them, has by now become a prominent feature of our economic structure. It was the Boston Associates who first hit upon the scheme of delegating the actual management to agents and underlings, with all the features of absentee ownership as we know them today. In the mills they set up, concentrating every stage of manufacture at one site, and eventually under one roof, we find the original model of what is now a distinguishing feature of the American scene, the great mass-production industries. Even in the handling of labor problems they were far ahead of their contemporaries, especially in the beginning of the period dealt with here, offering standards and services that were on many grounds comparable to those sought by trade unions today.

And yet despite the novelty and originality of their undertakings, the Boston Associates were far from being mere speculators, who enjoyed taking risks. Everything was calculated in advance, sometimes with such caution that the entrepreneurs, like Francis Cabot Lowell, were amazed only to find that the profits exceeded their estimates. "Keep in shoal water," was one of the favorite maxims of the Boston merchant. In urging Timothy Wiggin to come in on some deal, Amos Lawrence assured him that he would take *no risk*. Whenever real risk was involved, as in the establishment of the Beverly Cotton Factory, or the construction of the New England railroad system, the state was invited to share in the venture. If the profits were large enough to attract public attention, the Boston merchants justified their gains by describing the enterprise as a gamble, but this form of self-deprecation was solely for public consumption. To entertain the notion that an Appleton or a Lawrence would engage in a financial transaction dependent upon chance or unknown contingencies would be to misjudge the breed.

Certain accidents of history, to be sure, gave scope to the talents of these strategically placed businessmen: such as the fact that this was a new country with boundless resources and powers of expansion; that as a people we were profligate with our natural wealth; and that the nineteenth century saw the spread of the industrial revolution to the whole of the Western world. But the Boston merchant capitalists did more than embrace these opportunities, they joined forces to embark on massive undertakings, and then, closing up their ranks, held off all outsiders and newcomers. There was an exclusiveness, a sense of the realities of class power, an assumption of aristocratic privilege among the Boston Associates that for over half a century made their control of New England life almost absolute—even though they alone did not own all the mills, all the banks, all the commission houses, and all the insurance companies in the area. As a group they were stronger than any individual manufacturers or bankers, stronger than any rival group of operators, for there was rarely dissension among them. Through the preponderance of their weight in business, finance, and politics, they were effectually monopolists.

Writing from observation in the early 1830's, when the textile industry was still young, de Tocqueville expressed the opinion that

the manufacturing aristocracy which is growing up under our eyes is one of the harshest which ever existed in the world . . . the friends of democracy should keep their eyes anxiously fixed in this direction; for if ever a permanent inequality of conditions and aristocracy again penetrate into the world, it may be predicted that this is the channel by which it will enter.

Fortunately for their peace of mind, the Boston merchant-manufacturers were no friends of democracy, and could contemplate the process described by de Tocqueville not only without concern but also with some satisfaction at having contributed in large measure to this significant turn of affairs in their century.

Chapter VII

LORD OF THE LOOM

> Money-making having become a
> virtue, it was no longer con-
> trolled by the virtues, but
> ranked *with* them, and could be
> weighed against them when any
> conflict occurred.—JAMES TRU-
> SLOW ADAMS

IT IS not difficult to understand the reverence, almost amounting
to awe, with which Nathan Appleton was regarded by his contemporaries. In the first place, he owned a large fortune, sure
sign of a well-spent life. But his merits went beyond mere
shrewdness in business affairs; he was well informed on public
questions and widely read in many other fields, even a bit of
a theoretician. In this last role, close as he was to the industrial
revolution sweeping the United States during his lifetime, he was
able to stand off and measure some of its more general implica-
tions in a manner that throws considerable light on the patterns
of American life today.

For all his wealth, his private life was unostentatious; he was
kind and generous to his family, warm and considerate to his
chosen friends. His son Thomas Gold Appleton once told a
friend that he loved his father as much as five hundred fathers

were ever loved. None of Nathan's children dared mention anything sad at the dinner table, lest their tender-hearted parent spoil the soup with his tears. Men esteemed him even when they disagreed with him violently. Appleton's break with Charles Sumner on the slavery question caused Sumner to be ostracized by Boston's leading social lights, but except on this one subject Sumner never qualified his admiration of the textile magnate, referring to him always in letters to Franz Lieber as *Nathan der Weise.*

His upright private character sanctified Appleton's great wealth in the popular mind; as a corollary his great wealth made virtues common to many men and women seem more than life-size. To add to his stature, his means of acquiring a fortune were held unexceptionable by the standards of his time. Yet the methods of acquisition of an Appleton cannot always bear too careful scrutiny. Some men must pay to enable another to grow rich; those from whom he buys, those to whom he sells, and those who labor for him all contribute their mite, however small individually, to the piling up of a fortune. Collectively too the people can be made to deliver; legislation either to exempt favored interests from taxation or to impose taxes on others for their benefit works in the same direction. After a long acquaintance with the commercial society of New England, Emerson wrote that "the ways of trade are grown selfish to the borders of theft, and supple to the borders (if not beyond the borders) of fraud." In his eulogy of Lawrence, which was also an apology for his own life, Appleton hotly denied Emerson's imputation, attributing to the merchant a most delicate sense of honor, but the facts of his own business career, no less than Lawrence's, lend truth to the charge.

Whatever our ethical appraisal of these business methods may be today, there can be no doubt that Appleton made a personal contribution to the nation's industrial development, giving it the special form and direction it has maintained up to our own time. The possibilities of the modern corporation for large-scale manufacture, with a capitalization running into the millions, had first been exploited by Francis Cabot Lowell. Nathan Appleton, however, brought the corporate device up to date by showing how finance capital in banks and insurance companies could be drawn upon in the early stages of incorporation, how stock holdings could be dispersed by selling out to the "public," and control retained by divorcing management from ownership. What he was able to do for textiles, others did for steel, automobiles, and hundreds of other products manufactured today. For better or worse, that is the pattern of American industry, and it is because Appleton helped bring it about that he holds a more important place in American history than has hitherto been accorded him, or even than he claimed for himself.

During the early years of the American republic, a manufacturer was rated somewhat lower in the social scale than a merchant, the term "manufacturer" connoting a skilled mechanic who had gone into business for himself, a man like Samuel Slater, for example, rather than an entrepreneur. Hence when George Mc-Duffie in a speech in Congress in 1832 referred to Nathan Appleton as "one of the largest manufacturers in the United States," Appleton disclaimed the title. "I have no other claim to that character than what arises from my having invested property in some manufacturing establishments. My occupation through life has been that of an importing and exporting merchant," he explained to his fellow Representatives. Appleton was correct in a sense; he was an investor, a merchant, a banker, an absentee owner, a man in fine whose relation to the textile industry was purely financial. He had no closer connection with the actual weaving of calico than J. P. Morgan, later, with the forging of steel. The corporate structure of which he and his friends availed themselves, with its delegated responsibility through the officers to the agents, put him at a considerable remove from the grimier processes of industry.

It was as a banker, as a man to whom others entrusted their funds for investment, that Nathan Appleton was able to assume leadership in the textile industry, prefiguring the role that finance capitalists were to play in the great industrial corporations formed at the beginning of the present century. In his own time his views on banking were esteemed even more highly than his pronouncements on the cotton manufacture. After his death Edward Everett said that "there was no person in the community who understood the subjects of banking and currency better than Appleton." Indeed it was in his role as a banker that Appleton at length resolved the long and bitter conflict between the old merchants and the rising manufacturing interests of New England, bringing both groups finally to join forces in a great drive toward industrialization.

Nathan Appleton's quick intelligence and business acumen brought him at an early age to a position of influence in Boston mercantile circles, where, although opportunities were not wanting for any young man with the same qualifications, the best opportunities were reserved as a rule for the happy few with the proper antecedents. Neither did he gain his entree into the Boston social and business hierarchy by marriage, as many another ambitious outsider did. His father was a poor but respectable farmer, Deacon Isaac Appleton of New Ipswich, New Hampshire, whose family had long been settled in New England. Born on October 6, 1779, Nathan was the seventh son, and one of twelve children. Later in life these obscure origins, so unequal to the aristocratic pretensions of a Boston magnate, gave him some uneasiness, for he sought the services of a professional genealogist, who obligingly discovered a noble English ancestor for him in the person of William de Appulton, way back in 1326.

Happily unaware of this patrician strain, Appleton as a boy cheerfully helped with the farmwork and attended the local schools, where he was an excellent student, standing always at the head of his class. At the age of fifteen he passed his examinations for entrance into Dartmouth College, but, changing his plans suddenly, he renounced further scholastic ambitions for a career in trade.

A New England farm provides a meager livelihood for a man with twelve children, and even more limited prospects for seven sons. Nathan's elder brother Samuel thought to find broader opportunities in the wild lands of Maine, where two years of pioneering cured him permanently of any taste for farming. Returning to the neighborhood of New Ipswich, he opened a small store, in which a certain success led him to try his fortune in Boston. Here Samuel set up shop in 1794, starting modestly as a jobber, buying cloth at auction and selling it to country traders and peddlers. It has frequently been remarked that as soon as a New England youth made a small place for himself in the business world he was not content until he had shared his good fortune with all his brothers. Samuel Appleton began by taking in young Nathan, then "a fresh, vigorous, bright-eyed lad, just turned of fifteen," who arrived in Boston in the fall of 1794, with all his belongings in a bundle handkerchief.

The training of an apprentice shopkeeper, like that of a young merchant in the larger counting rooms, was rigorous, though not exhausting: he must learn to write business letters in a clear, round hand, without making errors or unsightly blots; he must copy the accounts exactly and eventually learn to keep the accounts himself; he must deliver goods purchased and keep track of everything sold or received. But above all, he must acquire the skill or art of buying cheap and selling dear. An apt pupil, Nathan soon became indispensable to his brother, and by the time he was twenty took sole charge of the business when Samuel went to Europe in 1799. In the following year Samuel offered him a partnership, the firm to be known as "S. & N. Appleton, Importers," a title several cuts above the jobbing with which Samuel had originally started out.

Like the Lowell operatives later, Nathan Appleton wasted none of his time after working hours. Having discovered that Eliphalet Hale, a man who resided at his boarding place, was familiar with double-entry bookkeeping, he persuaded Hale to teach him the then new method of keeping accounts in his spare time, and was the first in Boston to use it in a commercial house. Aware of the gaps in his education, he boarded for two years at the home of one Mr. Sales, in order to learn French, and mastered the language enough to speak and write it with some fluency. Meanwhile he neglected no opportunity to make friends with men of position or talent; at Mr. Sales' house, for example, he made the acquaintance of Henry Higginson, of the great Salem merchant family; and at Dr. Aspinwall's hospital in Brookline, where he was inoculated for the smallpox in 1798, he began a lifelong friendship with Joseph Story, then a Harvard student, but destined to become a famous law professor, a Supreme Court justice, and the high priest of New England conservatism.

Once he acquired the standing of a partner in the firm, Nathan too began voyaging to Europe to buy goods, making his first visit to Liverpool late in 1801. He transacted no business on this occasion, however, for the Peace of Amiens had been signed while he was on the high seas, and young Appleton, then only twenty-two years old, was astute enough to recognize that while war creates scarcity and justifies high prices, peace has the opposite effect. American merchants described the Peace of Amiens as a "national calamity."

Although their little importing business flourished, the Appleton brothers were not immediately admitted into the circle of great Boston merchants who dominated the social and business life of the city. It was not until 1808 that Nathan Appleton brought himself favorably to their attention by acting energetically in their behalf as well as his own. Like them a buyer of foreign goods, he had to pay for his purchases in British pounds, which were a fairly steady medium of exchange, although not backed by specie during the Napoleonic wars. On the other hand, whatever he sold in America would be paid for in the uncertain paper of country banks, which even in normal times was worth less than its face value, while in times of money pressure it was cleared at the Boston banks only after long delay and at a considerable discount. The Boston Exchange Office had been set up as a clearing house for this fluctuating paper money, but in 1808 it fell into the hands of an unscrupulous character, and once more bills of the country banks were held up for payment. Thereupon Nathan Appleton stepped in to halt this financial blackmail; by applying to prominent businessmen in Boston he raised $10,000 as a legal fund with which to bring suit against any banks that refused to clear their notes within a few days. The country banks were quickly brought around by the mere threat of multiple suits. Nathan Appleton had shown himself a man to be relied upon, a fact that the Boston merchants remembered when another crisis confronted them.

Until they transferred the larger part of their interests to manufacturing, the Appletons' merchant profits were to depend in great measure on the continental war intermittently raging in Europe. For this reason, bitterly as the New England merchants denounced the Embargo and Non-intercourse Acts, in the intervals between the lapse of one measure and the passage of another, they did fairly well, owing to the shortages created by these very measures. In 1809, for example, Nathan's cousin, William Appleton, also an importer, considered himself worth $4,000; in 1811 he estimated his fortune at $10,000, and in 1813, $60,000. Despite the confusion attending the Jefferson-Madison policy, Samuel Appleton thought the business prospects fair enough in 1809 to dissolve the partnership with his brother and go to Liverpool to establish himself there for a period of many years. Nathan then formed a partnership with another brother, Eben, and one Daniel P. Parker, but kept in constant communication with Samuel, even during the War of 1812, on the subject of their common business interests.

Nathan Appleton was in England on the business of Appleton & Parker from June, 1810, to May, 1811, during part of which time it was legally possible to send shipments of goods home, making large purchases for the account of himself and other Boston merchants. A presidential decree had set February 2, 1811, as the last day on which intercourse with Britain would be permitted, but the merchandise ordered by Appleton arrived at British ports too late to be shipped before the day set by the President. According to Appleton's testimony before a congressional committee in 1812, some of these goods were therefore sent to Boston in the following spring and summer by way of

Halifax and Montreal, which tangled them up in another legal snarl.

On March 2, 1811, Congress had passed an act forbidding any importations from Britain under penalty of forfeiture of vessels and cargo, unless—and this was the crucial point—Britain revoked her oppressive Orders in Council, whereupon the ban on importations would automatically be lifted. War against England was declared on June 18, 1812, but the news did not reach London until the thirtieth. On June 23, however, the Orders in Council were revoked, and immediately merchandise ordered by American merchants was loaded on vessels and prepared for shipment. William Appleton, in England at the time, ordered £30,-000 worth for various Boston firms, including his cousins'. Despite the declaration of war, these shipments were permitted to proceed on their way to American ports, under British license against capture up to September 15.

But to make confusion worse confounded, the declaration of war had suspended the operation of the Act of March 2, 1811, so that the merchandise, though sent in good faith, became subject to confiscation by the government of the United States on its arrival. Court and presidential action, however, made it possible for merchants to recover their cargoes by posting bonds for their appraised value and paying the import duty. This they proceeded to do with alacrity, for the merchandise became immensely valuable on the outbreak of hostilities. Gallatin, the Secretary of the Treasury, in whom was vested the right to remit these forfeitures, if he saw fit, proposed retaining enough of the bonds to give the government the advantage of the great increase in the value of the cargoes due to the war, that is, to hold on to the war profits. He was impelled to do this as much by the poverty of the Treasury as by the desire to curb profiteering.

A measure of Appleton's rising importance in the merchant community can be gathered from the fact that he was chosen as one of two Boston delegates to go to Washington and plead for the remission of these forfeitures before the Ways and Means

Committee. On November 25, 1812, he appeared before the committee and testified about the goods he had ordered in England the previous year. When asked about the connection between the importations from England and the illegal traffic with the British forces in the Spanish peninsula, he first denied that the same merchants were engaged in both, and then admitted, as if under adroit questioning, that "a very large portion of the goods lately imported on account of the merchants of Boston, were imported by those engaged in the exportations to the Peninsula." If this had been all the committee members were able to extract from him, he would have done his Boston friends no service. But the most important part of his testimony, and the most pertinent to the investigation, concerned the extra profit made on the shipments in consequence of the declaration of war. On this point he could not be shaken. "The extraordinary profit beyond that of peace and free intercourse," he maintained stoutly, "is about 5 to 10 percent."

The chairman of the Ways and Means Committee, Langdon Cheves, was so impressed with Appleton's modest claims that he led the fight in Congress to remit the forfeitures in their entirety, crying:

I would rather see the objects of the war fail—I would rather see the seamen of the country impressed on the ocean and our commerce swept from its bosom—than see the long arm of the Treasury indirectly thrust into the pocket of the citizen through the medium of a penal law.

Cheves was seconded by Calhoun and Lowndes, and a law was passed to return the amount of the bonds posted by the merchants, thus restraining the administration from doing what the merchants incontinently practiced on the public. For Appleton's testimony had been exceedingly disingenuous, as indicated by letters he wrote to his brother Samuel at this very period, in which he boasted of profits ranging from 112½ to 125 percent on the cost of the cargoes. The frail honor of a merchant is always in a state of suspension when he deals with his government.

The truth of the matter was that the New England merchants looked on the administration at Washington rather than the British government as their enemy. Along with the growth of his business Appleton had acquired a full-blown set of Federalist principles, and to a Federalist Great Britain offered far more liberty—or shall we say protection?—to his class than the "tyranny" of James Madison. The moneyed men of Boston refused to sanction Mr. Madison's War, even though it brought them wealth beyond that enjoyed by any other section of the country —indeed, as Samuel Eliot Morrison says, at the expense of the rest of the country. Operating under license from the British navy, they furnished supplies to Wellington's army on the peninsula at a gratifying profit; they carried on a brisk trade with Canada, and, since the British blockade was not effective north of New York, they succeeded in bringing in some shipments, which, at the prevailing high prices, could not but be remarkably lucrative. The Peninsular trade alone brought such high prices that five million dollars arrived in America (most of it going to Boston) in the first six weeks of the war.

While New England prospered during the War of 1812 the rest of the country suffered from hard times, with the result that most of the specie in the nation was concentrated in the Boston banks. The Federalist merchants who controlled these banks— and by 1813 Nathan Appleton had joined that select group as a director of the Boston Bank—showed their pique at the administration by refusing to contribute to any of the war loans, all of which failed in consequence. In order to meet its bills the government then issued large quantities of Treasury notes, the first paper money circulated under the Constitution without coin to back it up. When the war ended, all the banks in the country suspended specie payments except those of Boston, where huge cash reserves kept their banknotes at par. In fact, profitable investment for this great hoard of specie was so hard to find that Nathan Appleton and his associates graciously consented to subscribe to the loan of 1815, authorized by Congress to refund a large block of outstanding Treasury notes.

Alexander J. Dallas, who had by then become Secretary of the Treasury, apparently did not appreciate the generosity of the Boston bankers. To their great displeasure, he arbitrarily set a price of 95 in Treasury notes for 100 in bonds, which was far above the market value of the notes, and said he would accept no offers below that figure. Nevertheless, the cool reception of his proposal caused him to revise his plans. Taking a grim revenge on the New England financiers for their obstructive tactics during the war, he agreed to accept the depreciated paper of other sections of the country, at their face value, for the loan, and at a parity with Boston's sound money. This, as Henry Adams wrote, paid a premium to insolvency, and drained the New England banks of most of their specie. To make matters worse, Dallas also paid debts incurred by the government in the same depreciated currency, thereby prolonging the money crisis. Nathan Appleton, who had led the movement to maintain specie payment in the Boston banks, considered this procedure little short of criminal. As he wrote in a pamphlet on currency and banking many years later, Dallas "refused to use the power, given him by Congress, to redeem the public credit in the legal currency; but negotiated his loans in the most discredited currency of the day, which he passed off in payment to the public creditors as a fulfillment of the contracts of the government." These remarks reflected a very specific sense of injury, for Appleton had offered to subscribe to the 1815 loan at 92 in Treasury notes, only to be turned down curtly by Dallas. A year later when he presented a claim on the government for $2,000, Dallas had again offended by offering to pay him off in the shin-plasters of insolvent banks. The lesson in all this was not lost on Appleton; thenceforth he was known as the foremost advocate of a stable currency and sound banking in the land.

In his attacks on Dallas, Appleton spoke not only for himself, but for the whole Boston commercial community, which had now for several years admitted him to their councils. Comparative newcomer though he was, his pronouncements had unusual authority in those parochial circles, perhaps because within the larger group of merchants he represented a smaller but powerful clique consisting of himself and his brothers, Samuel and Eben, his cousin William Appleton, their various associates, and a few years later, two other rising suns in the business life of the city, Amos and Abbott Lawrence. Individually the men in this smaller group could have exercised little power; collectively their wealth and talents were significant, and might become formidable.

Nathan Appleton was the first of these new men to be admitted to a share in their far-spreading enterprises by the old Boston merchant hierarchy. As the stock of goods held by the firm of Appleton & Parker dwindled after the beginning of the War of 1812, and an effective embargo made smuggling more risky, the partnership was dissolved in 1813, and Nathan found himself with little to do. Estimating his fortune at $200,000, a nice round sum for the time, he contemplated retiring to a life of study and leisure on a moderate income. But alluring prospects for profitable investment soon involved him in a great variety of enterprises. With his flair for finance, it was a natural step for him to invest some of his funds in the Boston Bank, of which he became a director. But since he would not buy government bonds, there was some danger that a large part of his money would lie idle. Indeed, six months after the War of 1812 began he wrote to his brother Samuel in Liverpool, "I know of nothing to lay out money in with any profit or advantage."

In this frame of mind, he was prone to take a flyer with two merchants of the old guard, Patrick Tracy Jackson and Francis Cabot Lowell, in the Waltham project. On his trip to England in 1811, he had visited Edinburgh, where Lowell was sojourning at the time. In an autobiographical note Appleton described their meeting:

We had a good deal of conversation upon the subject of the cotton manufacture, and he told me that he had determined, before he returned, to make himself fully acquainted with the subject, with a view to the introduction of it at home. I urged him to do so, with an understanding that I should be ready to cooperate with him in such an undertaking.

But while Appleton's interest in the project was undoubtedly sincere, he did not permit it to run away with him at first. Indeed, his original investment seems to have been made almost as a favor to a business associate, for when Lowell and Jackson approached him on the subject in 1813:

I told them, that, theoretically, I thought the business ought to succeed, but that all I had seen of its practical operation was unfavorable. I was therefore willing to take $5,000 of the stock, in order to see the experiment fairly tried . . . and would make no complaint if I lost the whole.

Despite this boast Appleton was not the man to throw even the small sum of $5,000 to the winds without giving it another thought. He did, in fact, follow the consummation of Lowell's plans with great attention. When the installation of the machinery at Waltham was held up, he was "quite impatient with the delay," Kirk Boott observed. And when at length the power loom was set in motion in the fall of 1814, he hurried to the mill and sat in wonder by the hour watching the wheels go round.

Appleton's intention to retire from business did not survive the end of the war. He held to his original decision only in this sense that whatever he embarked on thereafter was in effect to be managed by others, while he drew profits as a silent partner, or a stockholder, limiting his labors to a general supervision of the enterprises. In this way he set up B. C. Ward & Company in 1815, after giving his partners to understand that since he had put up the capital, he would do none of the work. His conversion of B. C. Ward & Company from an importing concern into a commission house for the sale of Waltham goods, as described earlier, was a brilliant stroke, and one that immediately gave him a commanding position in the most profitable end of the manufacturing of textiles. Letters to his brother at this period indicate the reasons for his flagging interest in importing. On October 24, 1817, for example, he complained to Samuel that English sheetings were fetching low prices. "Our Waltham and other American goods have superseded them entirely." And in December he boasted of further progress: "Our Waltham cottons increase in demand. We have raised the price to 28 cents—and are unable to execute all our orders." By May of the following year he was in a mood to give up importing altogether: "I agree with you that importing English goods is a miserable business."

The immediate success of the Waltham mills led him to increase his investment to $26,000, but other business interests were simultaneously absorbing his funds. In 1818 he helped found two of Boston's greatest financial institutions, the Suffolk Bank and the Massachusetts Hospital Life Insurance Company. In the bank venture he was associated with his cousin William Appleton, Patrick Tracy Jackson, Ebenezer Francis, a wealthy East India merchant, and the four Lawrence brothers, Amos, Abbott, Luther and William, who like Appleton himself were casting about for sound investments for their importers' profits. In the life insurance company Appleton acted directly for the first time with three of the richest and best-known of the merchant princes of the East India and Northwest trade, William Sturgis, Ignatius Sargent, and the magisterial Thomas Handasyd Perkins.

It was Appleton who devised the famous Suffolk Bank System, by which any New England bank that left $5,000 on reserve deposit with the Suffolk could have its paper redeemed at par. Some two hundred took advantage of this service, giving the Suffolk $1,000,000 in working capital on which no interest was due, beyond its paid-in capital of $1,000,000. The Massachusetts Hospital Life Insurance Company also had large sums of money available for investment purposes. A director in both institutions, Appleton was now in a position where he could grant credit to his friends, and withhold it from others. He was strategically placed to direct the flow of all this accumulated capital to one enterprise or another, the more so as his cool head and dependability had won him universal respect from the moneyed men of Boston.

With these vast financial resources behind him, Appleton was ready to go forward in the manufacturing of cotton textiles. In later years, because of the success that attended most of his undertakings, Appleton tried to give the impression that he was one of the key figures in the Waltham venture. It would be closer to the truth to say that he only began to have confidence in the project after Lowell had established it as a sound business proposition, when the cloth began rolling out in quantity, and the profits of the selling agency reached a respectable figure. But if he was only one of the lesser architects of Waltham in 1813, he was definitely the prime mover in the foundation of the town of Lowell in 1822.

His knowledge of costs in the manufacture of sheeting enabled him to estimate the cost of making another article of common use, printed calico, which he realized could be produced more cheaply by the Waltham methods than the goods imported from England. Armed with these figures, he and Patrick Tracy Jackson had no difficulty raising capital for the Merrimack Company from among the Boston merchants. For those who wished to make the investment, but lacked the liquid capital, it was possible, if they belonged to the right circles, to borrow the sum needed at the bank or insurance company. Nathan Appleton very likely took advantage of these resources himself, for his original investment of $180,000 in the Merrimack Company was too large to have been paid out from his personal funds, unsupported by any loans.

Since such loans were quickly repaid from the profits of the Boston Manufacturing Company and the Merrimack mill, it was a simple matter to borrow money from the same sources, or to raise funds by selling stock in the older corporations when new mill projects were planned. In the twenties and thirties Appleton helped launch and held large blocks of stock in the Hamilton, Appleton, Lawrence, Boott, and Prescott companies in Lowell, the Taunton Manufacturing Company of Taunton, the Cabot Manufacturing Company of Chicopee, the Cocheco Manufacturing Company of Dover, the Stark Mills of Manchester, and several others. Appleton himself served as president of several of these corporations, and as director in most of them. Directors' meetings were at first held in the towns where the mills were located, but as the original investors grew old and infirm, it became customary to hold them at either the Appleton or Lawrence counting rooms in Boston, where in any case policy was decided upon. Not all the mills paid the high dividends of the Waltham company in its early years, or of the Merrimack over a long period, but profits from one could generally be depended upon to make up for losses from another, while Appleton could depend on his selling agency for a constant source of revenue.

If this agency had proved lucrative when B. C. Ward & Company handled the sales of only the Waltham company, it was immensely more so when the output of other mills was added to its list. In 1828 Mr. Ward retired from the firm, and a new partnership, under the name of J. W. Paige & Company, was set up by Appleton and other large stockholders in several of the Lowell mills. Unlike the earlier partnership, which had handled a general commission business, the new agency was devised to handle the sales of these mills and nothing else. On October 20, 1828, Paige and Appleton wrote to Patrick Tracy Jackson: "The subscribers propose to form a partnership under the firm of J. W. Paige and Company for the purpose of taking upon themselves the disposition of the Waltham, Hamilton, Merrimack and Appleton goods . . . on the following terms": namely, 1¼ percent on the Merrimack output and 1 percent on all the rest. No competitive bids were invited, and the terms stood as dictated. This new selling agency, however, assumed more functions with relation to the cotton industry than its prototype; it studied the needs of the market, designed the patterns

of the fabrics to be made, developed a selling program, financed
current production when necessary, and advised on every problem except those of the actual manufacture.

By the time the first Merrimack mill was completed, Nathan
Appleton was a great nabob in his own right. He had built himself a fine house, had a handsome equipage, and "enjoyed all of
the comforts and elegancies which wealth could furnish," as a
younger contemporary wrote. The life of leisure to pursue his
studies, which had appealed to him as a younger man, had to
be foregone as his business interests multiplied, even though he
participated only as an investor or promoter. The demands of
this occupation were not so exacting that they took up all his
time; he was able between times to travel, read widely, write
articles and pamphlets, entertain visiting notables, and place his
ripe experience at the service of his state and nation.

The shift of capital from merchant shipping to manufacturing
that took place during Appleton's career did in fact call for new
men and new ideas in politics. The day of the merchants who
clamored for free trade, the era of extreme localism was approaching its end during the twenties, while the rise of industry
opened new horizons, and put the role of government in a new
light. Nathan Appleton was a transitional figure in this development, bridging the two eras as well as the two systems. As a
businessman he hastened the movement of merchant capital from
ships to mills, and exploited all the possibilities of finance capital
for industrial development; in politics he moved steadily away
from the states'-rights, free-trade position held by the Boston
Federalists during the War of 1812 to the notion of a strong
central government and a high tariff held by all the textile magnates in the forties.

Nathan Appleton had small political ambitions, but when he
was chosen by the other great merchants of Boston to represent
them in the State Legislature or in Congress, it was because of
their faith in his ability to voice the businessman's point of view.
His first elective post was to the Massachusetts General Court

in 1816. Appointed chairman of the Committee on Finance by the speaker, he made his maiden speech in opposition to a specific tax on insurance companies, in which he was to have large and profitable investments. He was returned again to the legislature in 1821, 1823, 1824, and 1827.

In those artless days of the young republic, there were few to challenge the right of a businessman to take part personally in shaping laws for the advantage of his own financial interests, the revered founding fathers having set the pattern for this. After the democratic upsurge of the twenties and thirties, however, the question was frequently raised as to whether men should be permitted to legislate on a matter in which they stood to gain financially. Nathan Appleton never had any qualms about this. Answering the charge that he ought to have abstained from voting in Congress on the Tariff of 1842 because of his large mill investments, he wrote to the editor of the *New York Evening Post:* "In voting for the Tariff of 1842, I thought . . . that I was promoting the interests of every individual in the United States . . . I . . . was . . . and am now in as good a situation to form an impartial opinion as yourselves."

And yet by his own admission he was not elected to Congress by the ruling caste of Boston because of his impartiality in 1830 and 1842, when the tariff was to be debated. As Winthrop wrote in his memoir of Appleton, he "was selected for the candidacy, and induced to accept it at these particular times, with a special view to his ability to grapple with the questions . . . impending." Appleton's claims to speak for the Boston merchants were so imposing that when he first ran for Congress in 1830, Alexander Everett, who had mistakenly supposed that he was to have the nomination, withdrew in haste on learning that Appleton had been designated. "I can have no pretensions in opposition to you or to any candidate proposed by our common friends," he wrote to Appleton with becoming modesty.

Appleton's first campaign was not without heat, nevertheless, for the leading citizens of Boston itself were divided between the diehard East India merchants who clamored for free trade, and the great investors in manufactures. The free-trade candidate, according to his son, Colonel Henry Lee, felt that he was steam-rollered by the protectionists who favored Appleton: "Of course . . . no violence was offered, nor could a man of his birth and position be looked down upon by promoted shopkeepers; but as far as they dared and as they could, the then rich sellers of dry-goods showed their ill-will."

Still Appleton was probably selected as a candidate to speak for the tariff because his views on the subject were fairly moderate at that time. He had, to be sure, stood behind Francis Cabot Lowell in 1816 when that successful lobbyist obtained the first protective tariff ever passed in this country. But in October, 1820, Appleton's name appeared with that of Daniel Webster and Abbott Lawrence as sponsor of a series of free-trade resolutions adopted at a meeting of merchants held at Faneuil Hall.* As late as 1827 he was still not extravagant in his demands for protection, as evidenced by a letter he wrote on August 16 to Mr. James Lloyd, a Merrimack Company stockholder:

. . . and having myself, as you are probably aware, heretofore considered the duty on cottons even greater than was necessary for a full[?] encouragement of the business, and having always been opposed in principle to the general[?] forcing system advocated by Mr. Clay and others . . . I am perfectly satisfied that the business of manufacturing cotton, including the printing of calicoes, can be carried on in this country to as good advantage as in England in ordinary times, as the material is cheaper and the wages of labour, considering the larger proportion of female labour . . . scarcely if anything higher.

It was not for his mills, he declared, that protection was needed, but for the smaller mills, which were not organized on the basis of large-scale production. It is true that his brother Samuel was interested in at least one small mill, at Peterborough, New Hamp-

* Later Appleton claimed that his signature had been appended to this broadside by mistake, but the possibility of error seems fairly remote, as he was even then so prominent a personage that his name could not have been used in vain.

shire, which may have aroused greater concern in Nathan for the lot of the small manufacturer than the corporation mills generally showed. But it must have occurred to many as a result of such reasoning that if the tariff merely provided protection for certain small mills, it would at the same time multiply the already sizable profits of the large mills. Hence when Appleton took his seat in Congress he played down his earlier arguments on the low unit cost of labor in the New England cotton factories, and took another line.

His first speech on the subject, given on January 31, 1832, was a laborious discourse, poorly delivered, and would have aroused little attention but for the fact that it became the target for the livelier oratory of George McDuffie of South Carolina. McDuffie used the classical free-trade arguments, describing the tariff as putting an intolerable burden on the agricultural South. In responding to McDuffie's thrusts Appleton showed a little more spirit than in his maiden effort. The Southerner had called him a manufacturer. It was not as a manufacturer that he desired protection, Appleton said, but rather as an employer of labor, whose high wages depended on the tariff. He then restated Webster's thesis that protection had been foisted on New England, against her will, in 1816. Massachusetts, he protested, "is not the author of the protective system; she has opposed it at every stage." This was a curious bit of casuistry from a man who was very familiar with Francis Cabot Lowell's part in obtaining the insertion of the minimum principle in the tariff of 1816.

But though all this was bolstered up by figures, and despite his introduction of "an exhibition of the cotton manufacture" in Congress, Appleton was less useful to the group seeking protection on the floor of the House than he was in caucus. Invited to serve on a committee with John Davis, later Governor of Massachusetts, to outline a new tariff bill, he helped to frame a measure "making everything free which did not interfere with our own productions." The days when favors would be exchanged among various interests desiring protection had not yet come. Practically all the committee's suggestions were embodied in the Tariff of 1832, to Appleton's great satisfaction.

His contentment with a job well done was doomed, however, to be short-lived. The tariff of 1832 had consequences he had not foreseen, consequences that affected the thinking and attitudes not only of Appleton but of all the New England merchant-industrialists. In spite of reiterated charges that she had forced the protective system down the throats of unwilling New Englanders, South Carolina passed the Nullification Ordinance, defying the government to collect duties to which she was opposed. The situation was explosive and, although President Jackson resolved it by threatening the use of force, a less provocative tariff was hurriedly pushed through Congress in the session of 1833 to blunt the edge of South Carolina's intransigeance. Nathan Appleton himself declared in the course of the debate on the Compromise Tariff: "The only ground after all on which the immediate and hurried action of this House can be justified is that it is necessary to the preservation of the Union."

The preservation of the Union had indeed by 1833 become the shield and shibboleth of those same Northern merchants who twenty years earlier had played with the idea of secession at the Hartford Convention. The tariff was dear to their hearts, to be sure, and they would never cease to clamor for it, but, tariff or no, business could still be carried on at a profit, if other factors remained equal. The threat of disunion was another matter, endangering as it did all the commercial ties between North and South. As bankers and shippers to the Southern states, as purchasers of cotton raised in the South, as producers of the manufactured goods the South must buy, the Boston magnates shuddered at every threat to these delicate trade relationships. Hence from the thirties up to the Civil War they were prepared to give way to the South on every point of disagreement in order to hold the Union together. Charles Sumner charged that the New England merchants yielded to the South on slavery in the hope that someday they would be able to slip through a tariff as well. But it is extremely interesting to note that while up to 1832 some of them had described slavery as an unmitigated moral evil, the Nullification Ordinance was effective blackmail; thereafter, they submitted meekly to every encroachment of the slave power, reserving their greatest odium for a small but growing number of idealists in the North who felt that no compromise was possible with traffic in human beings.

Neither adverse tariff legislation nor a prolonged slump in business checked the expansion of the textile industry. Although the Compromise Tariff of 1833 provided for a gradual reduction of duties to 20 percent in 1842, a rate that provided revenue but no protection, business prospects seemed good enough for Appleton to help promote still another company at Lowell, the Boott Mills, in 1835. When the panic of 1837 broke, the Merrimack Company passed its dividend for only one year, resuming in 1838 with a lavish 40 percent, 3 percent in cash and 37 percent in a stock dividend. On this watered stock the dividend rate continued high, never falling below 7 percent, and rising to as much as 20 percent during the next ten years. On the basis of such profits, therefore, Nathan Appleton and others among the Boston group were able to draw on the money reserves in the institutions they controlled to finance two more large ventures in 1839, one in Lowell and another in Manchester, New Hampshire. This milking of the older established corporations for purposes of expansion, coupled with continued distress throughout the country, eventually made the cotton industry feel the pinch of hard times, too. Dividends were cut or passed entirely in the newer factories and, in the drive to lower expenses, wages were reduced in all the corporation mills in 1841.

The protectionists chose to attribute this deplorable state of affairs solely to the low duties, and therefore when new tariff legislation was due to come before Congress in 1842, they descended upon Washington resolved to win back what they had lost. Robert C. Winthrop, second only to Daniel Webster as the florid orator of the counting houses, was then the Boston representative in Congress, but just as the tariff debate was due to come up in May of that year, personal affairs obliged him to resign. Not a moment could be lost in appointing the right sort of man to take his place. As Appleton naively put it:

> The public looked to either Abbott Lawrence or myself to fill the vacancy. Mr. Lawrence was appointed commissioner . . . to settle the Maine boundary question . . . so that I found myself under an almost unavoidable necessity of consenting to take the place, which I did very reluctantly.

Called in as a pinchhitter, Appleton saved the day, for the 1842 tariff, restoring the duties almost to the level of 1832, passed the House of Representatives by a very narrow margin. An indignant correspondent wrote to Abbott Lawrence berating Appleton for his inconsistency:

> This gentleman . . . has published communications upon the impolicy of having very high duties, and yet he held up his hand in Congress in favor of the tariff of 1842 . . . carried by a majority of only one vote, which led someone to remark that "Mr. Appleton was the gentleman who always wrote right, but voted wrong."

Charges such as these drove Appleton to restate his theories on the subject of the tariff. In 1844 he published his most thoughtful essay, *Labor, its Relations in Europe and the United States Compared,* in which he developed the labor argument for protection from the point of view of theoretical economics.

Starting with Locke's axiom that labor is the only source of wealth, he went on to say that "whatever exists under the name of property, wealth or capital, is, therefore, the result or representative of previous labor—an accumulation not wanted for the present, but put aside for future use." He followed this up with the frank acknowledgment that wealth was power. "Its possessor is the object of envy and flattery, while, in its original humble state of labor, it is passed by almost without notice." Then in a sudden burst of democratic enthusiasm, the more unexpected as coming from a Boston merchant in whom suspicion of the people was deep-rooted, Appleton drew the inevitable comparison between the opportunities in his own happy land and those in the caste-ridden system of the old world.

> Ours is a great novel experiment in politics and civilization. . . . It is an attempt to equalize and improve the whole mass of population, by elevating the lower portions from their usual abject state and depressing the higher, in dispensing with a privileged aristocracy. The process consists in the higher reward and higher estimation of labor.

The free-trade doctrine, he added, was based on the Malthusian theory of population constantly exceeding the means of supporting life, which drove wages down to the lowest level. Without capital to give employment, labor in Europe was impotent, incapable of accumulating wealth, and therefore any increase of wealth went exclusively to the owners of capital. But in America the situation was wholly different because of high wages and vast areas of unsettled land:

> With us labor is in fact the great accumulator. It goes to work without difficulty on its own account; it is therefore perfectly clear that that legislation which gives it its fullest scope, is with us most productive of wealth. . . . The protective system rests as its basis on the principle of an enlarged field for labor, resulting from that legislation which restricts or shuts out the competition of the cheaper and more degraded labor of Europe.

Ricardo, Senior, McCulloch, and other economists of the free-trade school were therefore wrong in opposing "legislative interference" in aid of industry, for the experience of the United States proved the beneficial effects of such legislative action on all classes of society. But "legislative interference," Appleton implied, should only operate through the protective tariff and only against "foreign labor." American labor did not need to invoke aid from the legislative branch to protect its standards.

By a shrewd association of thought, Appleton then went on

to shift the responsibility not only for protection but also for high prices from the manufacturers to labor. Even though the protective system seemed to give "labor too great an advantage, in the power of levying a contribution in the prices of the commodities consumed by capital," capitalists need not complain, he said, for

with us labor and capital are so mixed together, that, in the general prosperity resulting from an active well-paid industry, capital is sure to get its share. All writers on political economy recognize the high reward of labor as indicating the highest measure of general prosperity.

This proposition that labor through high wages levied "a contribution on the high prices of commodities" represented quite a shift from Appleton's earlier view that the unit cost of labor in the Lowell mills was lower than that in the English mills. But more important still is the confident statement by a leading businessman thus early in the game that a high standard of living for workers in itself guaranteed profits to capital. With great clairvoyance Nathan Appleton saw this as a major difference between the American and the European economies. It was in fact what permitted the United States to emerge as the leading capitalist power of the world over a hundred years later, when the shortsighted policies of the European business class had driven one country after another toward socialism.

But discerning as some of the judgments in this pamphlet were, the low-tariff advocates were not convinced by the labor argument. In 1846 the Democrats were back in power, determined to undo the mischief perpetrated by the Whigs in the tariff of 1842. To fortify the arguments of the protectionists, and confound their opponents, Nathan Appleton hurried into print with another pamphlet on the whole question, *What is a Revenue Standard? and a Review of Secretary Walker's Report on the Tariff.*

The first premise of this pamphlet was that cotton textiles

were the most important article of American manufacture, and the one "which exhibits the greatest triumph of the protective policy." The *New York Evening Post* had charged that the minimum duty on coarse cottons was a severe tax on the clothing of the poor. Even while conceding that the manufacture of coarse cottons was so well established that it could survive without a tariff, Appleton denied the allegation of the newspaper editor by introducing a totally new theory: it was the *consuming public* that needed the protection of the tariff, for if the duty were lifted on coarse cottons, Britain would flood the country with an inferior type of goods, far dearer *intrinsically*, than the sturdy cloth made in the United States.

But Appleton was not content to save the improvident poor from the consequences of careless shopping; there was still the labor argument to be brought forward once more, buttressed by figures from the experience of Lowell itself. Secretary Walker had charged that the tariff was class legislation, designed not to increase wages, but to assure the manufacturing capitalist of larger profits than could be made in agriculture or commerce. To this Appleton replied that the tariff of 1842 had had a direct effect on the wages in the Lowell mills: "Now we find on inquiry of the different agencies at Lowell, that the average earnings of the operatives have increased full one-third since the disastrous year 1842, or from $1.50 to full $2.00 per week for females, exclusive of board."

To at least one historian of the tariff issue, Professor Stanwood, this argument was incontrovertible. But the wage picture in the corporation mills was not quite so simple. Francis Cabot Lowell had established the wage of $2.00 a week exclusive of board in 1815, and despite the tariffs of 1816, 1824, 1828, and 1832, each higher than the last, despite Nathan Appleton's claim that coarse cottons were not even in need of protection, the average wage had never increased. The amount of output required of each worker for the same wage had, on the contrary, increased steadily over the same period. Other factors besides low duties entered into the decision to make a wage cut in 1841, and other factors besides the tariff brought about the restoration of those cuts. Moreover, between 1842 and 1846, when Appleton published his reply to Walker, actual money wages in the textile mills again fell below the 1841 level, and at a time when the industry was enjoying unexampled prosperity.

Appleton's position at the apex of New England's economic life lent such authority to his statements on the tariff question that he was constantly being asked to furnish data in support of his position. In 1844 Horace Greeley approached him: "I am to debate the tariff question at Newburgh on Friday next, and am greatly in want of information on these points which I hope you may be able, as I am sure you will be willing, to supply." Daniel Webster, who had abandoned his early free-trade principles after the Boston magnates gave him their political and financial patronage, also came to look on Appleton as the sage of the protectionists. During the session of 1846 Webster wrote to him for material:

The state of the Tariff bill at Washington is such, that we shall need the advice of our best informed and most prudent friends . . . and I write this, to bespeak your attention, and to express the hope that we may hear from you and your neighbors as fully as possible. . . . I think we ought not to let the occasion pass, without attacking the whole principle of the bill, and exposing the follies of its detail. Pray take the trouble to book me up in these respects. Since 1840 I have not been brushed up, on Tariff subjects.

Respectful inquiries such as these, from leaders in politics and journalism, made Appleton, who was essentially a modest man, adopt a rather oracular tone in the conclusion to his *Review of Secretary Walker's Report*. Should Congress ignore his advice to retain the current tariff rates, he predicted: "Before the second year shall come round, the currency will feel it, the party in power will feel it, the labor of the country will feel it, or we are no true prophet."

But despite these gloomy prognostications, the tariff reductions went through. The party in power, to be sure, lost the next presidential election, but the tariff remained unchanged until 1857, when it was lowered still further. Nevertheless the country did not go to the dogs. The Merrimack Company, of which Appleton was president, continued to thrive even without high duties, earning an average of over 11 percent from 1846 to 1856, while the Amoskeag Company averaged over 19 percent for the five years from 1846 to 1850. Appleton was no true prophet, but he certainly was a canny investor.

Although his views on the tariff show some development, Appleton's opinions on financial matters were fixed throughout his active life. Hard money, a sound and stable currency, sustained by strong banks with a large capitalization, were the tenets of his financial credo, and he stood by them regardless of pressure from political or business allies. On other issues he changed his mind, or was not averse to expediency, but he never wavered in his belief that the promise on the face of a banknote, to pay in specie the sum thereon indicated, should be inviolable.

The two greatest obstacles to sound banking practice, in his view, were the failure of the government to redeem its paper money in specie, and the proliferation of innumerable state banks with insufficient capitalization and a tendency to issue banknotes recklessly. On the first matter he had tilted with Secretary of the Treasury Dallas in 1815; to deal with the second on a regional basis he had set up the Suffolk Bank System. Feeling that the code of the banker should be even more immaculate than that of the merchant (if that were possible), he lashed out again and again at Nicholas Biddle, head of the Second Bank of the United States, for provoking one financial crisis after another in order to force President Jackson to renew the bank's charter.* It was certainly not cricket for the financial leader of the country to revenge himself on a stubborn President to the extent of hurting other financiers.

Appleton's principles with regard to currency and banking were standard in financial circles until very recent times, when

---

* There is an excellent discussion of Appleton's part in the struggle over the Second Bank of the United States in Schlesinger's *Age of Jackson.*

the idea of "managed money" gained general acceptance. The banking practices he helped inaugurate, however, have not been outmoded to this very day. Largely owing to his influence, the Boston banks and insurance companies, bound together by interlocking directorates, commanded a pool of money that could be drawn upon by favored interests for any promising venture from the Atlantic to the Great Lakes. Unlike Vanderbilt and the other Robber Barons later, neither Appleton, nor any one man, controlled this vast hoard; it was at the disposal of a group of associates who could encourage one line of expansion and veto another, very much as the Morgan and Rockefeller interests work today. Without pushing himself forward, and acting always in concert with a select band, Appleton nevertheless paved the way for financial and industrial monopoly in this country.

Appleton's business labors were already in the thirties limited to promotional activities, directorships in corporations, and silent partnerships, leaving him time to write little essays not only on subjects in which he might be presumed to be expert, but also to launch out into fields where angels fear to tread. As Veblen puts it:

There is no branch or department of the humanities in which the substantial absentee owner is not competent to act as guide, philosopher and friend, whether in his own conceit or in the estimation of his underlying population—in art and literature, in church and state, in science and education, in law and morals.

As the master mind of the textile industry, Appleton consented to write the article on cotton manufacture in the United States for Franz Lieber's *Dictionary*, which he later expanded and published separately as *The Introduction of the Power Loom*. But this and his financial writings were too close to his business interests to qualify him for the academic kudos he seemingly craved. A Boston man was expected to be learned in some field quite remote from his ordinary concerns. Appleton therefore delved into the study of the comparatively new science of geology. During a trip to Europe in 1836–37, he spent some time in Switzerland examining rock formations, and on his return published his findings in his usual didactic style: "The theories of glaciers and icebergs have been introduced to account for their striae with the accompanying alluvium, but with little satisfaction to a careful observer, I think." Other careful observers, however, found more satisfaction in the theory, by now a commonplace to geologists, which may have led Appleton to abandon this particular line of inquiry. It was not at any rate because of this contribution to scholarship that Harvard College conferred on him the honorary degree of M.A. in 1844, and LL.D. in 1855.

His later years were devoted to other researches. Shortly before his death he ventured into print with his views on theological matters, publishing the correspondence between himself and an English clergyman in a pamphlet entitled *Original Sin and the Trinity*. "I do not profess to be a theologian," he wrote in this pamphlet, "although the Christian theology has been with me rather a favorite study." Theologian or not, he was a stubborn Unitarian, staunch in defense of what has been called the "Boston religion." His satisfaction with the way God and the world had treated him was fervent enough. "It would, in my opinion," he wrote at one point, "be great presumption in any man, to say he could point out any specific improvement over the existing state of things."

And consoled by this thought, he prepared calmly to meet his Maker, telling a friend in one of his last days that he was not fearful of the future: "I believe I am not afraid of anything." He suffered probably less than any other Boston merchant of his time from a sense of guilt because of his great wealth, and therefore did not indulge in any ostentatious display of benevolence, contenting himself rather with "doing his share" in public causes without any publicity. Even in giving charity he preferred to work with his associates, as part of a group.

A picture of Nathan Appleton as a bloated capitalist grinding his heel into the necks of downtrodden workers would be the grossest caricature. The testimony of his contemporaries concerning his kindly character was unanimous. And yet it was during his time, and largely through the form he gave to the corporation mills, that the distance between owners and operatives became so great, and their interests so seemingly disparate. It was of his textile companies that the term "soulless corporation" was first used in American journalism.

When Nathan's cousin and business associate, William Appleton, died, all his eulogists agreed that "he was passionately devoted to the accumulation of wealth." Nathan Appleton, on the other hand, told Winthrop toward the end of his life that he feared the world would think him "peculiarly devoted to money-making. . . . Yet nothing is more untrue. . . . Accident, not effort, has made me a rich man." It would be unfair to Appleton's real talents to acquiesce in this modest judgment. The establishment of B. C. Ward & Company as a selling agency was no accident. There was no accident in the success of the Suffolk Bank System, or in the complete and exclusive development of the city of Lowell by Appleton and his associates, or in the extension of the corporation mills to other New England centers, or in the application of capital owned or controlled by the Boston Associates to one type of venture after another: factories, canals, railroads, banks, insurance companies. It is impossible to believe that Nathan Appleton, with his penetrating intellect, did not know what he was doing, although it is conceivable that he did not understand its full import.

Like all absentee owners today, Nathan Appleton's connection with matters such as hours, living and working conditions was only incidental to his financial relationship to the textile industry. It was his role to float securities and set up corporate organization, not to establish labor policies. These he took over from Francis Cabot Lowell and, in the brief hour of greatness of the town on the Merrimack, enlightened labor policies attracted a superior type of operatives.

As Appleton's investments grew more diversified, his knowledge of actual working conditions in the mills became more secondary. In the early days at Lowell he had spent much time there, but as the industry expanded he visited the town only rarely, merely to act as cicerone to some distinguished foreign visitor. The atmosphere in Lowell had changed in the meantime, but he was not aware of the difference. How the ten-hour movement in the forties struck him is hard to tell, for his opinion is nowhere recorded, neither in his letters nor in any of his publications. But if he considered that paying wages for work done was an act of charity, it followed that any complaint about those wages or conditions of work could only be described as the basest ingratitude, no less than biting the hand that fed you.

Chapter VIII

THE ART OF BECOMING A MILLIONAIRE

SHORTLY after the death of Abbott Lawrence in 1855, a German pundit named Randolph Anders published a fascinating little brochure entitled *Der Weg zum Glück, oder die Kunst Millionär zu Werden (The Road to Happiness, or the Art of Becoming a Millionaire)*, purporting to be a translation of certain moral maxims bequeathed to Mr. Lawrence by a rich uncle. It was by adhering rigidly to the principles here set down, said Herr Anders, that the late Boston Croesus had found fortune and/or joy. As a matter of fact, the great textile magnate possessed no written manual to guide him through the mazes of an acquisitive society, nor did he have any rich uncle to help him on his way, although the German "translator" may have had in mind Abbott's older brother Amos. Nevertheless, there is no doubt that both Lawrences knew the art of becoming a millionaire, an art for which they had the temperament, the self-discipline, the ability to master exacting techniques, and the will to learn from older adepts. Though they neither wrote nor inherited any handbook for beginners in this field, we may, by studying their lives, get some notion of the peculiar skills that enabled them to win their hearts' desire.

It was Nathan Appleton who first welcomed the Lawrence brothers to the ranks of the rich and powerful in Boston society.

Perhaps because he saw his own career duplicated by them, perhaps because he too had once been mortified by the disdain of the great burghers, Appleton went out of his way to be cordial to Amos and Abbott Lawrence, particularly to the latter, for whom he felt almost paternal regard. How helpful he must have been to this younger contemporary is indicated by Mrs. Abbott Lawrence in a letter she wrote him after her husband died: *"You, of all others, stood by during the many trials which darkened our horizon."*

Whatever these many trials were, they were not of a financial nature. The story of Amos and Abbott Lawrence, their birth and education, their early business ventures and quick success, was strikingly similar to that of Nathan Appleton, even to the relationship between the two brothers, which paralleled that between Nathan and his brother Samuel. Like the Appletons, the Lawrences were descended from respectable English artisans who had formed the bulk of the original settlers of Massachusetts; and like Nathan Appleton, Abbott Lawrence later in life procured a much more elegant pedigree, originating from one Sir William Lawrence in the twelfth century, with which to confound the snobs.

As business partners the brothers Lawrence made a fabulous team, Amos contributing the measured, practical qualities needed to build a solid fortune, and Abbott the lively spirit and engaging manners that won friends and influenced people. An inspired bookkeeper, Amos could tot up three columns of figures as fast as another man could add one. During most of his active business life he was rarely far from his shop or counting room, while Abbott, a more extroverted type, traveled around for the firm, either as puchasing agent or salesman.

Happily these differences complemented each other in their business affairs, but on other grounds, in spite of a strong attachment between the two brothers, their temperaments clashed. Having renounced drinking, smoking, and the theatre at an early age, Amos convinced himself that all those who indulged in such vices were doomed to bankruptcy and "moral ruin."

Abbott, on the contrary, was far from being a blue-nose. "Exquisite wines" were served at his dinner table, as Longfellow wrote in his diary; and another contemporary remarked that when a large group of congressmen came on from Washington to attend the funeral of John Quincy Adams in 1848, Abbott Lawrence "liquored the company at his own expense," since for the moment a local prohibition ordinance was in effect. One term in the Legislature made Amos wash his hands forever of politics, while Abbott enjoyed political strife and particularly political power. Even in their charitable bequests the brothers betrayed their different natures. On the whole, Amos gave away more money than Abbott, over $700,000, a huge sum at that time, but for the most part it was donated in small sums, in the "crisp, new bills" that were later to arouse a spirit of emulation in John D. Rockefeller. The bounty of Amos often took the form of gifts of clothing, or bolts of material, or even Sunday-school tracts, each expenditure and its recipient being noted carefully and precisely by this benevolent bookkeeper. Abbott, on the other hand, preferred to make lordly gestures, like a donation of $50,000 at one time, which was certain to receive world-wide publicity.

For all their differences, however, the Lawrence brothers had one ruling passion in common: they were frankly determined to be rich. When a correspondent suggested to Abbott that he lower his commission rates, he replied emphatically, "If you are troubled with the belief that I am growing *too rich*, there is one thing that you may as well understand; I know how to make money, and *you* cannot prevent it." Although no statement of Amos Lawrence on this point is available, his son Amos Abbott Lawrence may be taken to reflect his father's views. Writing in his diary in his senior year in college, the young Lawrence, who was hardly likely to suffer want even if he never did a stroke of work, made a straightforward confession of faith: "To be rich would be my delight. I consider it an oyster-like dullness, and not a pious or enlightened way of thinking, that makes some despise riches." With such aims and endowments, the Lawrence brothers moved almost resistlessly toward the accumulation of vast wealth.

Amos Lawrence was born in Groton, Massachusetts, in 1788, one of five sons of a farmer who had been an officer in the Continental Army. After serving his apprenticeship as a clerk in a Groton store, Amos set out for Boston in 1807, with twenty dollars in his pocket, "to learn a few tricks of the trade," as he put it, before returning to his native town to go into business. A glimpse of Boston's thriving trade, however, disposed him to match his wits against the shrewd operators of the big city, and he soon set up shop for himself in Cornhill Street as a dealer in drygoods. A few months later his father mortgaged the family farm for $1,000, which he lent to Amos to buy goods. No sooner had the young storekeeper exchanged the bills his father had given him for specie, than the bank on which they were drawn failed. This narrow escape impressed Amos so deeply that he made it a rule thereafter never to give credit to any man who offered his father as bondsman for the loan.

Before long, finding that he needed an assistant, Amos sent for his brother Abbott, then a boy of fifteen, to be his apprentice. Abbott had received but little formal education, having spent only a few months at the Groton Academy after finishing his studies at the district school, but he was a smart, teachable boy. He had been a leader among the farm lads of Groton, whether in mischievous pranks or in breaking through the deep snowdrifts that blocked the roads in winter. Even as a youth he was known as a sharp trader; when bartering toys and playthings with his schoolmates he always got the best of the bargain. Under the stern discipline and method of Amos, however, Abbott's high spirits were soon directed into businesslike channels. Hoping to guard him from the pitfalls to which youth was exposed in the great city, Amos also urged him to spend his leisure hours in study, in order to "supply the deficiencies of his early education," as Nathan Appleton wrote. Since in those early years the brothers kept shop from 7:30 A.M. until 7:30 P.M., this was almost as full a day as the Lowell operatives were to know later.

In his first year's business in Boston, Amos made $1,500 profit; during the following two years, 1808–09, he earned over $4,000, despite the difficulties of obtaining goods from England. The greater the difficulties, however, the greater the rewards, it would seem, for during the next five years, although congressional action and the War of 1812 interrupted all legal commerce, he made over $50,000. As a rule, Amos Lawrence kept the most careful accounts of his business affairs, as well as a diary; nevertheless, "but few details of Mr. Lawrence's business from . . . [1810] until 1815 are now found," his son wrote in a memoir. "Suffice it to say, that, through the difficult and troubled times in which the United States were engaged in the war with England, his efforts were crowned with success." The rise in price of English cotton goods from 17–20 cents a yard to 75 cents a yard, which made smuggling extremely profitable, probably had much to do with this success.

In the old Boston directories Amos Lawrence is set down as "shopkeeper," or "dry-goods dealer." On January 1, 1814, however, he put up a capital of $50,000 and took his brother Abbott, who had then served out his apprenticeship, into the firm with him, assuming now the dignified title of "merchant." The mettlesome Abbott had proved himself worthy of his brother's esteem, no doubt, as Amos passed over his other close kin in selecting a partner.* But like many highstrung men, Abbott Lawrence was easily depressed. Early in January, 1814, just as his prospects seemed brightest, the "Bramble" news reached Boston, and plunged him into despair. The British schooner "Bramble" had arrived in Annapolis on December 30, 1814, bringing official reports of Napoleon's overwhelming defeat at Leipzig in October,

---

* During the War of 1812, however, Abbott's high spirits could not be quelled, and he joined the New England guards, not for the defense of the country, be it understood, but for the defense of the state of Massachusetts against the Federal government. Later on, in order to wear the cloak of a patriot, he boasted of having applied for a commission in the regular army before the war ended, but no evidence exists to support this claim.

as a result of which all the coastline of Europe save France was opened to British commerce. British control of European ports, coupled with an even more effective embargo of American ports, put through Congress by Monroe's party, spelled the end of high prices and of that illegal traffic which had made forehanded young Boston merchants rich in so short a time. There was panic in the counting houses at the threat of peace, as in 1802, after the Treaty of Amiens, and Abbott "looked on himself as already bankrupt," before the partnership with his brother was a week old. Confident that the scarcity of goods would continue for a while, Amos was more level-headed; he offered to dissolve the partnership if Abbott wished it, and to pay him five thousand dollars at the end of the year as well. On seeing his brother so composed, Abbott grew brave as a lion, and vowed that "come what might, he would not swerve from the contract."

The Lawrence brothers, prototypes of the modern American businessman, knew the value of speed in transacting their affairs. The moment the War of 1812 ended, Amos sent Abbott to England on the "Milo" to buy large quantities of cloth. Landing at Liverpool, Abbott was the first man off the ship; he traveled post-haste to Manchester—where the British textile manufacturers were exceedingly glad to see him—placed his orders, hurried back to Liverpool with his purchases, and saw the merchandise safely on board for the return trip of the vessel in which he had come. In the record time of 84 days after his departure, the goods he had bought for A. & A. Lawrence were delivered in Boston, the first to arrive after the war's end; because of the long pent-up demand for English textiles, they were disposed of within a week at enormous profit.

At that time the Lawrences handled all varieties of textiles, coarse and fine, cotton or wool. But in the following year the tariff of 1816 made the importation of sheeting and shirting so unprofitable that they dropped that item, turning instead to domestic mills for their source of supply. American woolens still seemed unlikely to supersede the English product, however, for Abbott Lawrence told a young manufacturer at this period to save his money and quit making flannels, as they could be imported much more cheaply than he could make them.

Making money hand over fist, the two brothers soon began looking about for profitable investments for their cash surplus. But most of the old Boston merchants turned a cold shoulder to these parvenus, excluding them from a share in blue-chip ventures such as shipping, banks, and insurance companies. It was at this point that Nathan Appleton provided them with an opening wedge into Boston's financial citadel by inviting them to participate in the foundation of the Suffolk Bank in 1818. They were soon prominent stockholders in the Massachusetts Hospital Life Insurance Company as well. The skill with which they weathered the panic of 1819 must also have earned them the grudging respect of the older shipping magnates. Thanks, no doubt, to the foresight of Amos, the Lawrence brothers avoided making large commitments and kept their capital in liquid form at a time when large numbers of businessmen all through the country were over-extended. As business revived during the twenties, they began expanding once more, until at the end of the decade the firm handled almost every conceivable article of commerce.

The sale of imported cloth continued to figure large in their business, but by 1830 they also imported and sold copper, tea, coffee, hides, indigo, madder, and other dyestuffs, as well as porter, stout, wines, and gin. (It might be ruinous to drink gin, as Amos thought, but not to sell it.) Aside from their importations, the Lawrences at this time also had a sizable commission-house business in domestic textiles. And with all their connections at home and abroad they had gradually come to handle a large shipping business to England and the Continent for Southerners.

In addition to this great variety of activities the partners owned stock in a warehouse company and in the Boston & Roxbury Mill Dam, and had made some sound investments in real estate. Possessing large sums of liquid capital, the Lawrences also carried on a kind of banking business, advancing money to manufacturers with whom they had dealings, and lending a certain proportion of their money out on mortgage. Such banking services permitted them in some cases to charge a higher commission rate than other houses, while mortgage foreclosures enabled them to take over promising enterprises at low figures. Eventually the Lawrences gained such a reputation for buying up distressed companies that ventures of various kinds which had run into difficulties were offered to them unbidden.

The rise of A. & A. Lawrence to the position of the first commission house of Boston within fifteen years was the success story of the day. For this Amos was largely responsible, for despite all the many ramifications of the firm's business, he never lost sight of first principles in trade. In a letter to Lambert Dexter, his London representative, in 1829, he wrote: "We hope you will not spare John Bull in prices—bring him down to the lowest point. . . . We shall have need of some good bargains." If he knew how to buy cheap, he was no less expert at selling dear. One of their customers around this time complained of an overcharge in *anticipation* of the passage of the tariff of 1828. This of course Amos promised to remit, in accordance with his code, which obliged him also to make good whenever customers accused the firm of supplying imperfect goods or short measure. Still, out of those little acorns great oaks grew.

Alert as they were to every business opportunity that impinged on their interests, the Lawrences did not overlook the rising textile industry in New England, once the domestic manufacture of cloth proved to be feasible. But in this field, they waited for others to make the first experiments, joining in the venture only after they caught the glint of gold in the threads woven by American looms. Indeed Abbott Lawrence played a leading role at a large meeting of Boston merchants in October, 1820, when strong resolutions were passed denouncing the tariff because it favored domestic manufactures unduly. A year later, however, the Lawrences changed their tune, as their firm began advancing credit to the Amesbury Company, a flannel factory, which Abbott only recently had declared to be an impractical venture. Before the end of the decade they had acquired most of the stock in the company, Amos becoming treasurer and general agent, while

Abbott emerged as one of the most zealous champions of protection in the land.*

Soon these proselytes acquired an added reason for their conversion to the principle of protection when they took over the exclusive selling agency of a textile mill in Salmon Falls, New Hampshire, which produced both cotton and woolen fabrics. In 1827 Abbott attended the Harrisburg Convention, called by the Pennsylvania Society for the Protection of Manufactures, as one of seven delegates from Massachusetts; and served on a committee that urged Congress to increase the minimum duty on printed cottons. From this time forward he was in fact tireless in the great cause, giving himself, his time, and his money without stint. During the course of the debate on the tariff in Congress in 1828, for example, Edward Everett, then the Boston representative in Washington, called on him for help. The measure that meant so much to the manufacturing interests, Everett feared, would not win a majority of votes in the House; he made bold to suggest, therefore, that five or six manufacturers come to the capital and entertain wavering congressmen at dinners with "wine and champagne." The expenditure of $1,500 and Abbott Lawrence in person at these feasts would clinch the vote, Everett concluded. Responding promptly to this plea, Lawrence had the satisfaction of seeing the tariff measure passed substantially in the form he wished.

The tariff of 1828 made investments in domestic manufacture more desirable than ever, and where but in Lowell could the largest returns on such investments be won? The Lawrence brothers for several years had kept their eyes on this thriving town, waiting for a chance to get their foot in the door. To men so resourceful and so affluent, this chance was not long in coming.

Like the Appletons, the Lawrences had strong family feeling, and

---

* The Lawrences in time chose to forget their early low-tariff position. Amos Lawrence's son, in writing of his father, passed it over altogether: "*Apart from all selfish motives*, he early became one of the strongest advocates for the protection of American industry, believing that the first duty of a government is to advance the interests of its own citizens." (My italics.)

no sooner had Amos caught a glimpse of the rich vein of ore in the Boston market place than he made it possible for all his brothers to cooperate with him in exploiting it. Abbott was the first to join him, in 1808; in 1809 his elder brother William, who had been destined to be a farmer, came to Boston when "his health broke down," and undertook the less arduous tasks of a shopkeeper under the guidance of the more astute Amos. In 1818, brother Luther, a struggling lawyer, the only one with a college education in the family, suddenly sprang into prominence by becoming a director of the Suffolk Bank, in which his brothers had a large interest. A place was also made for Samuel, the youngest brother, who entered into partnership with William in 1822. The firm of W. & S. Lawrence, later known as W. & S. Lawrence and Stone, was originally in the importing business, but by 1825 had become interested in domestic manufactures, principally woolens.

In that year they took over the selling agency for a small woolen mill in Lowell, which was owned by one Thomas Hurd. Hurd's mill was one of the very few pieces of Lowell property with water rights not held by the Locks and Canals Company, having been established on the old Pawtucket Canal since 1818. During the early years of the town's growth Hurd continued to operate his factory, but as business declined during the second half of the twenties, he was forced into debt. As selling agents for the mill, W. & S. Lawrence gave him $45,000 in advances and on May 8, 1827, took a mortgage on his property for $55,000. Although they were not unsuccessful, it is highly improbable that William and Samuel could have advanced $100,000 in cash to Hurd without some assistance from their wealthy brothers.

When Hurd failed in December, 1828, owing $370,000, William and Samuel took over the property on the mortgage, reorganizing the mill in 1830 under the name of the Middlesex Manufacturing Company, with a capital of $100,000, the exact amount of the money Hurd had borrowed from them. Sam stayed on in Lowell as the company's agent, and W. & S. Lawrence retained the selling agency in Boston, after the model of the great cotton mills already established. Even though the Middlesex had only between 60 and 80 operatives in 1830, it was the largest factory for the weaving of woolens in the country at that time. The Lawrences installed the most modern machinery, hired more hands, and increased production steadily.

Small as this enterprise was, it gave the Lawrences the foothold in Lowell they had been planning for. The methods they used were not however regarded with universal esteem. As one of their contemporaries remarked acidly: "When less prudent neighbors were shipwrecked they were able to profit by their disasters." Among the Boston Associates, however, the Lawrences' Yankee shrewdness earned more homage. Having made a breach in the walls, the brothers were now to make a grand entrance into Lowell by the front gate.

While the firm of A. & A. Lawrence continued to flourish, there was a distinct downward turn in business all over the country from 1826 to 1830. General activity was sufficiently depressed to make money somewhat stringent, and many small textile mills went out of business as their bank loans were called. Nevertheless, the Boston magnates were able to raise a million dollars in capital to float the Appleton Company at Lowell in 1828, a low point in the national economy. But as the recession continued into 1829, it was difficult to go on raising more and more funds in such large amounts. And yet there was still more water power available in Lowell, which the original founders had no intention of letting go by default to someone who might offer real competition. Whoever invested in Lowell mills must have the proper alliances, be large of fortune, and hold the correct business and political views. By 1828 the Lawrences fitted this bill precisely.

After a brush with the "aristocracy" of Boston in the early twenties, when he had been thwarted in his design to put up some undesirable buildings at the lower end of Boston Common, Abbott had modeled his behavior more closely on their standards, and was beginning to be accepted as one of them. Already in 1826 the Lawrence brothers were so conscious of what Boston might think of them that they chided their old father for becoming involved in a church quarrel in Groton, reminding him of the prominence of their name. To make his social position even more secure Abbott had married the daughter of Timothy Bigelow, distinguished as Speaker of the Massachusetts General Court, member of the Hartford Convention, director in several Boston banks, and a relative of the Barings of London. Nothing could have been more *bon ton*, moreover, more unreservedly Federalist, than the opinions of the two Lawrence brothers on all issues.

Fully aware of the situation in Lowell, and conscious of their eligibility as large investors, the Lawrences were now in a position to stipulate the conditions on which they would consent to embark on manufacturing on a large scale. The business recession reached its lowest point in 1829, when "several establishments in this country, operating with insufficient capital, were prostrated. The Merrimack . . . made no dividend that year," wrote Nathan Appleton in his history of the textile industry. "During this period of depression," he continued, "Messrs. Amos and Abbott Lawrence were induced by some tempting reductions in the terms made by the Proprietors of the Locks and Canals, to enter largely into the business."

Another factor in the corporate set-up at Lowell that may have given the Lawrences some uneasiness was also disposed of satisfactorily around the same time. This was the unlimited liability clause of all the corporation charters in Lowell, by which every stockholder might be called upon to discharge all the debts of a company, the amount of stock he held bearing no relation to his degree of liability. In the early days at Waltham and Lowell, the Boston Associates had not been averse to this provision, since fear of being liable for huge debts kept out the small fry, but as the number of stockholders in the corporation mills increased, unlimited liability seemed too great a risk to those who did not participate actively in the management of the enterprise. A rise in the number of business failures in 1829 made the problem more acute, and in 1830 the leading Boston businessmen induced the Legislature to pass a limited liability act by raising the old cry that "capital would leave the state" unless this were done promptly.

Now at last Amos and Abbott were ready to plunge heavily into the manufacture of cotton textiles in Lowell. In 1830 they took large blocks of stock in the Suffolk and Tremont companies, which were set up in that year; in 1831 they made a similar investment in the Lawrence Company. They were the principal stockholders in the Boott Mills, established in 1835, and in 1839 they helped launch the Massachusetts Cotton Mills. Nor did they limit their interests to Lowell. In 1831 they were active in promoting the York Manufacturing Company at Saco, Maine, and at one time or another they held some stock in practically all the corporation mills in New England. Like Nathan Appleton, they took over the exclusive selling agency of all those mills in which their interest was large, adding to their earnings from this source by acting as purchasing agents for the raw cotton needed. From the early thirties on, wrote Appleton, "their business, as selling agents, was on the most extensive scale, and their income from all sources large in proportion."

Thus with their entrance into the Lowell project the Lawrence brothers took another long step on their road to fortune.*

Soon after their emergence as great textile manufacturers, Amos Lawrence, whose health had always been delicate, began to suffer from such serious dyspeptic attacks that he retired from active participation in the firm, not without keeping his eagle eye on all the multifarious family interests. Abbott therefore moved up to the head of A. & A. Lawrence, Samuel and William watched over the affairs of the Middlesex Woolen Company, while, to guard the Lawrence interests in Lowell further, brother Luther moved to the textile town when he was chosen president of its

* Although they had made their way into the cotton manufacture at a comparatively early date, they were in no sense pioneers in the industry. Their attitude toward "innovations" was in fact one of suspicion, as can be seen from a letter Abbott wrote to his nephew in 1851 when the latter tried to interest him in the manufacture of linen cloth: "We must wait a little before we take up new things . . . look into it thoroughly . . . we must be careful how we move, for we cannot afford to try experiments that may prove expensive."

newly established bank. Although the weight of the Lawrence influence also won him his election as mayor of Lowell in 1838, poor Luther never learned to watch his step; while showing some friends through the plant of the Middlesex Company in 1839, he fell into a wheel pit and was killed instantly.

Abbott's increased responsibilities on the retirement of Amos did not fulfill all his need for action. He had long been attracted to the idea of entering politics, for which he felt qualified by his business experience, his wide acquaintance, and his address in handling people. Starting at the bottom of the political ladder, as a vote distributor in Boston, he rose to hold various elective offices in the city government, until in 1831 he was made a member of the Common Council. Occasionally Lawrence's yearning for higher political preferment was chilled; after a visit to President Adams at the White House in 1828, for example, he wrote to his brother that he was resolved never to be a politician. But this was only a passing mood. At a fairly early stage in his career Abbott Lawrence came to wield great power behind the scenes in the new Whig party, having learned all the tricks of handling a political machine. Indeed, in the middle thirties John Quincy Adams called him "the most leading man of Whig politics in Boston."

To begin with Lawrence knew how to use his wealth as an instrument of power. He was in the habit of contributing sums of money to the party chest, which, although they might seem insignificant today, were probably as large or larger than those given by any other capitalist of the time. As the Adams campaign against Jackson got under way in 1828, he pledged $100 on the part of his brother and himself for Adams, and promised to do anything required of him to bring about Jackson's defeat. In 1832 he offered to contribute $400 to the Clay campaign in order "to save our common country" from Andrew Jackson.* Besides

---

* His campaign contributions were always for some very definite purpose. Mr. Stuart Mitchell, curator of the Massachusetts Historical Society, tells me of having seen a check Abbott Lawrence gave to the Whig Party in 1852, which was endorsed on the back: "To beat Sumner."

giving liberally out of his own pocket for party purposes, he knew where more funds could be obtained as well as Roscoe Conkling did forty years later; for when Edward Everett informed him in 1828 that money-raising for the presidential campaign was not going well, Abbott answered that custom-house appointees should be taxed for the good fight. Alive to the usefulness of a favorable press, he advised editors, rewarded faithful journalists with money and jobs, punished the recalcitrant, and commanded space in prominent journals for whatever he wished to affirm or deny. At times he even established newspapers to carry on a particular crusade, as when he helped found the *New York American Advocate* in 1831 to plump for a higher tariff.

The journals he controlled followed the waverings of his opinions obediently. When the Compromise Tariff was passed in 1833, for example, with its gradual reduction of duties on imports, he was at first extremely dejected, thinking that his investments at Lowell would suffer. So great was his fright that he temporarily slipped back to the old principles of the Hartford Convention; much as he "deplored" the separation of the Union, he cried, "better that than ruin the entire country by making the concessions here proposed to the South." Only when Clay wrote to reassure him did his anxieties subside. On March 26, 1833 he answered that Clay's letter had helped remove "any prejudices that might have existed. . . . The newspaper press is now silent here upon the subject, and will remain so. I know the editors well, and have taken pains to place the whole subject upon true ground."

His growing influence in the party machine did not gratify his lofty ambitions, however, and he hankered for greater triumphs and higher office. In 1834 the opportunity to shine in the national capital came to him when Nathan Appleton refused to run again for Congress. The nomination then went as a matter of course to Abbott Lawrence, despite the charges of his opponents that he had too little education and too much money to be a proper representative of the Boston district. During the campaign he showed his political suavity when questioned by the Abolitionists as to his views on slavery in the District of Columbia; decrying slavery as a great moral evil, he promised to give the problem careful study, but insisted that if elected he must be "free and untrammeled." There was nothing in this to alienate the votes of the Abolitionists, but in any case Lawrence's election was never in doubt, as he was the choice of the merchant-manu-facturers, whose divine right to select the Boston representative in Congress had not been challenged up to that time.

It needed only a year in office, however, a year of intimate social intercourse with Southern statesmen, to end Lawrence's polite tolerance of the Garrison movement. In 1835 he appeared as vice-chairman of a memorable meeting in Faneuil Hall at which the "agitators of the slavery question" were denounced for "endangering the Union." Lawrence's sudden anxiety for the Union represented an unusually rapid turnabout for one who in 1833 had been quite willing to see the Union dissolved because an undesirable tariff measure was passed.

The change of attitude on Lawrence's part may have come about because after 1833 the South grew steadily more truculent toward those who would do away with her peculiar institution. One Southern newspaper, for example, had stated a new and dangerous principle:

Action, not words . . . is what we expect from the North, not pompous assertions of the right of discussion, not idle declamations on the evils of slavery. . . . Up to this mark the North must come if it would restore tranquillity and preserve the Union. . . . We urge our merchants therefore to extend their intercourse with Philadel-phia, and have none with places that show indifference to our rights and interests. Let Lowell be put first under the ban. Let us use none of her products.

This was grave indeed. Was Lowell to be sacrificed to a few fanatics? What was a moral principle compared to a paying in-vestment? After taking his stand against the Abolitionists at the Faneuil Hall meeting, Lawrence returned to Washington to find himself a social lion amongst the Southerners. He maintained and improved this position by voting to table a motion on the subject of slavery in the District of Columbia.*

Lawrence's first term in Congress seasoned him as a politician and taught him to conceal his underlying motives under the usual democratic platitudes. The rich man in politics has never been a popular figure. Amos once wrote to his son that "the open-mouthed lovers of the *dear people* are self-seekers in most instances. Beware of such." But, on another occasion, even Amos described himself as being one with the toiling masses: "We are literally all working-men; and the attempt to get up a 'Working-men's party' is a libel upon the whole population, as it implies that there are among us large numbers who are not working men." Up to his neck in politics, Abbott himself was obliged to be an "open-mouthed lover of the *dear people*," however he may have shared his brother's opinions and, by implication at least, to dissociate himself from the great capitalists he represented. Responding to an invitation to a dinner in his honor in 1837 after his first term in Congress, he said:

I have always kept in view in legislation those principles which would carry home to the MANY the greatest amount of prosperity and happiness, believing that the FEW can always take care of themselves. Who are the many? Are they not farmers, mechanics, traders, and laborers? And who are the few? Are they not the money-holders and money-lenders of the country? . . . The wealth of the country is founded in its labor, and in giving security to labor we protect the property of the whole country.

It was not, however, as a laboring man that Abbott Lawrence felt the panic that swept the country later in the year 1837. Since he and his brother were in the habit of advancing large credits to customers (at good interest) and had loans outstanding to various factories, their situation was exceedingly precarious for

---

* A few months later Garrison was attacked and nearly lynched by a mob of "gentlemen of property and standing" who had taken their cue from Abbott Lawrence and his friends at the Faneuil Hall meeting.

a while. Envious rivals gloated, somewhat prematurely, over the difficulties in which the Lawrences found themselves, and Abbott himself admitted that it was an experience he would remember with dread as long as he lived.

Fortunately for the Lawrences, the Lowell mills were but little affected by the crash. Although the Merrimack passed its dividend that year, the Tremont mills, in which the Lawrences were leading stockholders, came through with a dividend of 26 percent, including a 20-percent stock dividend. When caught in a tight place the brothers always knew just where to exert pressure to get out. "Their vigilance in looking after their debts secured their success," wrote one of their contemporaries.

Once the panic was over Abbott pursued his dual career in business and politics with his usual vigor. In the late thirties he went into partnership with William Appleton, Nathan's cousin, in the China trade. Not only were these ventures at sea profitable, but they gave Lawrence a social cachet in Boston merchant circles which all his other successes had failed to obtain. By 1840 his investments in the trade to China were so important that he called on the government to protect them from pirates in the China Sea. It was during his second term in Congress that he presented an appeal from American merchants in Canton for armed protection against marauders and for a commercial treaty with China. Previous attempts to obtain naval guarantees for Oriental trade had failed, but on this occasion President Van Buren obliged by ordering the United States East India fleet to Chinese waters.

The range and variety of Lawrence's interests were constantly increasing. Besides his ventures in the Oriental trade he owned ships that plied between Boston and Southern ports, others that went to South America. But he did not limit himself to ocean transportation. During the thirties he turned to the then new railroad business, becoming one of the foremost promoters of the Western Railroad, which was designed to overcome New York's advantage over Boston in access to the growing West. He was also one of the original stockholders in the Boston & Providence Railroad, and others in which the Boston Associates were active. Nevertheless Lawrence had more faith in real estate than in any other form of investment, and was always willing to buy more, "provided I can obtain on long leases to good tenants 8 percent per annum." His holdings of mill stock changed from year to year, depending on the state of the market, but it would seem from a note in his journal, dated January 3, 1842, that he placed more reliance on his commission-house fees than on stock dividends:

At this time all kinds of Manufacturing Stock are depressed and would sell at a great sacrifice if found in the market. I have no occasion however to sell and therefore shall hold on for the present— I have too lean [?] an amount however and intend to sell the first good opportunity the Nashua and Great Falls—Hamilton—Appleton, in short nearly all excepting the Merrimac of which we are not the Agents. Those I should sell in case we had not the Agency would be the Amesbury and Cocheco, neither of which are in a prosperous condition.

And then as an indication of his little confidence in manufacturing stock in general, he urges his executors, in case of his death, to sell a large amount of his mill stocks and invest in productive real estate or other *safe* properties. But he was too impatient to wait for his executors to do the sensible thing, for by January of 1843 he had sold out all but $110,000 worth of his stock in the textile corporations, which represented only one-tenth of his assets. Nevertheless, he continued to pose as spokesman for the cotton manufacturers, and especially for the operatives at mills in which his share was now quite small.

At the time he reduced his stock-holdings, late in 1842, the cash to his credit in A. & A. Lawrence and Company was $250,-000, a sum that cried out for profitable investment. This gave him leverage in all sorts of enterprises. For one thing, he might well disclaim the charge that he was a money-lender, but it was common knowledge that he always had large funds to put out at interest. The power to lend money or withhold it could be

used as a weapon, Lawrence knew, both in business and in politics. It must therefore have been a great source of satisfaction
to him when John C. Calhoun, the states'-rights champion of
South Carolina, approached him for a loan of $30,000 in 1845.
The terms on which Lawrence offered to help Calhoun are not
known directly, but can be gathered from Calhoun's own proud
letter of May 13, 1845, rejecting them:

My dear Sir, I received a few days since your letter of the 30th
April, containing the conditions on which you and your friends
propose to accept the offer of myself and my son to borrow $30,000.
On due reflection I have concluded to decline your proposal.

In offering to pay annually 100,000 pounds of picked cotton of
good quality or its value in the Boston market at the time, on the loan
of the proposed sum, my calculation was based on an estimate, that
at six cents the pound, we could spare that amount, after deducting
all expenses. As our means depended on cotton, I regarded it proper
to offer it as the basis on which our annual payment would depend
until the loan should be reduced. The offer was intended as a business
transaction and accordingly our engagement to be met with perfect
punctuality as well as the debt to be perfectly secured. Thus intended, I must decline your offer, because at 6 cents the pound (the
present average) we would not be able to pay as you propose $6,000
annually on the principle and interest in addition.

Whatever the interest rate, it was evident that Lawrence intended
the loan to be retired within five years, a quick turnover. But
there was another turn of the screw in the deal he proposed, as
Calhoun's letter indicates:

You must permit me to suggest another reason, which, if my impression is correct, would of itself compel me to decline. The impression your letter made on my mind is, that your offer is made from
a disposition to oblige me on the part of yourself and friends, and
that with some inconvenience to you and them. If I am right, as
greatly as I am indebted to you and them for your kind feelings, I
could not accept, for reasons which I feel assured you will duly appreciate on reflection. When I wrote you, I had supposed that a loan

might be effected from the state of [the] money market on terms mutually advantageous. It was only on that supposition that I could make the offer, or accept the loan.

Calhoun may have needed the money, and may have been willing to pay for its use at the usual commercial terms, but he was not going to give Mr. Lawrence his pound of flesh, nor take anything from him as a *favor*. A great cotton planter and slave-owner, he was in business as much as any Boston merchant, and he knew that no sound businessman lends money just to do another fellow a good turn.

As a matter of fact, although his fortune was still growing, almost of itself, having reached over a million and a half by 1845, Abbott Lawrence was at this very time preparing to launch a large venture that would drain most of his cash reserves. After several poor years the corporation mills all over New England had begun to show big profits, beginning in 1843. The Middlesex alone, of which the Lawrences were owners and agents, had paid 29 percent in 1843, in addition to a stock dividend of 11 percent. Prospects for all types of domestic manufactures looked very bright, and further expansion by the Boston Associates seemed to be indicated before other interests made their way into the field. But by 1844 Lowell's water power could no longer be extended to serve any new establishments, and it was necessary to seek for a factory site elsewhere.

This Abbott Lawrence had foreseen. As early as 1843, therefore, he deputed Samuel Lawrence and John Nesmith to buy up the water rights and the 100 farms along the Merrimack River at a spot near North Andover, as had been done at Chelmsford twenty years earlier. When the last sale was completed in 1845, a charter was obtained from the Legislature, incorporating the Essex Company to develop the area for factory purposes. Among the stockholders were Abbott, William and Samuel Lawrence, Nathan Appleton, Patrick Tracy Jackson, John Amory Lowell, and others among the Boston Associates. There were few new faces around the table despite the passage of the years. Abbott

Lawrence was the largest subscriber, taking 100 shares of stock at a thousand dollars a share. In July, 1845, work was started on the dam, and as the building proceeded, the Bay State Mills and the Atlantic Cotton Mills were incorporated, Abbott Lawrence being a large stockholder in both and president of the latter.

The connection of the Lawrence family with the development of the new venture made it inevitable that the town growing up about the mills should be called Lawrence. Lawrence was supposed to parallel the development of Lowell, but with improvements—improvements, that is, in the mill buildings, in the machinery, even in the boarding houses. There was to be no improvement in the pay or in the hours of work as compared with Lowell, otherwise Lowell would have lost its labor force to the new textile city. There were no innovations in the corporate structure or in the methods of doing business, or in the relationship between the directors, the treasurer, the agent, and the operatives. There was in reality nothing new except a certain mad haste in the construction, the use of shoddy materials, and an unbridled spirit of speculation that gripped the town for years. The development of Lowell under Kirk Boott and, indirectly, Nathan Appleton had been dignified, steady, orderly; the development of Lawrence was crude, thoughtless, boom-or-bust.

Abbott Lawrence was only indirectly responsible for this, since he was accustomed to delegating others to execute his large schemes. For in spite of his large investment in the new textile center, he could scarcely give it his exclusive attention. He had many other irons in the fire, and besides much of his time was taken up by political affairs. In politics his important local influence was gradually beginning to tip his ambition toward the highest political offices in the national hierarchy.

He had consented to run for his second term in Congress in 1839 only because of the pressure of his friends. In March, 1840, an attack of bilious fever caused him to resign his seat. Oddly enough, he recovered at the start of the presidential campaign, in which he immersed himself with passion, as now, after twelve long years, it seemed likely that the Democrats could be driven from office. Taking a leaf out of the book of the Jacksonians, the Whigs brought out their hard cider and their log-cabin symbols, flooded the country with songs and slogans for "Tippecanoe and Tyler too," and proved to their own satisfaction that they could outdo the Democrats in rabble-rousing and demagoguery. Abbott Lawrence was a tireless campaigner for General Harrison, the Whig candidate, seeing party workers from all the states, and spending money freely to beat Van Buren.

When at last all the cider barrels were emptied, and victory was won, Abbott Lawrence expected the successful presidential candidate to acknowledge his services by offering him the post of Secretary of the Treasury. General Harrison, however, proved to be wanting in gratitude, and the job went to another man. But Lawrence's aid to the winning party received flattering recognition from another source. "In February, 1841," Appleton remembered:

> Mr. Abbott Lawrence showed me a letter from Mr. Webster, who was to be Secretary of State under General Harrison, requesting that he, myself and another person whom he named, would come on to Washington previous to the 4th of March as he might wish for consultation and advice on the coming in of the new administration. Accordingly Mr. Lawrence and myself travelled to Washington and remained there about a week, during which we had many conferences with Mr. Webster.

If Lawrence was led by this to believe that his views on public questions would have some influence with the administration, he was speedily disabused. Harrison died after a month in office, and was succeeded by Tyler, who had been placed on the ticket in order to catch Democratic votes. As Tyler vetoed one bill after another desired by the Whigs, particularly a bill to recharter the Bank of the United States, the relations between the President and Lawrence grew more and more strained. Webster tried to mollify the Boston magnate by inducing Tyler to offer Lawrence the post as commissioner from Massachusetts to negotiate

the Maine boundary question with Lord Ashburton, but while
Lawrence accepted the assignment, he would not make peace.
On the contrary, he expected Webster to resign from the cabinet
in a rebuke to Tyler, and when Webster refused to comply
until he had completed certain diplomatic negotiations, Lawrence
decided that the Secretary of State merited public chastisement.

This he administered at the Massachusetts Whig convention in
1842; under his leadership the delegates passed a resolution of
"eternal separation" from the administration of John Tyler, and
went on record as favoring Henry Clay for the Presidency in
1844. The convention's action was doubly offensive to Webster,
both as a member of Tyler's official family, and as Clay's rival
for the Presidency. Webster could also take it as a grim reminder
that when a Boston magnate laid out good money for the support
of an impecunious statesman, he expected some consideration in
return. It was well known that on at least one occasion Webster
had been indebted to Lawrence for financial assistance.*

Since Lawrence held the money-bags, he had the whip hand.
The consequences of being estranged from him were brought
home to Webster very forcibly in February, 1845, when once
more the hat was passed among Boston financiers for their "fine
symbol and mantel ornament—costly enough to those who must
keep it," as Emerson described the black-browed orator. To
this second fund Abbott Lawrence pointedly refused to subscribe,
an omission so marked that Nathan Appleton took it upon himself to heal the breach between the two men. In August he induced Webster, who was really the injured party to the dispute,
to write a "propitiatory" letter to Lawrence, a letter carefully
edited by Appleton to give it an air of greater warmth and esteem.
As a result of this gesture, Abbott Lawrence consented to admit
Daniel Webster to his presence once more.

But this was merely a truce, to be maintained until political

* Lawrence was one of fifty Boston merchants who had raised $50,000 in 1835
to maintain Webster in public life. Edward Everett, who had started the money-
raising campaign, told prospective contributors that Webster was needed in
Washington to protect "our friends in Boston . . . their houses, their lands,
their stocks."

rivalry brought them into collision again. The unpopularity of the Mexican War, during the administration of the Democrat Polk, seemed to offer a good chance of a Whig victory in the presidential contest in 1848. After many disappointments, Webster, the perennial aspirant, hoped that this year would bring him the coveted prize, but he had shown himself to be "not dependable" shortly before the convention. He had swerved from the party line when he stated in the Senate that he would oppose the further extension of slavery or of slave representation at all times. Lawrence and his friends among the Boston Associates (many of whom were devoted to Webster) had been driven, on the other hand, into condoning the extension of slavery whenever the Southerners forced the issue. In retaliation, therefore, for this temporary exhibition of moral fervor on Webster's part, Lawrence crushed his presidential aspirations once more, and threw all the weight of his money and influence behind General Taylor.

The election of 1848 was the third presidential campaign in which Abbott Lawrence played a prominent part, but the first that saw him in the role of President-maker. What was more, he seemed to think that if he could make Taylor President, it ought to be simple to make himself Vice President. After all, General Taylor was an old man. . . . As early as March, 1848, a group of convention "fixers" began corresponding with Nathan Appleton about Lawrence's candidacy:

We are now ready to strike for *our* friend and *your* friend for the Vice-Presidency, and we write for the purpose of asking you to unite with us in furnishing the sinews of war . . . We must have strong men in Philadelphia [at the Convention] well known to politicians out of the state, to make an impression upon the convention and we . . . will be obliged to pay their expenses, to say nothing of their time.

But somehow it didn't come off. Even some of the Massachusetts delegates to the convention "spurned the bribe," and Millard Fillmore was named instead.

Concealing his mortification, Lawrence threw himself into the election campaign with undiminished enthusiasm, declaring at a great ratification meeting at Faneuil Hall in June that Taylor was the worthiest man to be named for the presidency since George Washington! In August he wrote to Nathan Appleton: "General Taylor is gaining every day. Tell ——— I hope he is ready to lend us a helping hand. I am willing to spend and be spent in the cause, but it would cheer me very much to have the countenance of the officials of this State in promoting the great cause of conservatism."

Such outstanding services to the winning candidate rated solid recompense, in the view of Lawrence and his friends. Nathan Appleton now expected this to be nothing less than the office of Secretary of State, or, failing that, the Treasury Department, but Taylor and his advisers, aware of popular clamor should a millionaire be appointed to such influential posts, passed him over for the important cabinet jobs. Abbott Lawrence's good friend, Jefferson Davis, urged that he be appointed Secretary of the Navy, but Lawrence considered this *infra dig*, and let it be known that he was not interested. In an attempt to placate his powerful supporters in New England, Taylor thereupon offered the textile magnate the highest office in the diplomatic corps, the Ministry to England. To Lawrence, as well as to his wife, and his nubile daughter, this was practically the only office within the power of the President to bestow that could have made up for the loss of the vice presidency. He accepted with alacrity, and departed for England even before the Senate had confirmed his nomination.

The Boston merchants took the appointment as a tribute to their occupation and their achievements, foreseeing with delight the improvement of their social status in London, the presentations at court, the opportunities to consort with persons of rank under the wing of a minister who was their close associate. Even old Amos, confined to his home by illness, and unable to take advantage of these rare privileges, who had looked with some disfavor on Abbott's political machinations, boasted a little now of "my brother, who is Minister to the Court of Saint James." The cries of jubilation that rose from Beacon Hill throats drowned out the sniggers of envious Democrats, who chortled over the anomaly of a free-trade country being represented at a free-trade court by a thorough protectionist.

Now at the apex of his career, Abbott in his fifties had borne out all the promise of his youth. His fortune, which he reckoned at over two million dollars in 1847, was one of the largest in the country. And in the fashion of the time, which allowed for no nuances of feeling toward successful men, he was spoken of as a paragon, the embodiment of all the noblest qualities, a veritable Chevalier Bayard. It was in such terms that Judge Story described him in a letter to Edward Everett in 1843: "I know of no one among us who now enjoys a more enviable reputation for integrity, intelligence, and public and private virtue."

Allowing for the bias of personal friendship in such eulogies, there was undeniably much that was attractive or engaging in Abbott Lawrence's personality. Nathan Appleton was not the only astute and hard-headed businessman who came under the spell of his "frank and conciliating manners." It is true that Abbott fawned on royalty and courted members of the peerage somewhat too assiduously, to the amusement of several Boston worthies, and yet he often exerted himself to be "democratic" and winning with men of humble station.

But despite his authoritative carriage, part of the baggage of a great Boston merchant, Abbott's volatile temperament, his political ambitions, and his appetite for wealth gave some concern to the "steadier" members of his own family. In 1842 his nephew Amos Abbott summed up his uncle's character in his journal: "He still grasps at money tho' he has more than a million and is the richest man of his age here: he loves power too and office. He does not grow better nor happier as he grows older." Even brother Amos, who up to 1844 had been a steady contributor to the Whig party chest, was at length disgusted by Abbott's greed for office. In 1848 he turned down a newspaper editor who had asked for a contribution to forward Abbott's vice-presidential ambitions, saying: "If my vote would make my brother Vice-President, I would not give it, as I think it lowering his good name to accept office of any sort, by employing such means as are now needful to get votes." Amos's squeamishness in this regard was not shared by Abbott, who was more realistic about the various means by which elections were won.

But something more than money, more than pressure on the custom-house officials and other beneficiaries of the spoils system was required to win elections. Aware that ideas were needful too, Abbott Lawrence learned to fire off resounding cliches as purposefully as any Fourth of July orator. De Tocqueville had pointed out that democratic communities had a natural taste for freedom, but that they had an even greater passion for equality. It was his consciousness of this passion for equality in the people that made Lawrence play down his aristocratic pretensions when in the political arena. Instead he posed as a "worker" or "laborer," though the most arduous physical task he ever performed, as Miriam Beard wrote in her account of the American businessman, was to sweep out his store in the morning.

Moreover, his love of the "dear people" did not extend so far as to make him relinquish any of his real power in government and industry. In 1853, when a new constitution was submitted to the voters of Massachusetts, a constitution extending the franchise for the first time since 1780 and limiting the influence of the merchant aristocracy in the state government, Lawrence pulled all sorts of wires, and made a deal with the Irish Catholic bishop of Boston to defeat the proposed change. The people who tended the machines in his mills might likewise desire certain changes in their working conditions, but Abbott Lawrence knew better than they what was good for them.

If there was any want of originality in the ideas he put forth, he played by ear with enough skill to overawe those who admired his success. This is exemplified perhaps best in his widely publicized letters to William C. Rives of Virginia, written early in 1846, just as a newly elected Democratic Congress was preparing to revise the tariff of 1842 downward. In these letters he used the well-known arguments of Webster and Clay, and the then lesser-known thesis of Horace Mann, without acknowledgment, to win over the South to the idea of a protective tariff. Echoing Webster, he wrote:

The American system was forced upon us, and was adopted for the purpose of creating a home market for the products of the soil of the South and West. We resisted the adoption of a system which we honestly believed would greatly injure our navigation, and drive us from our accustomed employments into a business we did not understand. We came into it, however, reluctantly, and soon learned that, with the transfer of our capital, we acquired skill in the use of it; and that, so far from our foreign commerce being diminished, it was increased, and that our domestic tonnage and commerce were very soon more than quadrupled.

Instead of combating the North on the tariff issue, wrote Lawrence, let the state of Virginia show that the South too could develop manufactures. But for this an educated populace was necessary, for without a certain level of education among the operatives, such projects would stand little chance of success. In developing this thought, Lawrence paraphrased the ideas of Horace Mann, who, after observing how much more productive the educated girls of Lowell were than illiterate immigrants, had published his famous report to prove that education had "a market value . . . it may be turned to pecuniary account."

But although Lawrence here spoke reverently of popular education, it will be recalled that he had always resisted any amelioration of the school system that would have to be paid for out of his own pocket. In fact, while he told Rives that "I am, therefore, clear in my convictions, not only of the duty, but the expediency, of introducing manufactures extensively into your State, with an expansive system of popular education . . ." it was to be taken with a grain of salt, for when the Virginia Legislature, and a committee of citizens from Richmond urged him to come down and show them how to do it, Mr. Lawrence was too busy, and his funds were otherwise engaged.

In a further and most important passage in these letters to Rives, Lawrence disclaimed any intention of obtaining special benefits for his own section of the country:

> I would not, if I could, have a tariff made for Massachusetts alone. If, however, there should be a new one, let our interests, with those of every other State in the Union, share that protection to which we are all entitled, and of which we claim our full share. I can with confidence assure you that we shall go upward and onward. We will work. If twelve hours' labor in the twenty-four will not sustain us, we can and will work fourteen; and at the same time feel that Congress cannot take the sinews from our arms, or rob us of the intelligence acquired from our public schools, established by the foresight and wisdom of our fathers.

If twelve hours' labor in the twenty-four will not sustain us, we can and will work fourteen. Can this remark have been intended for Mr. Rives, or for the Southern bloc that opposed high tariffs? Not by a long shot. Like many a similar innocuous reference in a political document, it was designed for home consumption. A year or so before the publication of these letters some of the young women in Lowell had started a drive to reduce the average working day from twelve to ten hours, a reform that had already been won for government employees and in certain industries. In the personal correspondence and the published papers of the Boston cotton magnates there is no reference made to the ten-hour movement, except in this one instance. But here it is clear: not only was the ten-hour day not to be discussed, but if the operators were stubborn in their demands, and if the tariff failed to pass as he desired, Mr. Lawrence would have no hesitation in imposing a fourteen-hour day.

On January 1, 1847, Abbott Lawrence wrote in his journal: "I hope to be able to bring my mind into a more truly religious state than it has been the past year. How great is the responsibility of a rich man!" In July he noted that his income for the past three years had been $120,000 a year, and that he was worth over $2,000,000. This vast wealth, coupled perhaps with some apprehensions about his true state of grace, brought him to the decision to offer some hostages to fortune. He therefore announced his intention to give $50,000 to Harvard College to establish a scientific school, the largest sum ever offered to Harvard by any living donor. All over the world men acclaimed this unexampled generosity, further proof, if any were needed, that virtue resided in great riches. Among the few who ventured to sound a sour note was the editor of an Albany newspaper, whose censorious remarks caught the eye of an English visitor:

That prince of manufacturers, Abbott Lawrence, has made a donation of $50,000, for the purpose of erecting suitable buildings, and endowing professorships, for a new department of education in the University of Harvard. . . . This magnificent gift of Mr. Lawrence is worthy of praise. How vastly better to do good in one's lifetime than to hoard up the shining dust. . . . And the inquiry has involuntarily arisen in our mind, from whence came this vast wealth? From the looms and spindles of Lowell. And this is one of those men who have besieged Congress for *protection*, so they might live. Was any of this trumpet-tongued charity made up from the sixpenny-a-week clippings from the wages of the weavers and spinners at Lowell? How many, many thousand extra hours of wearisome, life-wearing toil did it add to the over-wrought limbs and hands of the operatives, in order that *one man* may be gazetted as a great public benefactor?

Chapter IX

FAME: THE LITERARY MILL GIRLS

WHILE Boston textile magnates disdained the use of direct advertising, they showed great finesse in bringing their wares to the favorable attention of the public, acting as their own public-relations counselors with a skill that can scarcely be matched by the hucksters of our day. At comparatively small expense they were able to spread the fame of Lowell goods all over the world, and in the same breath acquire stature as benefactors of humanity. Willing members of the claque that applauded their every achievement included distinguished visitors from France and England, as well as Americans of some importance.

There were indeed so many difficulties attending the introduction of textile manufacturing into this country that the slightest success called for fulsome self-congratulation. Prominent personages were induced to wear garments made of domestic material in order to highlight the earliest performances in this field, as when George Washington for his first inauguration wore a suit of cloth made by the Hartford Woollen Manufactory. It is noteworthy, however, that Washington paid for the material out of his own pocket, a punctilious gesture that others did not see fit to imitate. After Abbott Lawrence began investing in the Lowell mills, he used to give away bolts of goods for a suit or a dress to key figures in the political and social life of the country, with the frank intention of building up good will. In some cases his efforts were unavailing. Dolly Madison, for example, on receiving such a gift from Mr. Lawrence, was extremely circumspect in her acknowl-edgments, leaving him uncertain as to whether she would indorse his products by wearing them.*

In another instance, involving a person less sensitive to the niceties of good breeding, Lawrence was more successful, for when he conferred a similar favor on Davy Crockett, the famous backwoodsman was outspoken, almost vociferous, in his expres-sions of gratitude. As a Jacksonian Democrat in Congress, Crockett had held little interest for the Boston merchant-manu-facturers; only after his rupture with Jackson in the early thirties did they make much of him, capitalizing on his homespun back-ground, and feeding his egregious vanity to obtain the most grati-fying publicity the town of Lowell had yet known. It was in Crockett's *Account of a Tour to the North and Down East,* one of the most popular books of the time, that he told of Lawrence's kindness in presenting him with a fine suit of domestic broadcloth, adding that "it was as good cloth as the best I ever bought as best imported." Then he went on to describe in great detail his visit to Lowell in May, 1834.

I had heard so much of this place that I longed to see it. . . . I wanted to see how it was that these Northerners could buy our cot-ton and carry it home, manufacture it, bring it back, and sell it half for nothing; and in the meantime, be well to live and make money besides.

After buttering up the manufacturers for their financial acu-men and industry, Crockett proceeded to praise them indirectly for the good looks and fine bearing of the operatives also, using for this his characteristic rustic imagery and humor:

We stopped at a large stone house at the head of the falls of the Merrimack River, and having taken a little refreshment, went down among the factories. The dinner-bells were ringing and the folks

* I am indebted for this information to Miss Katharine Anthony, author of the recently published *Dolly Madison.*

pouring out of the houses like bees out of gum. I looked at them as they passed, all well-dressed, lively and genteel in their appearance, indeed the girls looked as if they were coming from a quilting frolic. . . . I went in among the young girls, and talked with many of them. Not one expressed herself as tired of her employment, or oppressed with work; all talked well, and looked healthy. Some of them were very handsome; and I could not help observing that they kept the prettiest inside, and put the homely ones on the outside rows.

It is probable that not only the prettiest girls, but also the trouble-makers, were put on the inside rows, where they could not speak to visitors, for only two months before large numbers of them had gone on strike in protest against a wage-cut. But the manu-facturers did not rely on female pulchritude alone to sway the old bear-hunter; they prepared a table of statistics to prove to him that industrialism was "calculated not only to give individual hap-piness and prosperity, but to add to our national wealth and pros-perity." But lest the cold figures should fail of their purpose, Crockett was lodged and fed, "toted, toasted and praised to his heart's content" at the expense of the benevolent corporations. He returned to the Southwest an ardent protectionist, and ran for Congress once more on a high-tariff platform. But this conversion from his earlier Jacksonian principles proved unprofitable, since his Tennessee constituents, not having experienced Abbott Law-rence's hospitality, as Parrington says, did not give him a chance to cast a vote in Congress for a measure so pleasing to his Northern friends. These last had to remain content with the unqualified praise of their venture in Crockett's book, which through its wide circulation made Lowell and its girls a household word through-out the land.

The textile manufacturers also extended themselves in offering courtesies to visitors from abroad, many of whom included glow-ing descriptions of Lowell in their travel memoirs, as one of the wonders of the American republic. Beginning with Captain Basil Hall, in 1827, a whole succession of foreign tourists turned up year after year until about 1862, when the town finally ceased to exercise its former charm on the curious. At all times permission to visit the mills had to be obtained from the treasurer or the commission house in Boston; prominent persons, however, came armed with letters from Nathan Appleton, or from one of the Lawrence brothers, or, better still, with Appleton or Abbott Lawrence as guide and expositor. After enjoying the warm hospitality of these gentlemen in Boston, the visitors were all the more inclined to see Lowell through the eyes of the textile magnates, and if a slight exaggeration crept into their descriptions, it was of no more consequence than the flattering expressions one might use with regard to a host's progeny.

Captain Hall's *Travels in North America in the Years 1827 and 1828* was the first travel book about the United States to contain an account of Lowell, and in a way served as a model for those that followed. With the aid of Nathan Appleton, "his friendly guide," he saw Lowell as a magic city conjured up out of waste land. It could surely have been no accident either that Captain Hall interpreted the fine appearance of the operatives as a sign of the merits of the industrial set-up.

The whole discipline, ventilation, and other arrangements [he wrote] appeared to be excellent, of which the best proof was the healthy and cheerful look of the girls, all of whom, by the way, were trigged out with much neatness and simplicity, and wore high tortoise-shell combs at the back of their heads. . . . On the 13th of October, at 6 o'clock in the morning, I was awakened by the bells which tolled the people to their work, and on looking from the window, saw the whole space between the factories and the village speckled over with girls, nicely dressed, and glittering with bright shawls and showy-colored gowns and gay bonnets, all streaming along to their business, with an air of lightness, and an elasticity of step, implying an obvious desire to get to their work.

Another British traveler, Patrick Shirreff, visiting Lowell in 1833, came closer to the real reasons for the superiority of the mill operatives. In his *Tour through North America*, he drew a comparison between British and American textile workers that could not but be pleasing to the cotton magnates here. After describing the elegance and social graces of the Lowell girls, he went on to say:

The recent introduction of large manufacturing establishments, thin population, and ample reward of labor, account for the apparent comfort and propriety of the Lowell young women. The situation of the manufacturing class in Britain is very different; nurtured amidst poverty and vice, they toil in crowded and unwholesome factories from infancy, often disregarded by parents and employers, and attaining maturity ruined in constitution and in morals, with few of the sympathies of humanity.

The work of free publicity for the corporations was carried on even by the independent Miss Martineau, whose *Society in America*, published in 1837, had a wide circulation both in England and in the United States. The celebrated "blue" devoted considerable space in her book to an account of the factory system as practiced in the corporation mill towns. It was she who first circulated those highly exaggerated tales about the large numbers of girls who were "accumulating an independence" by working in the mills. So distorted was her view of such matters, and so elementary her economics, that in 1843 she wrote to the editor of the *Offering* urging that the Lowell girls agree to a reduction in the tariff and thus voluntarily accept a wage cut so that operatives in England might be able to raise their standards a little!

I have faith, that . . . you will rejoice in such a diminution of your very handsome earnings. If your manufactures should be reduced you will be satisfied with a supply of your real wants, and forego the rest rather than that thousands of willing and industrious girls should have the sole alternative of a life of shame, and blindness, and death before the age of twenty-five.

Although the American manufacturers may have resented Miss Martineau's views on the tariff, they could hardly have been put out by her suggestion that wages be lowered, since they were at the time in the process of doing that very thing.

And still the visitors kept coming to Lowell, "one of the most extraordinary towns in this extraordinary country," as Charles Augustus Murray wrote in his *Travels in North America in 1834, 5,6*. George Combe, the phrenologist, lectured there in 1838, and dutifully commented on the respectability and good health of the operatives. Lord Morpeth, later the Earl of Carlisle, came in 1840, under the wing of Nathan Appleton, and, while his impressions were not published, we know from his manuscript diary that he was very favorably impressed. The various Frenchmen who turned up likewise gave the town, its girls, and its industrialists a boost. Michel Chevalier was the first, but he was followed by Philarète Chasles and Léon Faucher in the forties, both of whom wrote with considerable interest of what they had observed. The girls were so accustomed to visitors that they were not unduly surprised when Mar Yohanan, a Nestorian bishop, walked past their looms in his flowing Oriental robes.

Certainly to those who could compare the American town to the dark, gloomy, wretched manufacturing cities of Europe, Lowell seemed like a workers' paradise. Its fashionable young women, its new buildings, free of soot, its "Italian skies," as someone described them, unclouded with smoke, all kindled the imagination of the stranger from abroad. Since the textile magnates were aware of its attractions for the stranger, the city was for a while the pet of the industry, and a "must" for every traveler who intended to report on the new society growing up on this side of the Atlantic. It was to be expected therefore that the most famous visitor of all, he whose books had pitilessly described all the horrors of the industrial revolution in his own country, should promptly be confronted with its blessings in the mills and boarding houses of Lowell. In his *American Notes*, Charles Dickens spared nothing and no one in the New World that struck him as strange or foolish or vile; but for Lowell he had only kind words, so that while the rest of the country smarted under his criticism, the owners and operatives of the textile city preened themselves all the more on his unqualified approbation.

Arriving at Lowell in the winter of 1841, Dickens was met at the station "by a gentleman intimately connected with the management of the factories there," who took him on a conducted tour of the mills and boarding houses. Nothing could be left to chance on such an important occasion. Only the best was to be viewed by the distinguished visitor with the powerful pen, only the finest mill and the best-appointed boarding house. And, except for one sly reference to the muddy streets, Dickens painted everything he saw in those sunbright colors he reserved for the happier scenes in his novels.

The girls, he found, were healthy, neat, and dressed in warm, serviceable clothes, with "the manners and deportment of young women; not of degraded beasts of burden," while their working quarters were as clean, comfortable, and well ordered as the work itself permitted. The hospital set aside for their use, the freshly painted boarding houses where they lived, also received words of praise. But Dickens' thoughtful guide had something even more astonishing to point out to him in the activities of the girls outside of their working hours. It was this that aroused Dickens' greatest enthusiasm:

I am now going to state three facts, which will startle a large class of readers on this side of the Atlantic very much. First, there is a joint-stock piano in a great many of the boarding-houses. Secondly, nearly all these young ladies subscribe to circulating libraries. Thirdly, they have got up among themselves a periodical called The Lowell Offering, "a repository of original articles, written exclusively by females actively employed in the mills,"—which is duly printed, published, and sold; and whereof I brought away from Lowell four hundred good solid pages, which I have read from beginning to end.

What! The operatives were not only virtuous, clean, healthy, pretty, well dressed and well paid, but they were literary too? This was news to a great many American readers of Dickens' book, no less than to his English and Continental audience. Surely there could be no valid criticism, on any grounds, of a system that favored such elegant accomplishments.

Nothing, in fact, contributed more to the esteem in which the Lowell mills and their owners were held than the publication of the *Lowell Offering*. An American in Paris, for example, attending a lecture given by Philarète Chasles, professor of comparative literature, at the Collège de France, was amazed and gratified to hear an hour's discourse on the merit and significance of the *Lowell Offering*. As an indication of what working women could accomplish for themselves in a young republic, Adolphe Thiers brought a bound volume of selections from the *Offering* to show to the French Chamber of Deputies. Georges Sand also saluted the literary debut of the mill girls across the seas, whose interests seemed to her so different from those of French textile operatives. In England Harriet Martineau wrote an introduction to *Mind Among the Spindles*, a collection of their choicest pieces, which was solemnly reviewed by the *Edinburgh Journal*. Though sparing of outright approval, the *Journal's* critic granted that "some of the articles, the verse as well as the prose, would appear as respectable efforts for females of any rank of life." In his *American Notes* Dickens had made a similar comment: "I will only observe, putting entirely out of sight the fact of the articles having been written by these girls after the arduous labors of the day, that it will compare advantageously with a great many English annuals."

By stressing the "rank of life" from which these literary efforts emanated, the foreign commentators showed their fundamental ignorance of the American scene. As pointed out earlier, the girls who worked in the mills and contributed to the *Lowell Offering* had the same family and educational background as their employers. They were natives of New England, and in the intellectual flowering of that region authorship was respected at all economic levels. The remarkable thing about their literary interests was not that they had them so much as the fact that they found the time and energy to indulge them. There is some reason to believe that it was the increasing pressure and monotony of their tasks that drove many of the girls to the pursuit of *belles lettres.*

Some critics, from that day to this, have tried to pooh-pooh the girls' literary accomplishments by stressing the small number who contributed to the magazine. It is true that the list of collaborators included only fifty-four names, and of these only one minor talent—that of Lucy Larcom—was fully developed later. But the active participation of fifty-four girls indicates a much larger proportion of intelligent and somewhat cultivated young women to be drawn upon. Many more had literary interests than had literary gifts. With all the facilities for study at our modern colleges, the number of students who write for the literary magazines there is not much greater.

Literary expression was no novelty to New England women of that period, for even in the remote villages from which the Lowell operatives came, there was generally a local authoress, whose essays, tales, or poems appeared in one of the many journals or annuals published for the delight and edification of other females. Lowell itself boasted of an *Album or Ladies' Commonplace Book* in the thirties, a *Ladies' Literary Repository*, and a *Ladies' Pearl* in the forties. As a rule, clergymen edited these periodicals, giving them the solemn and religious cast then commonly rated as a token of high literary quality. Although the first efforts of the Lowell operatives were likewise made under the guidance of their ministers, these men had the good sense to encourage less stilted compositions than were contained in most ladies' magazines then current.

The girls who were most interested in educating themselves had been organized in Improvement Circles for some years before they ventured into print. One of the most serious of these held its meetings in the vestry of the Second Universalist Church, whose intelligent and liberal minister, Abel C. Thomas, was the first to urge his young parishioners to write. His Improvement Circle met every two weeks to read and discuss manuscripts, some of which seemed so good that in October, 1840, it was decided to publish the best, with only slight revision by Mr. Thomas, under the heading of the *Lowell Offering*.

Six months later, in April, 1841, the Improvement Circle of the First Congregational Church, not to be outdone by the Universalists, brought forth the *Operatives' Magazine*. At least Lucy Larcom, who was then a Congregationalist, described its origins in this way, although the first issue states that it was edited by "an Association of Gentlemen of Different . . . Denominations." Denominational differences broke down completely when, in August, 1842, the two magazines were merged, while at the same time members of one Improvement Circle were automatically granted membership in each of the others.

"We did not receive much criticism," said Lucy Larcom when reviewing her early literary essays; "perhaps it would have been better for us if we had." The male editors, in fact, seem to have stood in some awe of the prodigies they had brought forth, stepping down after a short time in favor of young women who were or had been mill girls. Lydia S. Hall and Abba A. Goddard, who had graduated from mill work to become teachers in the public schools, took over the editorship of the *Operatives' Magazine*, while Harriet Farley and Harriott F. Curtis left the mills only when they became co-editors of the *Offering* after the merger.

When the first occasional numbers of the *Offering* began appearing, it was not intended that it should be the exclusive organ of the Lowell operatives. It was planned rather as a trial balloon, to be followed by a magazine with a broader base, *The Garland of the Mills*, made up of contributions from operatives all over New England. The interest aroused by the *Offering*, however, was so great that it began to appear regularly every month, and the original project was abandoned. Other magazines made their appearance in other textile towns—the *Olive Leaf and Factory Girls' Repository* of Chicopee, the *Factory Girl* of Newmarket, the *Factory Girls' Garland* of Exeter among others, but while these encouraged contributions from the operatives in their respective communities, they were as a rule founded and edited not by mill girls but by men interested in exploiting factory operatives for financial support.*

Like all aspiring writers, the girls were enchanted at seeing their modest compositions published. One of them crowed: "True, we had seen, or heard the articles before, but they seemed so much better in print. They appeared, to us, as good as anybody's writings. They sounded as if written by people who never worked at all!" This self-congratulatory note was justified by the warm reception their magazine was accorded. "Everywhere the Offering has been received with favor," wrote the editor in the issue of December, 1840. Papers had been sent from all over the country, she added, with a request for exchange privileges, and "letters from far and near have come to us, *postpaid* (without an exception), desiring information." With success the editors gained assurance, adopting a somewhat patronizing tone toward their confreres in the magazine field, as when they presented their compliments to the "boys" who ran the Yale and Dartmouth literary monthlies. So great was the interest in what they were doing that some of the most prominent figures in the intellectual life of the country were numbered among their friends and patrons: William Ellery Channing, John Greenleaf Whittier, Horace Greeley, Henry I. Bowditch, Maria Chapman, Elizabeth Peabody, and Emma Willard, among others.

The contents of the magazine followed the pattern of all such publications at the time, comprising poems, stories, descriptive sketches, and editorials, in all of which virtue was extolled and vice deplored with spirit enough to dispel any notions that the laborious occupation of the authors had led to any lowering of their moral standards. If this were all they had had to say, however, the *Offering* might have died stillborn. Happily most of the contributions reflected the life of the girls in their mills and boarding houses in a fresh and unpretending manner. "It is pleasant to find," wrote Dickens, in a very keen and significant appreciation,

* An exception to this was *The Wampanoag and Operatives' Journal* of Fall River, edited by Mrs. Green.

that many of its tales are of the mills, and of those who work in them.
. . . A strong feeling for the beauties of nature, as displayed in the
solitudes the writers have left at home, breathes through its pages like
wholesome village air; and though a circulating library is a favourable
school for the study of such topics, it has very scant allusion to fine
clothes, fine marriages, fine homes, or fine life.

Some of the sketches in the *Offering* furnish the best source
material we possess on the daily life of the operatives, while
many of the stories are thinly disguised "reporter pieces," describing the ambitions, the concerns, the difficulties of adjustment of country girls on their first contact with town life. In
style these articles were much less ponderously "literary" than
much that appeared in other ladies' magazines of the period,
possibly because, as one of their contributors wrote later, the
girls tried to model themselves on classical English authors such
as Addison and Goldsmith.

The poetry in the *Offering* was almost completely undistin-
guished. In this the models of the girls were Mrs. Sigourney,
Felicia Hemans, Hannah More, and other pallid poetesses of the
genteel tradition. Some of the girls claimed to have been influenced by Milton, Pope, and Cowper, but any resemblance to
the works of these masters was wholly imaginary. Occasionally
some simple and unaffected verses were printed, as for example
Lydia S. Hall's *Tomb of Washington*, which communicates a
very real emotion. Lucy Larcom, the most talented of all the
"literary" mill girls, frequently contributed stories and poems,
first to the *Operatives' Magazine*, and later to the *Offering*. She
was only nineteen years old, and had already spent eight years
in the mills when she wrote the *Sabbath Bells:*

> *List! a faint, a far-off chime!*
> *'Tis the knell of holy time,*
> *Chiming from the city's spires,*
> *From the hamlet's altar fires,*
> *Waking woods and lonely dells,*
> *Pleasant are the Sabbath bells.*

which, while a kind of pastiche of poetic cliches, shows the author as possessed of a fairly good ear. But this was merely an apprenticeship for Lucy Larcom. By seeing her verses in print she was better able to realize her own shortcomings, and after a few years she went on courageously to fill in the gaps in her education at an age when most women might have decided that it was too late.

The freest self-expression in the magazine, as always, belonged of right to the editors. Along with the responsibility of the position the editors took the bows, spoke in defense of the mill girls against their detractors, or scolded the operatives for their frailties. The intoxication they felt because of their role may be better understood when it is remembered that at this period only four other women in the United States were engaged in editorial work: Sarah Hale of *Godey's Lady's Book*, Cornelia Walter of the *Boston Transcript*, Mrs. Green of the Fall River *Wampanoag Journal*, and Lydia Maria Child of the *Anti-Slavery Standard*, all of them cultivated women of marked character and unusual ability. It therefore required no little daring for Harriott Curtis and Harriet Farley to undertake the management of the *Offering*, the more so as they lacked the education and middle-class background, the "connections," so to speak, of the others.

The poverty in which these two young women were reared belies the proposition so often put forth that the mill girls went to Lowell and the other corporation towns merely to raise money for a dowry or to buy finery. For instance, Miss Curtis, a descendant of Miles Standish, was born in Kellyvale, a tiny Vermont village where she grew up in the most straitened circumstances. Like so many women without other skills, she turned to writing to earn a little money, and before she went to Lowell had achieved some slight success as the author of one of the popular novels of the day: *Kate in Search of a Husband*. The earnings of a factory operative, however, were larger and more dependable than any she could expect from the writing of fiction. At Lowell she became a highly skilled harness-knitter, and was earning relatively high pay when she quit the mills to become an editor of the *Offering*. A vivacious, personable young woman, she was so forthright in her speech that "it made talk" in the town, as Harriet Hanson Robinson reported. Miss Curtis took charge of the subscription department of the magazine, wrote some of the editorial comment, and also contributed a novel called *The Smugglers*, which came out serially beginning with the issue of November, 1843.

Miss Farley's home background was equally poverty-stricken. Frank Sanborn, the friend and supporter of John Brown of Osawatomie, relates that his first feeling of compassion toward the poor was aroused by hearing that the Farley family had only potatoes and cream for breakfast, at a period when most Americans broke their fast with the equivalent of a five-course dinner. Harriet was a daughter of the Reverend Stephen Farley, a Congregationalist minister who held various parishes in New Hampshire. After bearing ten children, her mother gave up the struggle and became harmlessly insane. It was necessary for Harriet to make some financial contribution to the family at the age of fourteen, but while working at straw-plaiting, binding shoes, tailoring, and other trades that could be carried on at home, she managed to acquire a smattering of French, drawing, ornamental needlework, and all the "usual accomplishments." This was supposed to equip her for a teaching position, but she frankly did not want to be a teacher. The steady wages at Lowell were very attractive to a girl of this type; more, they were probably necessary for her survival. Commenting on her life in the mills, she wrote in a letter to Harriet Hanson Robinson in 1848: "I made good wages; I dressed economically; I assisted in the liberal education of one brother, and endeavoured to be the guardian angel of a lovely sister."

Harriet Farley quite clearly enjoyed occupying the editorial chair. In trying to convey edifying thoughts she flourished the editorial "we" like a sword, ever ready to be drawn in defense of the "character of the mill girls." It was, in fact, as the mill girls' advocate that she made her first contribution to the *Offering*, boldly taking issue with Orestes Brownson, one of the most formidable intellects of the period, who had impugned the morals of factory operatives.

Brownson was an extraordinary man, a friend of Emerson and the other Transcendentalists, a gifted writer and polemicist, a perpetual convert to new (and old) religions, a thoughtful and penetrating student of social questions. At the moment we are discussing he was a socialist, a temporary phase for him, but one during which he wrote several brilliant and prophetic studies of the capitalist system as it was developing in this country. In 1840 Brownson published two articles on the laboring classes in the *Boston Quarterly Review*, the organ he had established for the expression of his own opinions, and one of the truly noteworthy American periodicals of that time.

In these articles Brownson either willfully or through ignorance distorted the picture of life in the mill towns in one respect in order to point up the neglected rights of labor:

We pass through our manufacturing villages; most of them appear neat and flourishing. The operatives are well dressed, and, we are told, well paid. They are said to be healthy, contented, and happy. This is the *'fair side of the picture'*; the side exhibited to distinguished visitors. There is a *'dark side,'* moral as well as physical. Of the common operatives, few, if any, by their wages acquire a competence. . . . The great mass wear out their health, spirits, and morals, without becoming one whit better off than when they commenced labor. . . . What becomes of them then? Few of them ever marry, fewer still ever return to their native places with reputations unimpaired. *'She has worked in a factory,'* is sufficient to damn to infamy the most worthy and virtuous girl.

And where go the proceeds of their labors? asked Brownson. To a man who is

one of our city nabobs, revelling in luxury; or he is a member of our legislature, enacting laws to put money in his own pocket; or he is a member of Congress, contending for a high Tariff to tax the poor for the benefit of the rich; or in these times he is shedding crocodile tears over the deplorable condition of the poor laborer, while he docks his wages twenty-five percent.

It is doubtful whether Miss Farley understood the larger issues involved in Brownson's article; at any rate, she chose to pass them over lightly. The accusation of immorality brought against the girls was, however, clear and unmistakable, and not to be borne. For the December, 1840, issue of the *Offering* she wrote the leading article, signed A Factory Girl, in which she refuted this charge with high indignation. Brownson was a slanderer, she cried, and must "prove his words, if he can."

It has been asserted that to put ourselves under the influence and restraint of corporate bodies is contrary to the spirit of our institutions, and to that love of independence which we ought to cherish. . . . We are under restraints, but they are voluntarily assumed; and we are at liberty to withdraw from them, whenever they become galling or irksome. Neither have I ever discovered that any restraints were imposed upon us, but those which were necessary for the peace and comfort of the whole, and for the promotion of the design for which we are collected, namely, to get money, as much of it and as fast as we can. . . . It is these wages which, in spite of toil, restraint, discomfort and prejudice, have drawn so many worthy, virtuous, intelligent and well-educated girls to Lowell and other factories . . . strange would it be, if in money-loving New England, one of the most lucrative female employments should be rejected because it is toilsome, or because some people are prejudiced against it. . . .
But it may be remarked, "You certainly cannot mean to intimate that all factory girls are virtuous, intelligent, etc." No, I do not; and Lowell would be a stranger place than it has ever been represented, if among 8,000 girls there were none of the ignorant and depraved. Calumniators have asserted, that *all* were vile, because they knew some to be so.

Brownson was deeply wounded by this counter-attack, from a quarter where he least expected it. Replying to Miss Farley, he said:

I would put the plough into the hand of the owner and also the spindle and the loom. Your employers do not wish for this change. I wish you, the operatives, to be not only operatives but owners. . . . Do you not see that I am laboring for you against your employers? Do not then be caught in their trap. Do not war for your natural enemies against your friends.

Miss Farley's response to his article contributed to Brownson's disillusionment with radical reformism. As for Miss Farley, the controversy brought her some small renown. Brownson's very distinction, and the high regard in which he was held by many thoughtful people, aroused more interest than would normally have been the case. Besides her point of view was pleasing to Important Persons. The Factory Girl's identity, moreover, did not long remain a secret outside of the Improvement Circles.

Stephen Farley, Harriet's father, always on the edge of pauperism, in 1841 became one of the objects of Amos Lawrence's benevolence. As the "self-constituted Grand Almoner" of America, Amos had for ten years been distributing charity (in small amounts) on a huge scale. Always good for a touch by needy clergymen, he somehow became acquainted with Mr. Farley's circumstances and sent him a piece of woolen cloth for an overcoat. Since they were entering on the summer season then, an overcoat could hardly have been Farley's most urgent requirement at that moment, but he nevertheless sat down and wrote a letter of thanks to the Boston merchant. After expressing his acknowledgments, he proceeded to tell Lawrence about his next youngest daughter, Harriet, who "has been an operative at Lowell, about one half the time, for about three years. Her health, though not perfectly good, is better than it was while in her teens. She is one of the writers for the 'Lowell Offering' and composed the Review of Brownson."

For Amos Lawrence this was clearly the effect of casting bread upon the waters. Having befriended the father, he was no doubt gratified to learn that the daughter had taken a crack at Brownson, whom he classified with Emerson and Parker as dangerous radicals, unfit to teach at the Harvard Divinity School.

Within a year after he had received Mr. Farley's letter, Harriet was no longer an operative in the mills, but was living with Harriott Curtis in a little rose-covered cottage in the outskirts of Lowell, paid for out of their earnings as editors.

In spite of the wide interest in the magazines written by the mill girls, they were at no time a paying proposition. They were both, in fact, about to fold up in the middle of 1842, when William Schouler, owner and editor of the *Lowell Courier*, stepped in and bought them out, combining the two under the name of the *Offering*. The *Courier* was a Whig newspaper that was described by a radical of the time as "the pensioned press and political organ of the corporations in this city." Another rumor had it that the Locks & Canals Company had set Schouler up in business, and although this charge was indignantly denied by Schouler, in his newspaper and as representative from Lowell in the Massachusetts Legislature he championed the corporations' interests as effectively as if he had been well paid for it. The *Offering* could scarcely have been a profitable financial venture for him. It was, nevertheless, carried on for a year under this arrangement, with Miss Curtis and Miss Farley, assisted by Harriet Lees, as editors. It was then suspended for a month, resuming publication under the ownership of the Misses Curtis and Farley, while Schouler "took on the responsibility of publication," which probably meant that he did not press them for their printing bills.

Miss Farley's first signed editorial, which appeared in the issue of November, 1842, expressed her intentions in a manner that could have caused no uneasiness in the breasts of the textile magnates. Speaking of the operatives, she wrote: "We should like to influence them as moral and rational beings. . . . Our field is a wide one. . . . With wages, board, etc., we have nothing to do—these depend on circumstances over which we have no control." But having declared her helplessness in these important matters, she then went on to make one of those backhanded pleas for improved conditions that was to characterize all her editorials and bring the *Offering* under some suspicion among those operatives who were slowly growing aware of worsening conditions:

One thing we must observe . . . it is much easier to instill a feeling of self-respect, of desire for excellence, among a well-paid, than an ill-paid class of operatives. There is a feeling of independence, a desire to form and retain a good character, a wish to do something for others . . . which is necessarily connected with even "the root of all evil."

After a while, however, she began to appear sensitive to the charge that by washing her hands of corporation abuses she was in reality defending the corporations, for in the February, 1843 issue of the *Offering* she explained herself: "We would not be thought to speak favorably of corporations. We have nothing to do with them, farther than they affect the character of the females they employ." However, if wages were lowered again, she added primly in the April, 1843 issue, the girls must continue to show a ladylike decorum: "We could recommend to every girl . . . to render herself, by prudence and good management, as independent as possible of factories, and thus at such times leave their employment, instead of remaining to fly in the face of their employers." In the May issue her editorial was concerned with the problem of health, in answer to the oft-repeated accusation that work in the mills was physically injurious. If the girls fell sick, she claimed, they had only themselves to blame, for whatever sanitary laws were violated in the mills were equally violated all over New England. Nevertheless, she added a plea to the Merrimack Company to grant the "boon" of providing bathing facilities. A movement to reduce the hours of labor to ten was already gathering momentum in Lowell, but Miss Farley would not ally herself with it. "One more proposal . . . is that of a diminution in the hours of labor. Yet we do not make it. We do not think the operatives generally wish it, as it would, of course, be a farther reduction of wages."

One suspects that Miss Farley's readers among the operatives were inclined to take issue with this statement, for in the June issue she reiterated her pious wish for improvement. And in this editorial she made the only criticism of the corporations—a very mild one, to be sure—that ever appeared in the *Offering* while she was editor:

This extreme conservatism [about hours of labor] is the fault of the manufacturers, this dislike of change, and love of having all things go on as they have always done. This is probably because all projected reforms have been of such a nature as to effect immediately the pecuniary interests of those concerned. But reforms must come —some changes must be—and sooner or later there will be an alteration and retrenchment of the hours of labor.

But if reforms were inevitable, there was nothing a gentlewoman need do to hasten their coming. Continuing her monthly lecture, Miss Farley concluded:

Well-educated girls are not more fond of insult and oppression than are the ignorant, but they are less under the dominion of passion. . . . They would not easily be made the tools of aristocrats or demagogues. . . . They would not surround the City Hall in a mob, but, if wronged, would seek redress in some less exceptionable manner.

The truth of the matter was that although the *Offering* continued to print the compositions of working operatives, the editors, by stressing virtue, respectability, and gentility were beginning to lose touch with the girls who should have formed their audience. Now owners of a small enterprise of their own, they were inclined to see the "point of view" of the corporation heads, and knew without being told what would have displeased these remote and mighty characters. Miss Farley would never have accepted a bribe, but she was susceptible to "kindness." On October 17, 1843, she wrote to Amos Lawrence:

This letter will introduce to you Miss Harriott F. Curtis, who, with myself, has become a publisher of the Lowell Offering, which we intend to recommence the first of next month. Any advice or assistance from you will be gratefully received by her; and if you will sign for her a letter of introduction, or other recommendation, it may be of much service in her contemplated tour to some of our more southern cities. The interest you have heretofore expressed in the Offering, and your past kindness, has emboldened us to ask this renewal of favour.

What this past kindness may have been, beyond providing her father with the material for an overcoat, is not known, but she certainly had reason to be pleased with his present favor. Her letter is preserved among the Amos Lawrence papers, with a notation on the back in his own trembling hand: "*Gave her twenty dollars.*"

In the last years of its existence the *Offering* was more and more frequently charged with "toadying to the corporations." The owners, of course, were aware of the publicity value of the magazine, just as they were aware of the publicity value of the girls themselves. In Boston, literary attainments were highly regarded, and it must have given the Appletons and Lawrences a sense of ineffable virtue to have created a situation in which such things as the *Offering* could be. But astute as they were, they knew that the charm of the venture lay in the fact that it was *not* a house organ. That they never dictated anything that appeared in the magazine, or insisted that anything be suppressed is fairly certain, for there was a definite realism in the descriptions of life in Lowell in its pages (as Dickens had observed) that was at variance with the glowing pictures fabricated by the agents who went about the country engaging help. Even Miss Farley shrank from too rosy a view of the work and workers in the mills, as when in her review of Dickens' *American Notes* she charged him with some hyperbole. Very few boarding houses had joint-stock pianos, she wrote, only a limited number of girls subscribed to circulating libraries, and no more than one in fifty subscribed to the *Offering*.

This want of patronage among the mill girls may have been what led to the temporary suspension of the magazine in October, 1843. Who then were the regular subscribers? In the September issue Miss Farley referred to the fact that there were 300 subscribers in New York, and 100 in Albany. There were regular readers in every state of the Union except in the South, she claimed, which probably accounts for Harriott Curtis' trip to drum up trade in those benighted regions. But girls who, as the *Offering* itself stated, no longer attended church because they could afford neither the pew rent nor the conventional dress for such occasions would certainly not permit themselves the luxury of subscribing to a purely literary magazine.

Miss Farley's timid refinement, her failure to come to grips with the real concerns of the factory girls, was at no time more apparent than in 1845, the last year in which the magazine was published. The decline of the *Offering* coincided with the rise of a strong labor movement in the mill towns, organized in protest against long working hours, constant wage reductions, and crowded living conditions. The headquarters of this movement was Lowell; its leaders Lowell operatives, its first act was to petition the legislature for a ten-hour day. When this petition was rejected by a legislative committee appointed to consider it, Miss Farley registered only a spirit of resignation in her editorial column. Favorable consideration of the petition "could not have been expected in the present state of things," she wrote in the April issue, adding almost as an afterthought that "some respect" might have been shown to the petitioners, some "regard for the ease and comfort of the operatives."

This namby-pamby attitude exasperated the leaders of the ten-hour movement, chief of whom was Miss Sarah Bagley, a lively adversary. On July 4, 1845, Miss Bagley addressed a workingmen's meeting at Woburn, choosing the *Offering* as the target of her harangue. As the *Lowell Advertiser*, a Democratic newspaper, reported the affair:

Among the speakers was Miss Sarah G. Bagley . . . who was called out by some remarks in allusion to the Lowell Offering. She made some statements . . . which will do much to correct the im-

pression abroad that it is the organ of the "Factory Operatives"—
stating that she had written articles in relation to the condition of the
operatives, and their insertion had been invariably *refused!*

When this direct attack was brought to the attention of Miss
Farley, she hastened to write a letter of correction to the editor
of the *Courier*, denying that any article by Miss Bagley had ever
been rejected by her. If any had been refused, she added, it must
have been when Mr. Thomas was in charge of the *Offering*.

Miss Bagley, who had a keen sense of the value of publicity,
joyfully grasped the opportunity to keep the controversy alive.
Schouler was too closely bound up with the corporations to
grant her any space in his columns, but the editor of the opposition paper, the *Advertiser*, was glad to print anything that might
embarrass his competitor. On July 10 he published Miss Bagley's
rejoinder to Miss Farley, prefacing it with the remark that he
"never supposed that the editress of the Offering was conscious
that her publication was made use of by the corporations to
produce any erroneous impression in the community as to the
effects of the manufacturing system." Miss Bagley, however, felt
under no compulsion to "pull her punches." Cloaking herself in
the editorial "we"—which she enjoyed using as much as Miss
Farley—she directed her blows where they would inflict the
greatest pain:

> In looking over the Courier of Wednesday last we found our name
> in connection with the Lowell Offering, saying that we had never
> presented an article that had been refused since Miss Farley had been
> its editress. Well, as we did not say we had we do not see any chance
> for controversy. But we did say . . . that we had written articles
> for the Offering that have been rejected because they would make
> the Offering "controversial," and would change its "original design,"
> which was that there is "mind among the spindles."

She then went on to point out that controversial subjects had
not always been "studiously avoided," choosing as her example
the attack on Orestes Brownson, which, as everyone knew, had

been written by Miss Farley. The only question ever raised about material for the *Offering*, she added caustically, concerned the "propriety" of the controversy.

We stated that it had never been an organ through which the abuses of oppressive rules or unreasonable hours might be complained of. . . . We have not written this article to evince that there is "mind among the spindles," but to show that the minds here are not all *spindles*.

What the editor of the *Advertiser* and Miss Bagley were charging was so offensive to Harriet Farley's sensibilities that in her reply, printed in the *Advertiser* on July 15, she lapsed into the first person singular:

You say . . . that you do not suppose I am *conscious* that the Offering is used by the corporations to produce erroneous impressions; I do not think I am so unconscious of the impression it produces as you suppose me. The corporations do not take that lively interest in it that they have been represented to do. . . . It is impossible for the Offering to benefit the corporations only as it elevates the character of the operatives. . . .

Her intentions had been misrepresented, she exclaimed. All she had wished to do was to bring a little "cheer" into the lives of the factory girls. But if, in general, the tone of her letter was one of misunderstood virtue, it took on a more biting accent when referring to Miss Bagley:

I had ever before considered Miss Bagley and myself upon one side of that great question—what are the rights and capacities of the laborer? Not that I can do all the things that she can, for I cannot make a speech or talk politics, or speak of the factory system as she represents it, for it never seemed to me a "durance vile," or "Inquisition torture."

The controversy continued in the pages of the *Advertiser* for several weeks more, growing more and more acrimonious, until

Miss Bagley on August 7 called Miss Farley "a mouthpiece of the corporations," to which the editor of the *Offering* made no reply, taking refuge in a dignified silence.

But the genteel tone of the *Offering* was not enough to keep it going; it brought too little "cheer" into the lives of girls who were being driven harder all the time. The ten-hour movement was gaining momentum and winning new converts every day, especially among the more intelligent and better-educated operatives who had formerly taken such interest in the magazine. Miss Farley tried to recapture some of her old subscribers by modifying her views on the question of shorter hours. Whereas formerly her position had been that "we do not ask for a reduction of hours," now she emboldened herself to propose that the corporations shorten the working day by increasing the time for meals.

But this death-bed repentance came too late to do the *Offering* any good. Strong competition was entering the field. The redoubtable Miss Bagley had begun publishing an occasional number of *Factory Tracts*, consisting of material that had been rejected for the *Offering* by Mr. Thomas, particularly her own article attacking the "drivelling cotton lords," the "mushroom aristocracy of New England." And in October, 1845, a well-written, hard-hitting labor paper, the *Voice of Industry*, made its first appearance in Lowell, with Miss Bagley on its editorial board.

Miss Farley's organ for moral uplift collapsed two months after the *Voice of Industry* began publication. But her plaint that the corporations did not take much interest in her magazine had not passed unobserved in the proper quarters. In September Amos Lawrence gave her a substantial sum of money for her brother, a subtle means of expressing gratitude for her loyalty without laying himself open to the charge of tampering with the press. That it was so designed cannot be doubted, for if he had merely intended to help her brother he could easily have sent him the money directly, instead of using Harriet as an intermediary. The corporations employed the same oblique methods when the *Offering* was in severe financial straits in its last year, the Hamilton Company buying $1,000 worth of *back* numbers in order to avoid giving the impression that the magazine "is at present supported by the corporations or under their influence." Since the Misses Farley and Curtis were then proprietors of the concern, it is difficult to understand who else benefited by this generosity, unless it was William Schouler, who owned the press where the *Offering* was printed.

The *Offering* was not missed by the operatives when it suspended publication. As Amelia Sargent, a collaborator of Sarah Bagley, wrote in the *Voice of Industry*, only 52 girls subscribed to it in its last days, only twelve of them from Lowell, while one mill agent took 25 copies of each issue and another 20. In an editorial marking its passing, the *Voice of Industry* declared that the *Offering* hurt the operatives more than it helped them, while it had been unable to prove that factory life under the existing system was conducive to the expression and cultivation of the intellect. Miss Farley had meant well, but as Norman Ware put it, "she began by defending the operatives against attacks that were levelled at the corporations, and finished by defending the corporations at the expense of the operatives."

Chapter X

THE PICTURE CHANGES

WHAT had come over this idyllic scene of happy labor and well-rewarded capital, that participants like Sarah Bagley and others should now speak out with such inconceivable bitterness? Was Lowell no longer like a Spanish town with its conventual rules, where every girl went cheerfully about her duties, grateful for the benevolence that enabled her to earn a living without loss of virtue? Certainly the charm and novelty of the picture had dimmed by the forties. For one thing, the industry had leaped ahead, outstripping the most sanguine expectations of the original promoters. Changes of a fundamental nature were also to be seen in the corporate structure of the factories. The town itself, initially laid out with some reference to human comfort and dignity, had grown out of scale; some areas were already congested, and the centers of squalor could no longer be contained. For the first time the infallibility of the great nabobs was challenged when charges of incompetent management were brought up by one faction of stockholders because dividends took a temporary fall. The operatives were becoming less submissive under a constantly increasing pressure to keep up their wages and their standards. Within a space of less than twenty years the whole scene had changed radically. While Lowell was not yet the hideous mill town it was to become later, it was no longer the smiling manufacturing village that had impressed the visitors of an earlier day.

The startling growth of the textile industry in New England had been justified by the great demand for cloth arising from a greatly increased population. From the era of the first settlements, this country had never stood still, was never the same from one decade to another. During the three decades from 1820 to 1850 the population more than doubled, leaping from a little under 10 millions to over 23 millions. A constantly rising rate of immigration accounted for some of this increase, the rest being a consequence of a high birth-rate. The westward drive of a restless people continued unabated, western New York and Pennsylvania filling up during this period, while Ohio, Indiana, and Illinois became thickly settled, and the migration continued to the other areas of the "Old Northwest" and the "Old Southwest." Under the rough conditions of pioneer and farm life, the greatest need was not for the fine goods which for many years longer were still to be imported from abroad, but for the coarse sheeting and shirting, the cheap calicoes, drills, and canton flannels in whose manufacture Lowell was preeminent. When pioneers took root as farmers, and as farmers began to know prosperity, the demand for these sturdy cotton goods rose to heights unimaginable back in the twenties.

The vastly increased production of cotton cloth during this period can be attributed not only to a much larger population with a steadily rising standard of living, but also to changes in modes and the replacement of other materials by cotton. The linens, the wools, the linsey-woolseys that had so laboriously been woven at home, when they were not purchased at relatively high cost in the shops, were being replaced except for cold weather wear by the cheapest, most adaptable, most easily laundered material the world has ever known. The uses to which cotton was put as the century advanced were legion, and the needs of a growing country almost insatiable.

It was at this market in the North that the corporation mills aimed for the bulk of their sales. But there were other outlets as well. To satisfy the need for cheap cotton material for plantation slaves in the South, at least one mill in Lowell for a time turned out Osnaburgs or Negro cloth, as it was called, exclusively. Foreign trade absorbed some of the output also, South America and China providing the most profitable markets. In 1840 7½ percent of the total output was exported, and later in the decade Nathan Appleton considered the China trade so important that he attributed a temporary depression in the textile industry to unsettled conditions in China, causing interruptions to commerce. If an industry can but pay its expenses in the home market, economists maintain, foreign sales are pure profit. Up to the Civil War, however, the textile manufacturers for the most part relied on the expanding domestic market for their earnings.

With the extension of their textile plants from Waltham to Lowell, and then to Manchester, Chicopee, Taunton, York, Saco, and elsewhere the Boston Associates had helped to bring about an intense concentration of the industry in New England. Although by 1860 there were cotton mills in 29 states, New England had 70 percent of the capital investment, made 75 percent of the cloth, and 68 percent of all the cotton products in this country. The corporation mills alone had 20 percent of the spindleage in 1850, but their share of the industry was larger than this would indicate, since they turned out more yarn and cloth from each spindle and loom than any other factories in the world. Not only were there more textile mills in New England than elsewhere at this time, but the average mill was about twice as large. Rhode Island, Connecticut, and Pennsylvania, the largest rival textile centers in the country, operated into the forties for the most part on the family and contract system, which, although it called for smaller capital investment, could not take advantage of the economies in production in the highly rationalized factories of the Boston Associates.

The corporation mills also had the advantage of a cheap source of power in the swift-flowing rivers of the northern New England states. Tradition-bound mills around Philadelphia clung to the use of sluggish water power for decades after cheap coal from western Pennsylvania became available to provide steam power. Pennsylvania also produced a much finer type of goods than New England, since for many years it had been a center for immigrant weavers of a high degree of skill. Until Fall River began to come into prominence, therefore, early in the sixties, no textile center in the country could stand up to the combined strength of the mills controlled by Nathan Appleton, Abbott Lawrence, and their associates. Without exercising an absolute monopoly over the industry, they were stronger than all the rest combined.

And yet despite their dominating position in the industry, the Boston textile magnates were unable to keep the price of their product from falling steadily. Waltham heavy sheeting, which in 1816 sold for 30 cents a yard (an inflated figure because of post-war scarcity), declined gradually until in 1845 its price was 6½ cents a yard. Merrimack calicoes likewise declined from almost 18 cents a yard in 1836 to under 10 cents in 1849. However, except in food products during certain years, the general commodity level was falling off over the same period, more even than the wholesale price of cloth. According to no less an authority than Nathan Appleton, declining cotton-goods prices caused the manufacturers no loss because the cost of raw cotton fell concomitantly. Nevertheless, as the profit per yard shrank, it was necessary to increase production proportionately in order to avoid loss. Lower prices were in effect offset by larger volume of sales, which, in its turn, permitted economies in the manufacture.

Profits, as a matter of fact, continued at a high level on the average up to the middle forties, despite a serious slump in the industry from 1840 to the beginning of 1843. The Lowell mills never achieved the fabulous record of the Boston Manufacturing Company, whose investors recovered all of their investment after four years, but on the whole they did very well, the Merrimack earning an average of 12¾ percent annually, the Suffolk 14 percent, while the Hamilton and the Tremont each averaged 10½ percent for the same period. The Appleton, Lowell, Lawrence, and Boott mills averaged from 7 to 9⅞ percent, nothing to be sneezed at, the only bad actor in Lowell being the Massachusetts Mills, which, having started business on the eve of bad times, averaged only 5¼.

So great was the demand for the cheap textiles turned out by the mills of the Boston Associates that only a major depression was able to contract earnings appreciably. The corporation mills remained essentially untouched by the minor panics of 1819 and 1829, during which years the manufacturers proceeded with plans for expansion without misgivings. The panic of 1837 likewise gave the Associates only slight pause, for, like the crash of 1929, its effects were not fully felt until several years had passed, when the "hungry forties" were ushered in. But between 1840 and 1843 dividends in almost all the corporation mills were cut sharply, some, as in Chicopee, paying nothing in 1840, '42, and '43.

Now for the first time a muffled conflict began within the ranks of the great Boston capitalists themselves, who, while things were going well, had stood together like brothers. A loss of dividends is always a painful matter. Moreover, there were many more stockholders in the textile corporations in 1840 than twenty years before, men who had been drawn into the business because of the rich profits of those early days, and these new investors were interested in obtaining as high a return on their money as possible. It was habitual with the original entrepreneurs not only to re-invest their profits, but also to sell out part of their stock in the older corporations in order to float new companies. In this way the twelve initial stockholders in the Boston Company at Waltham grew to be 76 in 1830, with no one person owning more than 8½ percent of the stock. The board of directors, who settled all matters of policy, together held only 22 percent of the stock.

The funds realized through these sales of stock were then transferred to the Merrimack Company, and thence by the same methods to the other corporations in Lowell and elsewhere. In

1824, a year or so after its charter was granted, the Merrimack Company had some 70-odd stockholders; by 1845 there were 390. Breaking down this number by occupations, Thomas G. Cary, Treasurer of the Merrimack Company, described 46 as merchants and traders, 68 as "females," 52 as retired businessmen, 80 as administrators, guardians, and trustees, 23 as lawyers, 18 as physicians, 3 as "Literary Institutions," 15 as farmers, 40 as secretaries, clerks, etc., and 45 as manufacturers, mechanics, etc.

But this dispersion of stock was not as broad as Cary would have us believe. Stock ownership in the corporation mills was largely a family affair. Of the Waltham Company's stockholders in 1846, nine families long associated with the textile industry accounted for 43: the Appletons, Lowells, Lees, Abbotts, Jacksons, Lymans, Lorings, and Bordens. Various Appletons, Bootts, Cabots, Gorhams, Higginsons, Jacksons, Lowells, Lees, Lymans, and Thorndikes were represented in the Merrimack Company at its founding, and with their sisters and their cousins and their aunts, their in-laws, their guardians and trustees, and the cherished "Literary Institutions" endowed by them, accounted for a large part of the list submitted by Cary. All of these, at any rate, could be depended upon in any stockholders' meeting to uphold the decisions of the board of directors against any farmers, clerks, mechanics, etc., who might be dissatisfied with the conduct of the corporation.

For the control, or "management," remained always in the hands of the original promoters, mainly the Appletons, Lowells, Jacksons, and, a little later, the Lawrences, the chief figures among the textile magnates, whether their stock ownership was for the moment large or small. There could be no challenge to their authority except from within their own tight circle, which was more than content with the management as long as dividends were high and steady. "The rumour of your profits will make people delirious," wrote Harrison Gray Otis to a fellow director of the Taunton Manufacturing Company in 1835.

But when dividends fell, and in some cases were passed altogether in 1840 to 1843, these rapturous accents quickly changed to cries of woe. Unwilling to accept the explanation that hard times were responsible for the decline of mill profits, a group of dissident stockholders, calling themselves "reformers," began looking into the management of the corporations to discover whether they were being run with all possible efficiency. Although the lines were not clearly drawn, the reforming party consisted for the most part of those who received no salaries from the corporations and held no interest in the commission houses. Many of them had resisted the introduction of manufactures into New England as long as was feasible, as, for example, Henry Lee, Senior, who had run for Congress against Nathan Appleton in 1830 on a free-trade ticket. In 1842 Lee wrote a series of letters to a member of his family describing the activities of the "reformers." Unlike Appleton and Lawrence, Lee did not attribute the low dividends to the low tariff, but rather to the evils that had grown up within the corporations themselves, such as the extravagance and wastefulness of incompetent agents, who were selected on the basis of favoritism and nepotism. Raw materials, he pointed out, were not bought from the lowest bidders, but "orders . . . from Manufacturers for Indigo . . . usually are given to some of the connections or acquaintances of the Lowell agents or proprietors on the spot to solicit them not with reference so much as to their skill in buying as to favor individuals."

Lee and the other dissatisfied investors were prepared to go to some lengths to obtain reforms in the corporation management, even if this meant stepping on the toes of some of the leading figures in the industry. Their main attack was directed at the nephew and son-in-law of Francis Cabot Lowell, John Amory Lowell, who was one of the inner circle governing all the manifold interests of the Boston Associates. At that time John Amory Lowell held high office concurrently in eight of the corporations connected with the cotton manufacture; he was a director of the Amoskeag, Appleton, and Hamilton companies, treasurer of the Boott Mills, a director and agent for the purchase

of cotton of the Merrimack Company, treasurer and agent of
the Boston Manufacturing Company, director and agent of the
Massachusetts Mills, and president of the Lowell Machine Shop.
Four of these posts paid him $5,000 a year apiece, these substan-
tial emoluments being supplemented by "handsome trusteeships,"
as Amos Abbott Lawrence noted, and an enviable income from
banks, railroads, insurance companies, and the more prosperous
textile mills. The reformers seemed to feel that Lowell was making rather too good a thing of the textile business, especially as
his conduct of the Massachusetts Mills was far from satisfactory.
A new board of directors voted to reduce his salary (a rebuke
for which Abbott Lawrence kindly prepared him fifteen minutes
before the board meeting took place), but evidently decided not
to fire him, perhaps because his social standing made him useful
in spite of certain shortcomings. He was admonished but not
chastised; a Lowell could do no wrong.

The reforming party, by Henry Lee's account, seemed for a
while to be very energetic:

A *reforming party* has been at work with Wm. Appleton at its
head & sustained by Geo. Lyman, Col. Perkins, the Brooks, E. Francis,
H. Cabot, Geo. Howe—& nearly all the independent men who don't
get salaries & are not influenced by those who do— They have been
resisted by the combined power of Lawrence, N. Appleton, the Lowells & the Jacksons & their allies—but it was *ineffectual*. Salaries are
reduced. . . .

Besides reducing salaries in the higher brackets, the reformers
brought about changes in the methods of purchasing cotton,
which Lee said would save 3 or 4 percent on the capital of each
mill, as well as a revision of the credit arrangements, halting the
practice of extending long-term credits to poor risks.

But an equally important saving was made, upon the insistence
of the reformers, by reducing wages in the mills and increasing
the number of machines tended by the operatives. On this subject
Henry Lee was more explicit than any other textile magnate:

A *reforming Committee* last year visited R. Island & contrary to
their expectations it was found they paid lower wages & that one
woman worked 3 looms & some of them 4 looms by a slight reduction
of speed— This change, contrary to the opinion of some of our managers was made in our mills— Good Dr. Hobbs . . . tho't it could
not be done at first, but *suspension* of dividends at last drove him up
to it. . . . They found also that R. Island instead of using *fancy cotton* costing 3 cts more than plain—used a lower grade & made goods
of equal quality—that is the common sorts— This *"the girls"* object
to, & why? because . . . they could not run off so many yards &
therefore made a few cents a day less— However, Wm. Amory, who
is a reformer, tho' salary man; & Geo. Howe who is one also & a
Superintendent—set the example & now the Waltham & Lowell
[mills] have followed suit.

In a later letter Henry Lee wrote that he was sorry prices did
not stay down a year longer, "as the reformers might have been
able in that time to have made further changes and savings in
manufactures." The revival of business from 1843 on, however,
restored the faith of most of the investors in the management.
From 1843 to 1847 inclusive the Merrimack paid 81 percent,
the Amoskeag 96 percent, and the Tremont 63 percent, including
stock dividends. Stockholders are inclined to let well enough
alone when the pickings are good. At any rate, the nepotism and
favoritism of which Lee had complained went on as before.

But during the same period, wages continued their steady
downward trend. Henry Lee need not have taken credit for the
wage-cut and speed-up of the early forties, for it had been a
settled policy in the corporation mills ever since 1834. In that
year came the first lowering of piece-rates, presumably because
of lowered prices and improved mechanical techniques, despite
which many operatives suffered a loss in real wages. When prices
recovered quickly, however, making new highs in 1836, the wage-
cuts were not restored, a money crisis in that year furnishing
the excuse for fresh piece-rate reductions. For the Boston Associates, moreover, the money crisis was not serious enough to

halt the building of new mills, or prevent the declaration of handsome dividends.

During the forties, including the very prosperous middle years, wage-cutting continued, despite Nathan Appleton's statement that the operatives' earnings had risen as a result of the tariff. This rise was only a partial restoration of a larger cut earlier. And since piece-rates fell more sharply than average weekly wages, it is obvious that the mill girls were obliged to work harder to earn less pay at the beginning of this period than at the end. In the first half of 1842, for example, weavers, the most highly skilled operatives, earned an average weekly wage of $3.84 per week, or about $2.60 above board; in the last half of 1845, their average had sunk to $3.48 per week, or $2.23 above board. Other operatives, doing less skilled work, received an average of $3.40 in the second half of 1841, or $2.15 above board, and $2.76 in the second half of 1845, or $1.51 above their board. A Henry Lee might feel annoyed when the operatives objected to earning a few cents a day less, but leaving out the board charges, which the girls had come to regard as outside of their wages proper, the loss of a few cents a day might amount to as much as a 30-percent wage-cut.

What can explain this relentless pressure on wages, even in a period of prosperity for the industry as a whole? The fact was that cotton dividends had been declining consistently, falling from an average of 11.4 percent through 1836, to 9.7 percent from 1837 to 1846, and the latter figure might have been much lower if not for the great boom in part of the period. It must be remembered too that included in this average are steady earners like the Merrimack, which averaged 12¾ percent, and the Suffolk, which averaged 14 percent up to 1845. After 1847 the average took another plunge, falling to 5.8 percent up to 1859.

The decline in wages has generally been attributed to the decline in dividends, which in turn is said to have come about as a result of competition and overproduction. The theory here is that as competition drove prices down, the corporations could only make up the loss by increasing production, and that when the fall in prices was great enough to curtail dividends, stock-holders put pressure on the agents or managers of the factories to cut wage costs. Wages were, in fact, the only item in the cost of manufacture that was flexible, all other factors, such as plant, insurance, and raw materials being either rigid or beyond the power of the manufacturers to control. But it is not certain that lowered dividends came about as a result of the competitive element alone. The earlier high profits had been due in part to the fact that cotton manufacture was a new industry, which as it acquired skill could still make a handsome return on its investment when prices were lowered. In fact, the relationship between profits and prices can be exaggerated in this case, since dividends were high in the thirties, during the period of falling prices, and lower in the forties and fifties when prices had be-come fairly stabilized.

The importance of overproduction in causing prices to fall, and by the same process forcing wages down can also be ex-aggerated, since if there was overproduction it was inspired largely by the Boston Associates themselves, who launched one company after another almost up to the Civil War. They would scarcely have done this if the prospects for earnings seemed poor.

A more likely explanation of the dwindling returns on cotton mill stock, is suggested by Professor Vera Shlakman,* who points out that in the earlier years of the industry most of the operating profits were paid out in the form of dividends, leaving little or no depreciation reserves for needed repairs, new equipment, or machinery replacement. That this process of concealed obso-lescence continued through the forties is borne out by a letter Nathan Appleton wrote to the editor of the *New York Evening Post* in 1844: "As to dividends, the tendency always is to divide too much. . . . In general, the reserves are barely sufficient to cover the wear and tear of the machinery." If the machinery was not in first-rate condition, costs in that department had a tendency

---

* Vera Shlakman: *Economic History of a Factory Town, a Study of Chicopee, Massachusetts.*

to rise, a movement that exerted a powerful downward pressure on wages if dividends were to be maintained. To the stockholders there was no question but that dividends must be maintained, if (or until) the heavens should fall. Interlocking directorates and free exchange of cost information among the corporation mills enabled leading stockholders to persuade an agent to cut wages whenever his production costs rose in comparison with those of other corporations. This, in effect, was what the "reforming party" accomplished in 1842, its other economy measures being of only temporary duration. The agent was also impelled by the stockholders to make economies whenever a business crisis made the conservation of liquid capital necessary, as in 1836, when money was very tight.

Wage-cutting, it must be remembered, was begun in a period of great prosperity for the industry, was continued in years of depression, and went on unchecked in the subsequent boom. And when the final wave of high dividends subsided toward the end of the fifth decade, when repairs and replacements for obsolete machinery and plant could no longer be postponed, once again the ax fell on wages. Neither could dividends be kept up to their former high average, during the decade that followed. It was not competition or overproduction that brought about this state of affairs as much as poor business practices.

The changes that came over Lowell were implicit in its beginnings. Neat and ordered as the town seemed to the guided visitor, there was even from the first an area to which no one pointed with pride: the Acre, so-called, where the Irish immigrant day laborers who had dug the canals and helped build the dams and mills lived with their families. In the thirties about 500 persons lived in the Acre, in cabins seven to ten feet high, made of slabs and rough boards, turfed up to the eaves, with a window in one end and two small holes in the sides for air and light. Some idea of the crowding may be gathered from Seth Luther's statement in 1832 that he had seen one small house in the Irish quarter of Lowell, one-half of which was occupied by 72 persons.

While the building operations continued at a rapid pace, these men found fairly steady employment, but as development slackened, the day laborers were often reduced to destitution and even to beggary. Such abject poverty was a new element in American life; up to the thirties beggary was almost unknown. Visitors from abroad like Mrs. Trollope and Harriet Martineau were struck by the absence of mendicants, a familiar feature of the European scene. Having spent her childhood years in the town of Beverly, on the seacoast, Lucy Larcom had never been approached by anyone for alms until she went to Lowell in 1835, when "my childish desire to see a real beggar was gratified. Straggling petitioners for 'cold victuals' hung around our back yard, always of Hibernian extraction." Industrialism had already begun to mark its victims, and by the early forties poverty among laborers in the cities was a recognized phenomenon. The breach between the upper and the lower economic strata was growing broader all the time; the rich were richer and the poor poorer than they had been twenty years earlier.

In education, sympathies, and religion, the New England mill operatives undoubtedly felt far closer to the textile magnates than they did to the poverty-stricken Irish, even though they too worked for wages. But the Irish population kept increasing as the years went by; their children were growing up here, and their ranks were constantly being added to by waves of immigration, soon to reach a peak at the end of the forties, at the time of the Irish potato famine. Here, side by side with the girls who came down from the country to work in the mills for a few years, a labor pool was being formed, consisting of young women with no standards the textile manufacturers might feel obliged to respect.

But the Irish quarter was not the only crowded part of Lowell. After purchasing the several farms on which the future town was to be located, the Merrimack Company had placed its mills on the river's edge, its boarding houses nearby, and transferred the rest of the property to the Locks & Canals Company. A very small area was allocated for the use of shops, inns, and the houses and services of the population not engaged to work in the mills. The Locks & Canals Company sold choice land along the river and for company tenements to the whole list of corporations as they were chartered, but most of the property it owned within the city limits was allowed to remain idle. The result of this was to jam the sustaining population within a very small area, except for the more prosperous tradesmen and professional people, who took refuge in what were then the suburbs. Because the corporations left most of the land undeveloped, the town was unable to lay out any public parks for twenty years.

But with the setting up of the Prescott Manufacturing Company (later merged with the Massachusetts Mills) in 1844, all available mill sites were allocated. In the following year the Boston Associates therefore decided to sell out the 111 lots of land still remaining in the possession of the Locks & Canals Company. Unfortunately, this occurred too late to affect the congested pattern of the city for some time. In 1847 one observer, writing in the *Lowell Courier*, described a house in the center of town "occupied by one store and twenty-five different families embracing 120 persons, more than half of whom were adults. In one of the rooms . . . I found one of the families to consist of a man, his wife, and eight children . . . and four adult boarders. . . . By no means the worst case."

In contrast with the overcrowding in the rest of the city the corporations could point with pride to their white-frame or red-brick boarding houses, kept so neat and clean on their order. Nevertheless, the bedrooms in the boarding houses in the 1840's were far more cramped as sleeping quarters than they had been earlier. Six and sometimes eight girls frequently shared one room, with all their effects. Soon after the establishment of the first mills real estate values became so high that no more semi-detached boarding houses were erected, while some of those already existing were pulled down to make way for solid blocks of buildings, with narrow alleys between two rows. The loss of light owing to this change of policy was probably not important to girls who generally worked from dawn to dark, but the difference in ventilation, especially in the hot summer months, must have been very marked.

The open spaces between the mills were likewise doomed to go. The pleasing, almost formal arrangement of buildings in the mill yards did not last beyond the forties, when the need for more working space could no longer be met by putting up new structures, since the whole waterfront was now occupied. The solution was to link up the scattered buildings of one corporation after another until they presented a solid wall between the town and the river. By 1848 the Hamilton Company had filled in the space between two of its old mills and built another 320 feet long within its former area; the Appleton and Suffolk companies had linked up two of their mills; the Merrimack had completed a mill 350 feet long, and the Boott Mills had a new building under construction that was 510 feet long. When it is recalled that the original mills had been no longer than 150 or 160 feet, and stood detached from one another to give the inhabitants of the town a glimpse of the river and the countryside beyond, the effect of the later changes can be readily gauged. Once the closing-in process was completed, Lowell was well on its way to becoming the dismal, grimy concentration of factories and workers that we think of nowadays when we speak of a mill town—not a place for youthful adventure and enterprise, but a trap.

While the town was deteriorating in looks and in the amenities of life, the mills were also growing less agreeable as places of work. By the forties no one could possibly have pictured the mill rooms as "light and airy apartments." The report of Dr. Josiah Curtis to the American Medical Association in 1849 described conditions of which the operatives had begun to complain almost ten years previously:

In winter, for four months, when the windows are closed and generally double, each room has fifty solar lamps burning morning and evening, which assist not only in impairing the confined air, but also in raising the temperature frequently to 90 degrees Fahrenheit before closing work at night.

Even in the summer, many of the overseers kept the windows nailed down tight, despite the entreaties of the operatives, on the ground that by maintaining the humidity at a steady level, the threads broke less frequently. In all seasons the flying lint was a source of great discomfort, the more so as the corporations were deaf to all pleas to provide bathing facilities for the operatives. Their reluctance to offer this simple and inexpensive service seems strangely dogged, for, as the *Voice of Industry* pointed out in 1846, the one mill at Manchester that had a bathhouse never lacked for hands when the others were short.

Working conditions of this order made the girls restive, particularly since the long hours, combined with the speed-up, were beginning to tell on the health of many of them. Dr. Curtis' report had pointed out that when the operatives left the overheated mills in the evening, and rushed home to their evening meal with their wraps half undone, they were running the risk of goodness knows what pulmonary ailments. In the summer the high incidence of "bowel complaints" and dysentery was commonly attributed to the fact that the operatives put in two hours of work before breakfast.

The working hours were fifteen minutes a day longer in 1841 than they had been in 1829. They varied from season to season, but averaged almost twelve and a half hours a day throughout the year. Only half an hour was allowed for meals. Beginning in December and on through the winter the girls worked about eleven and a half hours; from April on through the summer, thirteen and a half hours. Some Southern slaves of particular skills had a shorter working day at this period, and even plantation slaves had an hour for meals. The despised British textile worker, whose low standards were so often cited to lend greater brilliance to the Lowell picture, had, by the forties, won a work week of 69 hours, contrasted with almost 75 in the New England mills, and six holidays a year as against only four in the Massachusetts mills.

But the mere length of the day was not the only trying aspect of the working conditions in the forties as compared with the twenties. As indicated earlier, the comparatively high cost of labor in the United States had made rationalization of industry obligatory. Any new device that could hasten the manufacturing process was speedily adopted, the original Waltham cam-driven loom, for example, being supplanted after a short period by the crank-driven loom, which was faster. This entailed an increased consumption of cotton, and gave rise to the many complaints of flying lint heard so frequently in the thirties. The noise and nervous strain on the operatives also increased proportionately, as every part of the machinery revolved more rapidly. But in the drive to increase production the human machines had to be speeded up as well; whereas in the twenties one or two looms were as much as any girl was required to tend, by the forties three or four were the rule.* A girl who was unable or unwilling to stand the speed-up soon felt the consequences in the amount of her pay, as piecework rates dropped steadily.

But speeding up the machinery and increasing the number of looms and frames to be tended did not achieve the result desired by the corporation managers, and so a third scheme for increasing production was devised: the premium system. The premium system granted bonuses to overseers and second hands who succeeded in getting more work out of the operatives than they were accustomed to do. This completely altered the relationship between the girls and their immediate superiors, with whom they had formerly been on easy, and often friendly, terms. New rivalries and new antagonisms were set up; the girls were afraid to stay away when they fell sick, fearful of falling behind one another, as some of the newer overseers were brutal and tyrannical, and took advantage of their position to play favorites. A

---

* In this connection it is interesting to note that as late as 1860, British textile workers were still required to operate no more than two looms.

letter on this subject was published in the *Voice of Industry* on December 21, 1846:

This "premium system" is a curse to us—it ought not to be tolerated. . . . Often have girls been so afraid of the "old man" they dare not ask to go out when sick, for they know he would have a great deal to say. Some girls cannot get off as much cloth as others; such ones are apt to be treated unkindly, and often reminded by the "old man" that "Sally and Dolly got off several cuts more the last four weeks; they come in long before the speed starts up and do their cleaning, and if you don't get off more next month I will send you off."

Even before the adoption of the premium system overseers exercised arbitrary power in interpreting the rules to which each operative submitted herself on taking a job in one of the corporation mills. Out of 107 discharges at the Hamilton Company in 1826–27, only 31 came after proper notice had been given by the girls on the one side or the management on the other, while all the rest were due to accusations by overseers of misconduct, mutiny, disobedience to orders, impudence, levity, dissatisfaction with wages, non-performance of duty, lying, misrepresentation, captiousness, or hysteria. A girl with some independence of spirit was sure to fall into one or another of these categories of misbehavior.

The rules could be made to cover almost every aspect of the operatives' lives, going far beyond the preservation of moral character, and becoming particularly irksome when designed to speed up production. The first known strike or "turnout" in the New England mills took place at the Cocheco Company in Dover, New Hampshire, in December, 1828, when, according to the *Boston Commercial Gazette*, three to four hundred girls "rioted" because of "restrictive regulations." Among these was a fine of 12½ cents imposed on "any hand arriving at the mill entrance after the bell stopped ringing." Other causes of irritation mentioned were the great powers of the overseers, and the ban on talking while at work.

During a turnout at Lowell in 1836, called in protest against a wage-cut, great emphasis was laid by the ringleaders on "dictation not only as to what they shall eat and drink and wherewithal they shall be clothed, but when they shall eat, drink and sleep." In 1845 some girls complained that they were watched at the end of the day to see that their footsteps "did not drag beyond the corporation limits." At that period, too, girls who were caught reading radical newspapers, or were known to be active in the ten-hour movement, were subject to immediate dismissal. The men who worked in the mills were told how to vote, under threat of discharge if they voted a ticket displeasing to their employers.

Having been "dishonorably" discharged from one mill, a girl could find no employment in any of the other mills controlled by the Boston merchants. Troublemakers found their names on a black list, which was in the hands of every factory agent, kept constantly up to date. As early as 1829 the Hamilton Company sent out a black list with the names of 17 girls guilty perhaps of "mutiny," "disobedience to orders," "dissatisfaction with wages," or "impudence to overseer." In 1842 the Middlesex Corporation put up a new mill and transferred a large number of its employees from its old mill. When they realized that they were now expected to tend four looms instead of three in their new jobs, seventy of the girls left, hoping to find work elsewhere in Lowell. But at all the other corporations in the city they were turned away with the statement that "they wanted none of the turnouts from Middlesex." The black list was so effective a way of disposing of malcontents that when the Nashua Convention was called in September, 1846, to discuss the ten-hour day, delegates were warned to "play the hypocrite" by pretending to be sick, "that you may attend the convention without having your name sent to the counting-house black-lists."

As the picture changed, less flattering accounts of Lowell began to be circulated, challenging the credibility of witnesses who saw the mill town as an abode of sweetness and light. As early as 1832, Seth Luther, the cud-chewing agitator for the short-lived

New England Workingmen's Association, went traveling about the factory towns delivering peppery talks on the evils of industrialism. Although Luther's vivid descriptions of the barbarities of child labor did not apply to the corporation mills, his remarks on how the Boston magnates influenced public opinion, maintained political power, and presented a solid front on labor questions, were very much to the point. Deriding Clay for a Senate speech extolling the charms of factory labor, as exemplified by the "light and cheerful step" with which the operatives went to and from their meals, Luther said:

> While on a visit to that pink of perfection, Waltham, I remarked that the females moved with a very light step, and well they might, for the bell rung for them to return to the mill from their homes in 19 minutes after it had rung for them to go to breakfast.

With the collapse of the New England Workingmen's Association, certain elements of the Democratic party reasserted their right to speak for the toiling masses. The *Lowell Mercury*, a Democratic newspaper, had in fact stated this position in 1831: "The old democratic party is the party of the working men; and the newspapers of that party have always been the advocates of the laboring people." The Democratic party was then as now made up of several discordant elements: Northern city workers and Southern slave-owners, among others. As leader of the Southern faction, Calhoun, for example, proposed a coalition between Northern businessmen and the slave-owners to keep down labor agitation as well as Abolitionist propaganda. The Democratic party in the North, however, was more inclined to pose as champion of the rights of labor against the big business element in the Whig party. It was undoubtedly for this reason that the *Boston Daily Times*, a Democratic newspaper, provoked a controversy about the health and morals of the Lowell factory operatives that has in effect been continued down to the present day. On July 13, 1839, the *Times* carried a long editorial describing conditions in Lowell in terms the very opposite of those employed by Crockett, Clay, and the foreign visitors.

The girls worked and lived in an unhealthy environment, said the writer; their hours were too long, their food poor and inadequate, so that they soon became "pale, feeble, and finally broken in constitution." He further charged that great numbers of loose women came to work in the mills, and that many innocent operatives were systematically seduced: "There has been created and there is now growing up in Lowell a manufacturing population whose tendency in, the scale of civilization, health, morals, and intellectually is manifestly downwards." It was this blast that gave Brownson the ammunition for his attack on the morality of the operatives in the *Boston Quarterly* the following year.

The challenging statements of the *Times* and Brownson did not go unanswered. No less a personage than the first mayor of Lowell after its incorporation as a city, Dr. Elisha Bartlett, took up the cudgels in defense of the operatives' health and morals.*
With an impressive misuse of scientific method, considering that he was a doctor, Bartlett compared the vital statistics of Lowell and Portsmouth, New Hampshire, than which no two towns in the United States could be more dissimilar, Lowell being only recently settled, and inhabited by a large, transient, youthful population, while Portsmouth was an old town, with a permanent population of all ages, and a long-established industry. The death rate in Portsmouth was higher than that of Lowell, Bartlett was able to prove, likewise the incidence of sickness, and from these unrelated figures the good doctor deduced that far from being detrimental to health, factory labor was actually ameliorative! He also dismissed the imputation of immorality as completely unfounded in fact.

Bartlett's whitewash only stimulated the controversy, being followed shortly by the article † of a "Citizen of Lowell" in the *Vox Populi*, who described Bartlett's reasoning as silly, his figures as distorted, and the man himself as the "servant of interested

---

* Elisha Bartlett: *A Vindication of the Character and Condition of the Females Employed in the Lowell Mills, etc.* Lowell, 1841.

† Later published as "Corporations and Operatives . . . a review of the 'Vindication' by Elisha Bartlett, M.D."

aristocracies." The "Citizen" named specific abuses: long hours, desperately hurried mealtimes, filth and vermin in the boarding houses.

Partisans of the corporations tried to refute criticism of this type by dwelling on the propriety and respectability of the girls, "approaching with some to the genteel," repeating the compliment so often that it ended by ringing hollow. From the remarks of several "disinterested" observers one was led inescapably to the conclusion that the Lowell operatives did not know when they were well off. But by 1845 propriety and respectability, even when it approached the genteel, had ceased to be the prime objectives of the mill girls. Concrete issues like health, job security, wages, and hours were beginning to loom larger in their minds than silk parasols or Navarino bonnets. More and more girls were coming to the mills, not to buy luxuries or accumulate a little nest egg, but under the compulsion of earning their bread. John Greenleaf Whittier, who spent six months in Lowell as editor of the *Middlesex Standard*, sensed this as soon as he arrived. His column of August 15, 1844, titled "The Stranger in Lowell," reads:

Not as a matter of taste and self-gratification have many of them exchanged the free breezes . . . of the country for the close, hot city, and the jar and whirl of these crowded and noisy mills. Nor am I one of those who count steady, daily toil, consuming the golden hours of the day, and leaving only the night for recreation, study and rest, as in itself a pleasurable matter. There have been a good many foolish essays written upon the beauty and divinity of labor by those who have never known what it really is to earn one's livelihood by the sweat of the brow. . . . Let such be silent.

In the early part of the century one of the most potent arguments for the use of women in industry had been that they would otherwise be "useless, if not a burden to society." It was also considered highly desirable from a moral point of view to keep female creatures from idleness and from the vice that idleness bred. As time went on, these Puritanical motives were played down, the corporations themselves encouraging the notion that work in a cotton mill was a "romantic sport," an idea that is entertained up to this very day in some quarters. Else how could the young ladies have had time to cultivate their minds, read Milton, translate Goethe, and write verses? The most literary of the Lowell girls, Lucy Larcom, who held herself aloof from all reform movements, found that she could accomplish this only by a sacrifice in wages, by taking a job that paid less than most of the girls earned. Another view was expressed by Catherine Beecher, after a visit to Lowell in 1845, when she stated categorically that literary activities could be carried on by mill girls only at a sacrifice to health, during "hours which should have been given to sleep."

To sum up, by 1845 the operatives in the corporation mills were putting in more time under less agreeable working conditions, turning out more cloth and receiving less pay than when the industry was first established. Less intelligent girls than these high-spirited New England farmers' daughters would have been irked by this state of affairs. Instinctively they were aware of what Professor Victor Clark, the historian of American manufactures, has stated as an axiom: "If a worker is producing more and working harder at the end of a period than at the beginning, and is getting practically the same wage, he is then not participating in the prosperity of the industry."

Other textile cities were noted for one feature or another, Manchester in England for its enormous size and output, Lyons in France for the beauty and fine quality of its silks, but Lowell had become world-famous for reasons other than these. Lowell's fame rested on two things: first, the socially responsible attitude of the mill owners, and second, the dignity and merit of the operatives, two factors which, as the textile magnates properly understood, were closely interrelated. Unfortunately the magnates saw their social responsibility only in terms of what was praiseworthy in 1823.

Hence, while in the twenties and early thirties they provided services and wages somewhat above the level of wages and working conditions in other industries, by 1845 these had fallen below the current standards. In the later period, moreover, the wages in many occupations for women were beginning to catch up with the earnings in the mills, so that other conditions would have had to be better in Lowell to make up for the narrowing difference in pay. The earlier benevolence of the mill owners toward their operatives had been assumed in order to win the tolerance of a dominantly agricultural community toward manufacturing. But, as the opposition to industrialism subsided, the pretense of benevolence only made actual conditions in the mill towns assume a grimmer aspect. At any rate, you could not count on high-spirited and intelligent New England girls to accept such a drop in their standards tamely. They were not deceived by the sanctimoniousness of corporation paternalism.

Chapter XI

UNREST

RUSTIC and ungainly though the mill girls were when they first arrived in Lowell and the other corporation towns, they brought with them a spirit of independence and a sense of equality with any man that resisted all attempts to proletarianize them. Coming fresh from the rural democracy, and constantly recruited from the same source, they had no tradition of fellowship with their employers such as had been common in the small-scale industry of an earlier day. Hence, when the absolutism of the corporations made itself felt either in a wage-cut or in new restrictive regulations, they quickly flared up in revolt.

Up to the 1840's these outbursts were spontaneous, unorganized affairs, more like an explosion of indignation than a strike as we know the term today. Thus, though they were carried on spiritedly for a few days they were inevitably abandoned by the girls without winning any concessions. Young women with the background and education of these textile operatives of a century ago could scarcely be expected to know how workers in other fields had banded themselves together to seek improvements in wages or working conditions.

Not that these more experienced workers had achieved better results up to this time. Organizations of journeymen among cordwainers, printers, carpenters, tailors, and others had come into existence at the end of the Revolutionary War, but, in spite of occasionally bitter strikes, had made few gains. This early labor movement was quelled when employers, joining forces in well-knit groups, invoked the law of conspiracy in the courts to ban the unions. In the late twenties there came a new drive to organize skilled workers, not only for economic ends but also for political action. Workingmen's parties were formed in several of the large cities, with platforms embracing a broad area of social reform, including opposition to imprisonment for debt, the end of the militia system, free universal education, and land reform, which, though fine principles in themselves, served rather to confuse their adherents than achieve definite working-class aims. Trade union organization on the purely economic level took another spurt in the early thirties, with 173 strikes occurring between 1833 and 1837; but this drive, too, petered out during the depression following the panic in the latter year, its dissolution no doubt hastened by one-sided court decisions.*

If at any time a group of workingmen held a monopoly of a certain craft, that is, if they possessed irreplaceable skills, indispensable in certain processes of manufacture, their bargaining position was of course much stronger whether they were unionized or not. The story is told of the first batch of English calico printers imported by the Merrimack Company, that when they reached Lowell they spurned the wages offered by the corporation, charging that a much higher rate of pay had been promised them before they sailed from England. Affronted by this deception, they all set off for Boston in a large wagon, with all of their effects and a band of musicians playing lively airs. As it was impossible to replace these skilled workers anywhere in the United States, Kirk Boott at once set out in his carriage to overtake them, agreed to their terms, and brought them back to the accompaniment of even more jubilant music.

* Among the champions of labor at that period was John Greenleaf Whittier, himself a journeyman printer by trade, who denounced Judge Edwards of New York for handing down an opinion that trade unions constituted a criminal conspiracy. Writing in the *Essex Gazette* for July 23, 1836, Whittier said: "To brand laborers as criminals for peaceably requiring an increase of their wages, we hold to be an outrage on the rights of man, and a disgrace to a community professing to be free."

The unskilled operatives in the mills had no such bargaining position; their like could be found in any New England village. But despite their want of skill or experience, despite their lack of organization, the mill girls, when tried too far, resorted instinctively to the only means of protest available to them: the concerted withdrawal of their services. Because of their impromptu character and brief duration, these protests were properly called "turnouts," rather than "strikes," which would have involved both premeditation and a greater class consciousness than the mill girls possessed.

Since Lowell was the "pet" of the textile magnates, the showpiece of the industry, conditions there were always a little better than in the other mill towns. It was for this reason that the first turnout in the New England cotton mills took place not in Lowell, but in Dover, New Hampshire, where there was no constant file of distinguished visitors to be impressed with happy, smiling faces. At the Cocheco Company in Dover, established in 1823, the terms of employment to which all operatives had to subscribe, were somewhat harsher than in Lowell, particularly the one that read: "We, the subscribers . . . agree to work for such wages per week, and prices by the Job, as the Company may see fit to pay, and be subject to the fines, as well as entitled to the premiums paid by the Company." For some years the privilege of exacting fines was not exercised, but late in December, 1828, a fine of 12½ cents was imposed by the management on any operative arriving at the mill entrance after the bell stopped ringing. In that season of the year the day's work began several hours before the sun rose, and some tardiness would seem explicable. Moreover, the fine was out of all proportion to the crime of being a few minutes late, amounting to over a third of a day's wage, exclusive of board. Outraged by this injustice, the girls remembered all the other indignities and vexations they had been enduring silently: the petty tyranny of the overseers, the rule against talking during working hours, the injunction against forming any "combination" without forfeit of wages, the requirement that they give two weeks' notice, without any corresponding agreement on the part of the corporation, the threat of being blacklisted.

They resolved that they would show their mettle. On the Friday afternoon after the fine was announced, between three and four hundred girls turned out, paraded about the town to the strains of martial music, and burned several casks of gunpowder. The management, not intimidated in the slightest, countered by advertising for several hundred "better-behaved women." What could the girls do next? They did not know. On the Monday following all but those who had been blacklisted returned to work, having accomplished nothing more than letting off a little steam.

The suddenness with which this outbreak took place is indicative of the long-suppressed resentment many of the operatives must have felt at the loss of their independence. Later flare-ups occurred because of the girls' struggle to keep their standards from being degraded further. Wage-cuts were the most frequent cause of dissatisfaction, although there were other causes as well. In May, 1829, 60 weavers left their looms in the Taunton mills because of an attempted wage-cut, and three factories were forced to shut down partially as a result, Taunton being a smaller textile center than Dover or Lowell. At another turnout in Exeter, New Hampshire, in 1834, girls who had "worked till 8 for pay till 7:30" won the agent's promise that the foremen's watch would be regulated in conformity with solar time. How well this particular promise was kept is not known, but the device, later resorted to in Lowell also, would seem to have been a favorite trick for squeezing out a little more yardage from the operatives at the end of the day.

Up to this time, however, no disturbances in Lowell are recorded, either because conditions there were superior to those in other textile centers, or because Lowell attracted what was then referred to as a "superior" type of operative, that is, a girl too well bred to make a public demonstration for whatever cause. But early in 1834, when wage-cuts were announced for the first of March in the Lowell mills, these pampered misses showed they could react as sharply to a loss in earning power as factory girls anywhere.* To temper the blow, the corporations had originally planned to reduce wages gradually, but when their intention became known, it gave rise to so much "untimely discontent" that they decided to "save all future controversy" by making the entire cut at once.

If there had been "untimely discontent" before this announcement, what followed could only be described as open rebellion. On February 20 the *Boston Transcript* reported the events in Lowell in some detail, using a tone of dignified regret at such goings-on:

> We learn that extraordinary excitement was occasioned at Lowell, last week, by an announcement that the wages paid in some of the departments would be reduced 15 percent on the 1st of March. The reduction principally affected the female operatives, and they held several meetings, or caucuses, at which a young woman presided, who took an active part in persuading her associates to give notice that they should quit the mills, and to induce them to "make a run" on the Lowell Bank and the Savings Bank, which they did.
>
> On Friday morning, the young woman referred to was *dismissed*, by the Agent . . . and on leaving the office . . . waved her calash in the air, as a signal to the others, who were watching from the windows, when they immediately "struck" and assembled about her, in despite of the overseers.
>
> The number soon increased to nearly *800*. A procession was formed, and they marched about the town, to the amusement of a mob of idlers and boys, and, we are sorry to add, not altogether to the credit of Yankee girls. . . . We are told that one of the leaders mounted a stump and made a flaming Mary Wollstonecraft speech on the rights of women and the iniquities of the "*monied* aristocracy," which produced a powerful effect on her auditors, and they determined to "have their way if they died for it."

* As indicated earlier, this reduction in pay was attributed by the corporations to a rise in the cost of raw cotton and a fall in the price of cotton goods, but when raw material costs fell and prices rose presently, the wage-cuts were not restored.

The treatment of the story by the labor press was naturally far more respectful. On February 22, *The Man*, a New York workingmen's paper, reported that the proposed wage reductions amounted to from 12 to 25 percent, and that there was nothing unseemly in the operatives' demonstration:

. . . the Yankee girls at Lowell are doing themselves much credit by their determined resistance of the attempt of their taskmasters to visit punishment upon them for the sins of Bankism. The run upon the Lowell Banks still continued, and the Banks had been obliged to send to Boston for specie.

On Saturday the militant spirit of the girls was still so strong that they issued a proclamation, a naive mixture of defiance and crude irony designed to hold their ranks firm.

Union Is Power

Our present object is to have union and exertion, and we remain in possession of our inalienable rights. We circulate this paper, wishing to obtain the names of all who imbibe the spirit of our patriotic ancestors, who preferred privation to bondage, and parted with all that renders life desirable—and even life itself—to procure independence for their children. The oppressing hand of avarice would enslave us; and to gain their object, they very gravely tell us of the pressure of the times; this we are already sensible of, and deplore it. If any are in want of assistance, the Ladies will be compassionate, and assist them; but we prefer to have the disposing of our charities in our own hands. . . .

All who patronize this effort, we wish to have discontinue their labors until terms of reconciliation are made.

Resolved, That we will not go back into the mills to work until our wages are continued to us as they have been.

Resolved, That none of us will go back unless they receive us all as one.

Resolved, That if any have not money enough to carry them home, that they shall be supplied.

Let oppression shrug her shoulders
And a haughty tyrant frown,
And little upstart Ignorance
In mockery look down.
Yet I value not the feeble threats
Of Tories in disguise,
While the flag of Independence
O'er our noble nation flies.

These brave sentiments were issued when the excitement was at fever pitch, some reports indicating that as many as two thousand girls had joined the turnouts. But the next day being Sunday, they all went to church and cooled off. Come Monday morning, all the operatives except those who had decided to return to their homes in the country began straggling back into the mills, and on March 1 the reduced wage scale went into effect without any further disturbance in Lowell.

But the fiat had gone forth from the Boston counting houses that wages were to be reduced in all the corporation mills at about the same time, and another textile town was soon to be heard from. Inspired by the events at Lowell, and having already had experience of a turnout in 1828, the girls in the Cocheco mills at Dover decided to protest the new pay-cut announced toward the end of February, 1834. They must have been aware, however, of the necessity for improved tactics, for on this occasion they bowed to the criticism of their earlier turnout by refraining from parades and fireworks. Even the local newspaper, which in so many company towns was under the thumb of the corporations, paid tribute to their dignified behavior. On March 8, 1834, the *Dover Gazette* gave a detailed account of the demonstration of the preceding days, ending up with:

In justice to the girls we feel it our duty to say that their whole conduct since leaving the mills on Friday morning has been marked with the strictest regard to propriety and decorum, and merits unqualified approbation.

Instead of forming processions and parading the streets to the amusement of gaping idlers, they have confined themselves for the most part within their respective boarding houses and seem impelled by no other motive than a firm determination to maintain their just rights, of which they believe it is in contemplation to deprive them.

Other less friendly newspapers, however, viewing any turn-out with alarm, no matter how peaceably conducted, referred to the girls' loose organization as a "riotous combination," and the young women themselves as "otherwise respectable." Evidently the demonstration involved large numbers of operatives, for the Cocheco Company advertised for 500 females to take the place of the turnouts, and, to avoid any misunderstanding, published the rules all employees must promise to obey. In answer to this the Dover girls published their own advertisement:

Girls on Hand. There are now 500 of us in the town of Dover, who are now at work for ourselves, but might easily answer the wants and wishes of the "Cocheco Manufacturing Company, at Dover, N.H.," excepting that we will not consent to work at the reduced tariff of wages to take place on the 15th of March instant, or even one mill less than the wages lately given. We would just say to our sex in the country that we are not to live here long without plenty of work.

On the Saturday afternoon following their walkout, six or seven hundred girls assembled in the courthouse to discuss their grievances and plan further measures. Without a dissenting vote the following resolutions were passed:

1st, Resolved, That we will never consent to work for the Cocheco Manufacturing Company at their reduced "*Tariff of Wages.*"

2nd, Resolved, That we believe the "*unusual pressure of the times,*" which is so much complained of, to have been caused by artful and designing men to subserve party purposes, or more wickedly still, to promote their own private ends.

3rd, Resolved, That we view with feelings of indignation the attempt made to throw upon us, who are least able to bear it, the effect of this "pressure" by reducing our wages, while those of our overseers and Agent are continued to them at their former high rate. That we think our wage already low enough, when the peculiar circumstances of our situation are considered; that we are many of us far from our homes, parents, and friends, and it is only by strict economy and untiring industry that any of us have been able to lay up anything. . . .

We view this attempt to reduce our wages as part of a general plan of the proprietors of the different manufacturing establishments to reduce the Females in their employ to that state of dependence on them in which they openly, as they do now secretly, abuse and insult them by calling them their "slaves."

After the resolutions were passed a committee of twelve was chosen to communicate the proceedings of the meeting to the operatives of the mills at Great Falls, Newmarket, and Lowell. It was also voted that funds be raised to pay the expenses of those who wanted to return home but lacked the wherewithal, and that the proceedings of the meeting be published in the *Gazette* and other journals opposed to "slavery" in the factories, to counteract the effect of reports that had appeared in unfriendly newspapers.

In spite of all this display of energy, the Dover girls returned to work at the reduced wages, when the mills reopened on March 15. And yet the demonstrations of 1834, both in Dover and in Lowell, had shown something of an advance over the haphazard demonstration of 1828. By withdrawing their funds from the banks, the Lowell girls had indicated awareness of the necessity of a war chest. The Dover operatives also went a step or two further in the approach to trade union problems: they had tried to broaden the base of their protest by seeking solidarity with the girls in other mill towns; and they had recognized the importance of favorable publicity and a friendly press—an advantage that American labor still lacks today. But it must be remembered that lessons learned by operatives in one year, or at one period, were not necessarily put into practice by the same girls when a new outbreak occurred. Most of them remained in the mills for only three or four years and, with such a constant turnover, not to speak of the blacklisting of known trouble-makers, it was impossible to build a permanent organization or maintain a consistent policy.

In the hour of dissatisfaction and revolt, therefore, the girls generally walked out first, and improvised some plan of action afterward. We see the pattern repeated in the turnout in Lowell in October, 1836, the largest and most prolonged in the mills up to that time, when the corporations made a fresh attack on wages by increasing the price of board. Demonstrations also took place at Dover, and, for the first time, at Chicopee, on the same grounds, but in neither place did the walkout assume such proportions or arouse so much interest as in Lowell.

By arrangement with the corporations, the boarding-house keepers had from the beginning charged the operatives $1.25 a week for board, which was deducted from their earnings at the counting house. Since the girls never actually handled the money paid for their board, they reckoned their wages in terms of the sum received after board was deducted. The rate of $1.25 a week per person was barely sufficient to cover the expenses of the boarding-house mistress; in fact, Lucy Larcom's mother, who was accustomed to setting a "good table," found it necessary to send Lucy to work in the mills at the age of eleven in order to make ends meet. To aggravate the situation, by 1836 the cost of living had risen so sharply that many boarding-house keepers would have been forced to abandon their leases if they had not been granted relief. The corporations therefore agreed to come to their rescue by lowering the weekly rent of their houses by 12½ cents per boarder, and increasing the amount deducted from the girls' wages for board by the same amount. Small as it seems now, the sum of 12½ cents weekly amounted to a five-percent wage-cut, on the average, and the girls said they would not take it.

Little Harriet Hanson, then eleven years old, was working as a doffer in one of the mills when the turnout was being discussed by the older girls in the spinning room. Strangely enough, the better-paid operatives, the weavers, to whom the cut represented a smaller proportion of their weekly wage, were the first to leave their places, walking out in such numbers that the overseers turned off the machinery. But, in the spinning room, Harriet observed that the girls were still undecided . . .

asking each other, "Would you?" or "Shall we turn out?" and not one of them having the courage to lead off, I, who began to think they would not go out, after all their talk, became impatient and started on ahead, saying with childish bravado, "I don't care what you do, *I* am going to turn out, whether any one else does or not;" and I marched out, and was followed by the others.

Between twelve and fifteen hundred girls paraded through the streets singing a parody of an old song, "I won't be a nun":

> *Oh, isn't it a pity, such a pretty girl as I*
> *Should be sent to the factory to pine away and die?*
> *Oh! I will not be a slave*
> *For I'm so fond of liberty*
> *That I cannot be a slave.*

Again their speakers recalled the valor of their patriot forebears: "As our fathers resisted unto blood the lordly avarice of the British ministry, so we, their daughters, never will wear the yoke which has been prepared for us."

A Factory Girls' Association was formed, which soon reached a membership of 2,500, and passed resolutions that all dealings with the mill owners were to be carried on through their union officers, and that any communication from the corporations proscribing any member or officer of the union would be ignored. Moral support for the turnouts came from the Third Annual Convention of the National Trades Union, then in session in Philadelphia, which adopted resolutions expressing the deep sympathy of organized labor for the operatives' struggle to maintain their rights. Unions throughout the country were urged in another resolution "to do all in their power to aid either by money or otherwise the females" who were "standing out against the oppression of these soulless employers." But while the convention itself sent fraternal greetings to the embattled operatives at Lowell, its Committee on Female Labor brought in a report—evidently prepared before the turnout took place—chiding women workers for not building *permanent* societies for mutual help:

> Is it not singular [the report ran] that females who would sacrifice their time and health to distribute tracts and collect moneys for the heathen could not devote a mite for their own oppressed country-women without the sacrifice of time and health? We do not object to these objects by any means, but while they are discharging the duties of humanity they should not overlook their own sex and kin.

This criticism was particularly apt in the case of the textile operatives, who, though regular contributors to Western missions, never dreamed of putting an equal sum into an organization to protect their own standards.

Hence, almost before the encouragement and sound advice proffered by the Trades Union Convention could reach the Lowell operatives, they had been starved out. The girls returned to work before the end of October, without a restoration of the wage-cut, and without a recognition of their "union," which evaporated into thin air. Their failure had at least one interesting consequence, reflecting the energy with which the corporation tracked down malefactors of little wealth. As Harriet Hanson Robinson wrote in her reminiscences of this period:

> The agent of the corporation where I then worked took some small revenge on the supposed ring-leaders; on the principle of sending the weaker to the wall, my mother was turned away from her boarding-house, that functionary saying: "Mrs. Hanson, you could not prevent the older girls from turning out, but your daughter is a child, and *her* you could control."

The widow Hanson, who had kept a boarding house for men in Lowell to support her four children, thus became ineligible to enjoy the "philanthropy" of the Boston textile magnates because of the depravity of her eleven-year-old daughter. A touch of privation would perhaps teach her to exercise sterner discipline over that scapegrace infant.

The turnouts at Dover and Chicopee at the same time proved equally unsuccessful. If the operatives learned anything from these brief flare-ups, it was that they were constantly losing status, without being able to halt the process. On the other hand, the mill owners, although at first a bit jumpy, soon realized that there was nothing formidable in these demonstrations. Indeed they considered the turnouts so slight a threat that they never invoked the conspiracy laws to stamp out these minor insurrections. Even when the girls won a small point, they did not know how to extract the fullest advantage from it, or build on it for future gains. At Amesbury, for example, in March, 1836, a brief turnout occurred among the operatives when they were told they must tend two looms instead of one, without any raise in wages. Marching to the vestry of the Baptist Church, they chose officers and passed resolutions in the usual vein, pledging themselves not to return to work unless all were taken back, or forfeit $5. According to the *Boston Transcript* of March 25, 1836, the agent, finding them determined to persevere, sent a written notice that they might come back. Presumably all the turn-outs were accepted without prejudice, but otherwise the conditions were as stipulated by the management, that is, each operative worked two looms for the former wage of tending one. In no case during this whole period did the textile workers succeed in getting a higher wage or a restoration of a wage-cut by the use of the turnout.

Except for the burning of a couple of barrels of gunpowder at Dover in 1828, these protests were far from disorderly or violent. The girls walked out of the mills, paraded about the town, made a few speeches, passed some resolutions, and returned to work peaceably at the end of a few days. And yet their restraint earned no praise. It was, in fact, considered somewhat comical, not to say scandalous, for females to draw attention to themselves in this unorthodox manner. Conscious as they were of the taboos of the society in this regard, the girls needed both great courage and a deep sense of wrong to bring them to participate in public demonstrations on the scale of the turnouts of the thirties. For this reason the large numbers of operatives involved—800 in 1834 and 2,500 in 1836—is very significant.

There is evidence to prove that the textile magnates believed the girls would more easily bear unpleasant conditions because they did not intend to stay more than a few years in the mills. Nevertheless, the willingness to risk so desperate a measure as a strike or a turnout suggests that large numbers of operatives did not feel free to return home whenever they wished, either because their families depended on their earnings, or because they themselves had no other means of support. So far as the rest were concerned, the question was simply how long their incentive to remain in the mills could survive the constant depression of wages and standards.

For almost seven years after the turnouts of 1836 few disturbances on the part of the mill girls were noted. These years coincided with a period of depression all over the country, following the panic of 1837, in which almost every industry suffered. Among city workers there was widespread distress caused by wage-cuts and unemployment at the same time that the cost of living rose in the most indispensable items. Since labor organizations do not as a rule flourish in hard times, the promising trade union movement of the early thirties received a blow from which it did not recover until the middle of the next decade. If men in better-organized trades were unable to maintain their standards, it is not to be wondered at that the unorganized textile operatives put up no resistance to wage reductions and the speed-up during those lean years.

The downward trend of wages in the corporation mills, begun in 1834, a boom year, went on relentlessly after the panic, even though the New England textile industry suffered less than other enterprises from its effects. Dividends remained high until 1840,

for example, and even in the two bad years following there were
no mass discharges of employees, indicating a sustained demand
for textile products. For the most part the girls kept mum during this period,* aware of real want elsewhere, which the textile
magnates conscientiously brought to their attention. In 1840, for
example, when a new wage-cut was to go into effect, Amos
Lawrence arranged to have a Lowell newspaper print a letter
from his son, then traveling in Europe, describing the dreadful
wretchedness of the working population in the slums of Naples.
Any operative who considered herself abused could draw the
obvious inference that compared with other places Lowell was
a workers' paradise.

But the moment a slight upswing in business was noted, new
outbreaks occurred in the corporation mills. In December, 1842,
after the passage of the tariff that was supposed to restore earlier
wage-cuts, a new reduction of 20 percent went into effect at
the Middlesex Mills in Lowell. The Middlesex had just installed
William Crompton's loom for weaving fancy woolen fabrics,
an innovation that was to triple their profits for several years.
The cut in wages, a piece-rate reduction, was justified by the
corporation on the grounds of improvements in the machinery,
but a contemporary newspaper gave the show away by stating
that the girls could make *nearly* as much, under the reduced rate,
as under the old wages, using the old machinery. Fifty of the
girls, feeling that "nearly as much" was not nearly enough,
marched out of the mills in protest, and 150 others agreed to
join them presently. But the opportunity for a larger demonstration never came, for the Middlesex immediately replaced the
turnouts with other girls.

A second flare-up in Chicopee occurred in 1843 on the announcement of new schedules providing for lowered piece-rates
and a further speed-up. It was the operatives at the Chicopee
Manufacturing Company who took the initiative, after several
fruitless sessions with the agent. On May 3 some forty girls,

---

* There was one turnout at the York Company at Saco, Maine, in 1841, with a
parade and music, but it excited little comment.

using a painted window curtain as a banner, "marched round the streets doing themselves no credit," as a townsman wrote in his diary. They then proceeded in orderly fashion to the Cabot Manufacturing Company to induce the operatives there to join them, but without success. The situation seemed ominous enough for two of the largest investors in the Chicopee mills, James K. Mills and Edmund Dwight, to come up from Boston to look into this breach of discipline. The following day there were more meetings, speeches, and parades, but the numbers of the turnouts had declined by half. A day later the strike was over.

The small numbers of operatives involved in the two incidents just described, compared with the hundreds who left the mills in the demonstrations of 1834 and 1836, would indicate that in the forties most of the girls had lost faith in the efficacy of the turnout as a weapon to protect their standards. Not only had they come to realize that these methods invariably resulted in failure, but many were conscious also that in the eyes of the public they lost caste by such action. Their middle-class status as daughters of yeomen was very dear to them, and seemingly the more so as the conditions of their employment tended increasingly to place them on the footing of a helpless proletariat. Unable to rely on the humanity of their employers, and frustrated in their own efforts to improve their situation, they began exploring other possible outlets for their discontent.

At this low ebb in the morale of the operatives, new hope came to them from an unexpected source, from idealists and dreamers who somehow flourished at that period despite the enormous materialistic development of the country.

The workings of the capitalist system at this period, it should be remembered, were generally considered automatic and mysterious, subject to immutable laws over which mere men had no control. The victims of industrialism were therefore assured by newspaper editors that no improvement in their lot could come about except through the "justice and mercy" of their employers. If this justice and mercy were vouchsafed, so much the better; if not, nothing could be done about it. The with-holding of justice and mercy, moreover, did not detract from the sterling moral qualities of employers whose upright charac-ter was fixed in the public eye not only by their possession of wealth but also by their distribution of largesse to the *deserving* poor.

During the thirties, however, the New England intellectuals grouped around Emerson, and calling themselves Transcenden-talists, began to apply another critique to the prevailing economic system. In their view the inequalities and injustices of the exist-ing order could not be defended as ordained from on high, nor could self-interest be glorified as the prime and ultimate motive of human behavior. Transcendentalists nowadays even spoke of the great Boston nabobs with some want of reverence, as when W. Ellery Channing wrote in the *Dial* that "the great art of being a merchant is to look wise and ride in a carriage."

While the Transcendentalists themselves offered no panacea for the world's ills, they provided a moral climate in which Utopian theories could thrive. During the forties three different Utopian groups sprang into prominence: the Brisbane Associa-tionists, the Owen Associationists, and the Land Reformers led by George Henry Evans. For the existing system, the Utopians had so little hope that they concerned themselves not at all with its amelioration, and only half-heartedly with the mitigation of its worst abuses, but quite simply with its disestablishment. They did not wish to reform society, but to transform it into some-thing else.

The Brisbane Associationists were followers of Fourier, who wished to reorganize society into phalansteries or cooperative colonies made up of about 1,600 persons, all of whom would perform the work of the community according to their aptitudes. Each phalanstery would be self-supporting, raising its own food and providing other necessities through handicrafts. The Associ-ationists led by Robert Owen differed from the Fourierists in that they planned to take advantage of modern industrial proc-esses, use the best machinery available, and offer the greatest variety of employment in their cooperative colonies even while relying on agriculture for their principal means of support. Nevertheless, Owen's scheme was a little less appealing than Fourier's, since it involved strict paternalistic management, in line with Owen's earlier experiments at New Lanark.

George Henry Evans, the leader of the Land Reformers, started out with no less idealistic a program: that of "rural republican townships," with inalienable land holdings and handicrafts producing goods only for use. Unlike the other Utopians, however, Evans altered his scheme until all that remained of it was the demand for free land from the public domain for all settlers.

Inveterate lecture-goers, the operatives at Lowell, Chicopee, Manchester, Waltham, and the other mill towns had heard the mellow voice of Emerson, the high priest of Transcendentalism, on the lyceum platform. They were also acquainted with the Brook Farm experiment, originally undertaken by a group of Transcendentalists in 1842 as a resort for "plain living and high thinking," and converted into a Fourierist Phalanx in 1844. Lectures on Fourierism or Associationism were often given in Lowell, and although most of the operatives realized that there was to be no escape for them back into the past these movements were trying to recreate, they recognized the evils the Utopias were designed to correct. The Land Reformers also aroused some interest, but the advantages of free land in the West must have seemed vague to girls whose fathers, though landowners, earned such a meager livelihood that their daughters were obliged to go to work in the cotton mills.

Nevertheless, the spirit of criticism manifested in these various Utopian movements of the forties was most stimulating to the more thoughtful operatives, who for some years had seen conditions in the textile towns grow steadily worse while they remained powerless to remedy them. For this reason they were willing to cooperate with the Associationist and Land Reform groups, even to the point of accepting temporarily the leadership of the woolly-headed gentlemen who guided them. On the other hand, the Utopians, though not fundamentally interested in actual working-class problems, were conscious of the necessity for having a mass basis for their movements, and were therefore willing to play along for a while with labor groups intent on immediate objectives. Later the Utopians were to abandon and betray the newly revived labor movement, but for the moment they furnished leadership that was desperately needed, besides providing a rallying point and a forum for the inexperienced agitators among the mill girls.

In addition to these allies among the intellectuals, operatives who were discontented with conditions in the mills found welcome support in the certain newspapers of the time. As mentioned before, the Democratic newspapers of the thirties and forties treated the aspirations of the working classes with considerable sympathy. In the *Advertiser*, for example, Lowell itself boasted of a prosperous Democratic newspaper, a lively competitor of the corporations' "tool," the Whig *Courier*, edited by William Schouler. The *Lowell Advertiser*, while opposing the corporation magnates on political rather than economic grounds, reported without prejudice on workers' activities, and always had space for the operatives' side of current controversies.

A dozen or so newspapers specially designed to attract readers among the mill workers in the various New England textile centers also came into existence in the early forties. The first of these, *The Factory Girl*, published in New Market, New Hampshire, in 1842, discussed wages and hours in its editorials, branded factory owners as monopolists, and in general warned tyrants to expect rough treatment. *The Factory Girls' Garland*, published in Exeter, New Hampshire, in 1844, pointed out that in some parts of "that detested dynasty, that hated anarchy, old despotic England," wages were higher and hours shorter than in "this free republic, this glorious country," and stated its belief that the worker had "a right to a livelihood, not a mere subsistence." The names of many of these papers show a singular poverty of imagination; among others there was *The Factory Girls' Friend* (later taken over by the *Voice of Industry*) as well as the *Factory Girls' Album and Operatives' Advocate*, both of which, as might have been expected from their titles, urged reforms in mill conditions.

As the factory controversy grew more acute, other papers, not allied to either of the national parties, or aimed solely at working-class readers, took their stand in defense of the operatives' rights and privileges. "Is it no harm," cried A. B. F. Hildreth, editor of the *Ladies' Literary Repository* of Lowell . . .

that thousands of females are enticed away from their homes and their friends by false pretences, by flattering representations, and congregate in manufacturing places to seek employment at the hands of soulless corporations, thereby enabling the corporations by an influx of help to dictate the terms on which they shall gain an existence?

And in 1845 an insipid weekly published in Chicopee, the *Cabotville Chronicle*, had a sudden brief blooming as champion of labor's rights until the editor was run out of town, presumably for offending "public morality" by the publication of a perfectly innocuous serial story.

This sort of high-handed action could happen in Chicopee, a corporation town pure and simple, in the hinterland, but not in a city of world-wide fame like Lowell. It was in Lowell that the most eloquent, the most professional, and the most widely read of all the labor papers of the forties appeared: *The Voice of Industry*. Originally published in Fitchburg, Massachusetts, by William F. Young, in 1845 it was combined with two other labor papers and moved to the textile city on the banks of the Merrimack. Here it was issued weekly by a publishing committee of three, consisting of Young, Sarah Bagley, and Joel Hatch. In its prospectus the journal described itself as the organ of the New England Workingmen's Association, and stated its aims as no less than the abolition of Mental, Moral, and Physical Servitude, in all their complicated forms, and the interests of the Industrial Classes. It also made a bid for the interest of those operatives with literary inclinations who had formerly supported the *Lowell Offering:* "The Voice will contain a Female Department, under the immediate supervision of the Lowell Female Labor Reform Association, and be supported by contributions from the Operatives of this city and other manufacturing towns."

The part that the mill girls played in the publication of the *Voice of Industry* was indeed impressive. Sarah Bagley was for a long time a member of the publishing committee, moving up later to be its editor-in-chief. After Miss Bagley left the paper, the name of Mehitabel Eastman, a Manchester factory girl, appeared on the masthead as co-editor. During most of its life Huldah J. Stone ran the Female Department, a superfluous section, in a way, since practically all the material published was directed at an audience of operatives, especially after the paper's type and presses were bought by the Lowell Female Labor Reform Association. But, unlike all other journals of the period addressed principally to women, the *Voice of Industry* avoided the mincing prudery, the saccharine pieties, and the rest of the Victorian nonsense then considered suitable for female readers. Operatives, for instance, were urged to attend the Boston meeting of the New England Workingmen's Association in May, 1846, "without false delicacy." Joint meetings of male and female branches of the Labor Reform Leagues were commented on in a matter-of-fact tone, while the speeches and reports of women delegates to the various Workingmen's Conventions were given equal coverage with those of the men.

When it is remembered that the first woman's rights convention was not held until 1848, the equal, or rather predominant, role of women—and more particularly the textile operatives—in the resurgent labor movement between 1845 and 1847 seems all the more remarkable. Harriet Farley had written in one of her effusions in the *Lowell Offering:* "With wages and hours we have nothing to do." It was precisely with the subjects of wages and hours that Sarah Bagley, Huldah Stone, Mehitabel Eastman, Mary Emerson, and all their followers thought they ought to concern themselves. As a first step, they concentrated their efforts on winning legislation providing for the ten-hour day.

In the Female Labor Reform Associations, therefore, the textile operatives for the first time had the equivalent of a union; in the *Voice of Industry* they had their own newspaper; in the Utopians they had allies among the intellectuals, and in the ten-hour movement they had a specific objective. Contrasted with the lack of leadership and plan from which they had suffered in the thirties, the situation in the middle forties seemed full of promise. Reforms would not now be long in coming, they felt, not in the form of a boon granted by their merciful employers, but as a right, after full and open discussion in the factories, in the press, and in the Legislature. If as a result of their activities the ten-hour day should be won, what was there to prevent them from marching on to other victories? Perhaps they could increase their wages to earlier levels, stem the eternal speed-up, recover their status as respected and self-respecting members of the community, and show that in the great industrial transformation that was changing the face of the country, female labor need not be a passive factor.

Chapter XII

THE TEN-HOUR STRUGGLE

THE Lowell Female Labor Reform Association had come into being one evening in December, 1844, when five mill girls met in a dim-lit room at the close of the long day's work and resolved to fight for the ten-hour day. Knowing that it would be no easy task to put over their program, they fortified themselves against discouragement by selecting as their motto: "Try Again." Presumably this group was to function as the ladies' auxiliary of the local Mechanics and Laborers Association,* a society of workingmen organized to bring pressure for general labor reform; but within an astonishingly short time the tail began to wag the dog. From these small beginnings, the Female Labor Reform Association grew within three months to a membership of over 300 operatives, and a year later claimed over 600 members in Lowell alone, with branches of various sizes in almost all the important textile centers in New England. At last the mill girls had a union to present their grievances and work for corrective measures. It was not a union in the modern sense, with the power to negotiate directly with employers, but no one doubted that it spoke for the operatives, even though it appealed only to public opinion.

* Not to be confused with the Middlesex Mechanics Association of Lowell, which received considerable financial support from the corporations, and was made up of technicians, overseers, superintendents, etc.

If the contributors to the *Lowell Offering* formed a kind of elite, the leadership of the Female Labor Reform Association constituted a distillation of that elite. Sarah G. Bagley, Huldah J. Stone, Hannah C. Tarlton, Eliza Hemingway, Mary Emerson, and Mrs. Quimby were not only able to write with some fluency and interlard their writings with quotations from the poets, but also wrote to some purpose. Of these intelligent young women, Sarah Bagley, president of the Association, was undoubtedly the most nimble-witted, the most energetic, and the most fertile in devising schemes to advance the cause of reform. "A common-schooled New England operative," as a contemporary described her, she was a native of New Hampshire, whence the most capable and enterprising girls were recruited for work in the mills. Arriving in Lowell shortly after the unsuccessful turnout of October, 1836, she had been employed for six and a half years at the Hamilton Corporation, and two years at the Middlesex factory.

As a member of one of the Improvement Circles she had been touched by the literary fever, contributing one article, "The Pleasures of Factory Life," to the *Lowell Offering* while the Rev. Mr. Thomas was still the editor. But after Orestes Brownson's series on the laboring classes came out in the *Boston Quarterly Review*, she began to revaluate those pleasures. Apparently she was not a little provoked by Harriet Farley's pious defense of the operatives' virtue, for her resentment against corporation abuses grew even livelier when Mr. Thomas rejected as "too controversial" an article she had written sustaining Brownson's thesis. Nor is it strange that the respectable clergyman should have found her contribution too saucy for the genteel pages of the *Offering*, for when the article was at length published in 1845 as the first of a series of *Factory Tracts*, issued by the Lowell Female Labor Reform Association, Miss Bagley stood forth as a militant radical. Calling on the operatives to join the struggle for better conditions, she thundered: "In the strength of our united influence we will show these *driveling* cotton lords, this mushroom aristocracy of New England, who so arrogantly aspire to lord it over God's heritage, that our rights cannot be trampled upon with impunity."

Her tone grew no milder after she assumed the leadership of the reform movement. In one of her articles in the *Voice of Industry*, for example, when referring to an agent who had threatened an operative with discharge because of participation in the ten-hour movement, Miss Bagley used terms that must have made Miss Farley shudder: "We will make the name of him who dares the act stink with every wind from all parts of the compass." * And again, reporting on a visit she paid to the State Prison at Concord, New Hampshire, she apostrophized a fine-looking prisoner incarcerated there for forgery: "You might have selected some game equally dishonest, that would . . . have made you looked up to, as a man of wealth. . . . You might have performed some 'hocus-pocus' means of robbery, without forgery, and passed as an Appleton, a Lawrence, or an Astor in society."

Miss Bagley also showed some talent as a public speaker, even though the role exposed her to the raillery of overbearing males and the titters of more faint-hearted maidens. Whether prepared or impromptu, her speeches aroused considerable interest, and were cited with liberal quotations in the press of the period. Quick to understand the need for organizing textile workers on an industry-wide scale, she urged that branches of the Female Labor Reform Association be established in all the corporation mill towns. So great was her prestige that one evening when she appeared before a large meeting of operatives in Manchester, New Hampshire, with a constitution for their acceptance, it was adopted forthwith.† The Manchester Female Labor Reform Association, thus brought to life, grew to a membership of 300

---

* Miss Farley's passion for "refinement" was not shared by all the country girls who worked in the mills. Even her close friend Harriott Curtis was said to be very outspoken. But in this respect Miss Bagley was less inhibited even than the male radicals of the time.

† This was especially remarkable since the poor girls had been obliged to listen to a three-hour speech by John Cluer, a well-known radical orator, before Miss Bagley could get their ear.

within a year, and developed a couple of ardent agitators in Sarah Rumrill and Mehitabel Eastman. When other branches were formed in Waltham, Nashua, Dover, and Fall River, Miss Bagley encouraged them to keep in close touch with one another by correspondence, and she further increased the sense of solidarity among operatives in the various mill towns by arranging to publish various tracts and papers on their common problems. It was also largely through her efforts that the Lowell Industrial Reform Lyceum was established—as a rival attraction to the more conventional lyceum, where "controversial" subjects were not discussed—to hear lectures by Robert Rantoul, Jr., George Ripley, Horace Greeley, and William Lloyd Garrison.

But for all her presumably masculine activities, Miss Bagley did not eschew all feminine accomplishments. When she and Huldah Stone went as delegates to the first convention of the New England Workingmen's Association in Boston, for example, they presented the society with a "large, tasteful banner," the handiwork of members of the Lowell group. To awaken interest in the purposes of the labor reformers, fairs and parties were frequently held, some of them quite elaborate. For the St. Valentine's Day Party in 1846 "eminent and distinguished speakers from abroad" were advertised, as well as a band, and "rich treat of fruit and other eatables." A special *Valentine Offering* was issued on this occasion, containing poems and articles like those in the *Lowell Offering*, but stressing reform. In preparation for an Independence Day celebration in 1846 Miss Bagley announced the formation of a Sewing Circle, "for the advancement of social improvement, and to prepare articles for their contemplated Fair," thus combining what might be called a study group with more utilitarian functions.

But the most significant accomplishment of this unusually versatile young woman was her leadership of the ten-hour movement of the middle forties, during its most active phase. She made Lowell for a few years the center of the movement, and the Lowell Female Labor Reform Association its spearhead. The idea that no one should be required to work for an employer more than ten hours a day did not originate with Miss Bagley. Labor groups had begun agitating for this reform as early as 1825, some of them, notably mechanics and outdoor workers, winning a cut in their long hours by means of effective strikes. The panic of 1837 interrupted this promising movement, but in 1840 it gained a new impetus when President Van Buren, courting the votes of Northern laborers, carried out a promise made earlier by Jackson and issued an executive order limiting the working hours of artisans in the public service to ten a day, without any reduction in wages. Some states followed suit, but by far the largest number of workers in the country still put in as many hours of labor a day as their employers could extract from them, large corporations being particularly uncompromising in this regard. It therefore became apparent to labor leaders that since corporations were granted broad, monopolistic powers by state legislatures, they could be forced to reduce working hours by action of the same legislatures that had sponsored them.

New England, a conservative stronghold, was in the rear of the development toward a shorter working day. Its principal industry was cotton textiles, and the cotton-textile magnates of Boston dominated its legislatures. Under their prompting, the Whig press of the time denounced the ten-hour movement as "Democratic humbug," and hammered away at the debatable point that reduced hours would necessarily entail reduced wages. On the other hand, since it was the textile operatives who felt the discomfort of long working hours at monotonous tasks most cruelly, no other group was better qualified to lead the movement for a shorter day.

English immigrant operatives at Fall River, with broader experience in labor agitation than native workers, took the initiative in this when they presented a petition for the establishment of a ten-hour day to the Massachusetts Legislature in 1842. This first petition, signed by 1,300 mill workers from Fall River, Mansfield, New Bedford, Attleboro, Taunton, and Newburyport, contained a rather general statement of grievances, among which was a plea for the abolition of child labor, that had supposedly been outlawed in Massachusetts in 1836. The Legislature took no action on this request.

Compared with the smaller textile towns, Lowell had always pointed with pride to its superior conditions, its large proportion of native-born operatives, its relatively small number of child workers. Nevertheless, the Lowell girls had long been aware of the unnatural strain in their long hours. As early as 1834 Charles Douglas, editor of the *New England Artisan,* had spoken to a large and sympathetic audience of Lowell mill girls on the advantages of the *eight*-hour day, in order to provide "ample time for mental improvement and for healthful exercise in the open air." During the next ten years the speed-up rendered the long working day even more onerous, and it would have been strange if the intelligent native operatives of Lowell had been willing to put up with conditions that recent immigrants in Fall River found intolerable. Hence the second petition for a ten-hour day, signed by 1,600 operatives, originated in Lowell in 1843. The petitioners asked for a law specifically enjoining corporations from requiring more than ten hours of labor a day from their employees. Such a law, the petition stated, was needed to safeguard the operatives' health, to give them time for "mental and moral cultivation" as well as opportunity to attend to their personal affairs. This plea suffered the fate of the first one.

In 1844 still another petition for a ten-hour day, signed by 1,000 operatives, was sent to the State House from Lowell, affirming that wages were being lowered, hours increased, and that operatives merited protection as much as corporations. The drive for reform of hours was assuming the proportions of a nuisance; it could no longer be ignored. By referring the petition to the next session, the Legislature nevertheless put off the unhappy day when the problem must be faced squarely, a postponement that gave both the corporation "satraps" in the Legislature and the leaders of the ten-hour movement in Lowell time to prepare their case.

One of Lowell's representatives in the Legislature at that time was William Schouler, proprietor of the *Lowell Courier*. The interests of labor at that period were considered of so little consequence that there was no labor committee in the Massachusetts House of Representatives, which therefore assigned the *Committee on Manufactures* to hold hearings on the ten-hour petitions. As the session of 1845 began, however, William Schouler, who had never before sat on that committee, was suddenly appointed its chairman by the Speaker of the House, an omen of great significance.

The reformers in Lowell now busied themselves feverishly in preparation for the hearings before the legislative committee, the first governmental investigating committee ever to inquire into labor conditions in American history.* It was at this time, shortly before the end of the year 1844, that the Lowell Female Labor Reform Association was organized to take advantage of this new opportunity. Fresh petitions were circulated through the mill towns by the Association, and over 2,000 signatures obtained, of which about 1,500 were from Lowell, and most of these from women. One of the Lowell petitions started off with the words:

> We the undersigned peaceable, industrious and hardworking men and women of Lowell, in view of our condition—the evils already come upon us, by toiling from 13 to 14 hours per day, confined in unhealthy apartments, exposed to the poisonous contagion of air, vegetable, animal and mineral properties, debarred from proper Physical Exercise, Mental discipline, and Mastication cruelly limited, and thereby hastening us on through pain, disease and privation, down to a premature grave. . . .

Heading the list of petitioners were the names of John Quincy Adams Thayer, Sarah G. Bagley, and James Carle. A measure of the new importance conceded to the women's branch of the ten-hour movement may be gained from the fact that the summons to testify before the legislative committee was addressed

---

* The Committee on Manufactures, before holding these hearings, had a rebirth as a Special Committee to Investigate Labor Conditions.

to Miss Bagley as well as to Thayer. On February 6, 1845, William Schouler sent them an official notice:

To J. Q. A. Thayer, S. G. Bagley and others:
A petition relative to a reduction of the hours of labor has been referred to the Committee on Manufactures, of which I am Chairman. By a resolution passed by the House, instructing said Committee to send for such persons and papers as may be necessary to make an investigation of the claims of said petitioners to an interference in their behalf, I would inform you that as the greater part of the petitioners are females, it will be necessary for them to make the defence, or we shall be under the necessity of laying it aside.

If Mr. Schouler supposed that maidenly modesty would keep the determined Miss Bagley from making a public appearance at the State House in Boston, he was gravely mistaken. When the committee hearings opened on February 13, she was on hand to give evidence, flanked by other operatives whose combined experience provided an interesting overall picture of the working life of a Lowell girl. The first woman witness was Miss Eliza R. Hemingway, who had worked two years at the Middlesex Corporation and nine months at the Hamilton. Miss Hemingway, a skilled weaver on woolens, earning top wages—from $16 to $23 a month exclusive of board—and required to operate only one loom, had less to complain of in these respects than most operatives. And yet her answers to the committee members' questions showed that discontent had spread to all levels. The working time was too long, she said; the mealtimes too short. The air in the factory was bad: over 150 persons worked in one room, for example, where 293 small lamps and 61 large ones burned morning and evening during the winter months. There was no day, she added, when fewer than six girls stayed away from work because of illness; as many as 30 had been known to remain at home on one day for that reason.

A Miss Judith Payne followed Miss Hemingway on the witness stand, with a story that points up many of the fallacious notions about the joyous lives of the factory girls. Miss Payne had come to Lowell in 1829, in the more leisurely days of the industry, in spite of which she had been obliged to go back home because of ill health after working a year and a half at the Merrimack Corporation. What is most interesting is that like many other girls she was driven by economic necessity back into the mills again after an absence of several years. In 1838 she returned to Lowell, where she had been employed at the Boott Mills ever since. Unlike Miss Hemingway, Miss Payne operated three looms, and earned only an average of $2.93 a week above her board, skilled though she was. In the past seven years, she testified, she had lost about one year altogether because of illness.

Miss Bagley, when called upon to testify, corroborated the evidence of the others. She had been at the Hamilton Corporation for six and a half years, at the Middlesex for two years, and had returned every year to her home in New Hampshire for a six weeks' vacation. Nevertheless, after three years in the mills her health had begun to fail, and during the last year she had been out one-third of the time because of illness.*

Realizing that Sarah Bagley was the leader of the malcontents, the committee members plied her with questions intended to embarrass her. If the girls were not obliged to work such long hours, what would they do with their leisure, she was asked. Their "intellectual, moral and religious habits would . . . be benefited," she replied; they would have time in which to cultivate their minds. For example, she explained, after the fatigue of the day's work, she had kept school in her room in the evening for girls who wished to make up deficiencies in their education. The way in which the committee was to pervert this particular bit of information was extremely revealing.

Another operative testified that she made as little as $1.62½

---

* In testifying before a legislative committee the following year, William Boott admitted that "The evils which constant employment and want of amusements are calculated to produce if persisted in too long, are, to a very great extent, counteracted by periodical visits to their friends." Clearly, even the corporations conceded that the long hours caused ill health, necessitating regular vacations, but at the operatives' expense.

a week above board, and evidence was brought forward to show that, among the few illiterates in the mills, wages were 18 percent lower than among the better-educated girls. Proponents of the ten-hour law also cited the example of England, supposedly so far in the rear of American developments, where the average working week was about 68 hours instead of over 72 and there were two more holidays a year than in the United States.

For the employers' side a whole battery of witnesses testified that the long hours had no ill effects on the operatives. One of these was Mr. Isaac Cooper, then representative in the Legislature from Lowell, who had formerly worked as an overseer at the Lawrence Corporation for nine years. The girls who worked in the mills enjoyed the best of health, said Mr. Cooper ingenuously, for the simple reason that they rose early, went to bed early, and had "three meals regular." Complaints about overheated factory rooms were misleading, he implied, since the mills were heated by steam pipes, and the temperature was regulated by a thermometer not to fall below 62 and not to rise above 68 degrees. Another witness declared that wages would necessarily be cut if hours were reduced, although earlier petitions had stated that "the long hours resulted in extorting much unpaid service from the laborer," implying that if wages were reduced further all incentive to work in the mills would be removed. Still another witness testified to the corporations' high regard for culture by saying that girls were permitted to leave before the evening bell in order to attend lectures, playing down the fact that they were docked for the time lost.

In view of this conflicting testimony the committee members were not satisfied that they had enough data to make a recommendation to the Legislature, and therefore it was decided that they all go up to Lowell to make a study of conditions on the spot. This was all they needed. They visited the Lowell Manufacturing Company and the Middlesex Mills and found them in apple-pie order: "Grass-plots have been laid out, trees have been planted, and fine varieties of flowers in their season are cultivated within the factory grounds. In short, everything in and about the mills and boarding-houses appeared to have for its end health and comfort."

The report of the investigating committee, written by Schouler, was therefore adverse to any ten-hour legislation. After weighing the testimony of witnesses on both sides, they decided that the health of the operatives was good. In any case, the report said, if a longer working day had ill effects on the employees of corporations, it would have equally bad effects on all other workers. But since the petition had called for legislation specifically restraining corporations, the committee could not in all fairness recommend that corporations alone be penalized. Besides, a shorter working day would result in reductions in wages, with which the committee did not care to be involved. As for analogies with other countries, the committee found them of negligible interest. Granting that hours were shorter in England than in the United States, they declared that comparison was inept because of vastly superior conditions in the Massachusetts mills: "Your committee returned fully satisfied that the order, decorum, and general appearance of things could not be improved."

But should the grass plots, trees, and flowers fail to allay discontent, the committee inserted a few sententious remarks in its report on the whole problem:

Labor in Massachusetts is on an equality with capital and indeed controls it, and so it ever will be while free education and free constitutions exist. . . . Labor is intelligent enough to make its own bargains, and look out for its own interests without any interference from us.

Nevertheless, despite their equal rank with capital, and their control over capital (could William Schouler have been reading Nathan Appleton on *Labor*?), the operatives were not to look to the legislature for redress of any grievances: "The remedy [for long hours] does not lie with us. We look for it in the progressive improvement in art and science, in a higher appreciation of man's destiny, in a less love for money, and a more ardent love for social happiness and intellectual superiority."

When this singular document was made public, cries of "Shame!" went up in all but the Whig press. The Boston correspondent of the Democratic *Lowell Advertiser* wrote on March 14, 1845: "I think the committee might have brought in a more satisfactory report, after sitting a fortnight or more. . . . Is it the business of the legislature to pass laws *only* for corporations, and not for those whose labor makes corporations valuable?"

The Lowell Female Labor Reform Association at its April meeting berated the committee for its "lack of independence, honesty and humanity," and singled out Schouler, the chairman, as its special target: "As he is merely a corporation machine or tool, we will use our best endeavors . . . to keep him in the 'City of Spindles' where he belongs and not trouble Boston folks with him."

In one particular detail Miss Bagley was able to show how the committee either withheld facts or distorted them for reasons of its own. She had testified that the operatives would use their leisure time to improve their minds, in evidence whereof she had cited the evening classes held in her room. From this the committee had drawn its own inferences: "Miss Bagley said, in addition to her labor in the mills, she had kept evening school during the winter months for four years, and thought this extra labor must have injured her health."

As a direct result of having alienated the Lowell Female Labor Reform Association, Schouler was defeated when he stood for the Legislature again in the fall, a remarkable circumstance when it is remembered that these women had no vote. On November 28, the *Voice of Industry* published a resolution passed by the Association at their most recent meeting:

Resolved, that the members of this Association tender their grateful acknowledgements to the voters of Lowell, for consigning William Schouler to the obscurity he so justly deserves, for treating so unjustly and ungentlemanly the defence made by the delegates of this Association, before the special committee of the Legislature, to whom was referred petitions for the reduction of the hours of labor, of which he was Chairman.*

But if the operatives did not forget an enemy, neither did the corporations forget a friend. On April 11, 1845, the *Vox Populi*, a Lowell newspaper of somewhat independent leanings, carried the following notice:

The great defender of the "vested rights" of corporations in our late legislature, Hon. Linus Childs, has been rewarded therefor in the shape of an appointment to the Agency of the Boott Mills in this city —with a salary of $3,500 per annum. This pays well. It shows, too, that if "Republics *is* ungrateful," corporations *isn't*.

Disappointed and indignant though they were with the committee's report, the militant operatives were not unduly discouraged. Not for nothing was their motto "Try Again!" Preparations were made for new petitions to be drawn up, with more names on them than ever; local organizational and publicity work was carried on in Lowell; branches of the Female Labor Reform Association were set up in other textile towns and a larger overall group, the New England Workingmen's Association, began meeting in frequent conventions to decide matters of general policy.

Indeed, these conventions were held so often that it must have been fairly bewildering to the mill girls to attempt to follow them all. A first preliminary meeting, held in Boston on October 16, 1844, assembled in response to a call by the Fall River Me-

---

* Schouler was, however, returned to the Legislature in 1847. But that was his last term as representative from Lowell, for in that year through the influence of the great Boston magnates he was offered the plum of Whig journalism: the post as editor-in-chief of the influential *Boston Daily Atlas*. He campaigned for Taylor for the presidency willingly enough, but in the end even his cast-iron stomach was turned by Webster's 7th of March speech in 1850. When he repudiated Webster, the Whig leadership, resolved to let nothing stand in the way of their lovefest with the slave interest, forced him to resign.

chanics and Laborers Association. Among the two hundred who attended there were strong delegations of working people from Lynn, Lowell, and Fall River, but these were quite overshadowed, in the reports of the meeting that have come down to us, by the presence of such well-known personages as the Associationist Robert Owen, George Evans and Mike Walsh, representing the Land Reformers, and a contingent of Fourierists from Brook Farm. That working-class problems were not wholly ignored is indicated by the fact that Robert Owen spoke to some point about the ten-hour day, which he had adopted almost thirty years earlier, with excellent results in production and morale, and no reduction in wages, in his mills at New Lanark.

A second preliminary convention, held in Lowell on March 18, 1845, to adopt a constitution for the New England Workingmen's Association, aroused even greater interest, with between 1,500 and 2,000 delegates present. Since the first meeting at Boston the Lowell Female Labor Reform Association had taken off to a good start, a development so promising that the new constitution specifically provided for the admission of female labor groups into the larger association on terms of equality. Responding to a welcoming address, the irrepressible Sarah Bagley addressed the meeting in behalf of the Lowell group and gave a report of its accomplishments thus far. But, despite the large labor representation, the Fourierists took over the convention after a bitter quarrel among the various Utopian groups.

It is difficult to explain this strange turn of affairs except on the ground that the Utopians were more articulate, more opinionated, and more impressive personally than any of the artisans, mechanics, or operatives among the delegates. The Utopians had the authority of their convictions, the pertinacity of zealots, the vanity of dreamers. Lacking any working-class basis, they nevertheless allied themselves with the working classes, then presumed to speak for them, and at length to dictate to them. The first result of their capture of the labor group was a sharp drop in attendance at the first regular meeting of the New England Workingmen's Association in Boston on May 28, 1845.*

Only thirty delegates, ten of whom were women, were present in the chapel under the museum in Boston, when the convention was called to order. The do-gooders had turned up in force, Robert Owen, Charles A. Dana, L. W. Ryckman, George Ripley, Wendell Phillips, Albert Brisbane, W. H. Channing, Horace Greeley, and William Lloyd Garrison being the best-known. Lowell sent a strictly labor group, including Sarah Bagley, Huldah Stone, and Joel Hatch of the Mechanics and Laborers Association, but the meeting was largely given over to the airing of their views by the foggy Associationists. Ryckman of Brook Farm advocated questioning candidates for office about their views on labor questions, which if his suggestion had been adopted, would have robbed the disfranchised women's groups of their effectiveness by stressing political action. Others, with an even more ambiguous attitude toward the grievances of the mill operatives, urged "measures of harmony and concord between the Laboring and Employing Classes," to quote Horace Greeley in the *New York Tribune*. Sarah Bagley was the only speaker who gave the equivalent of a trade union report to this convention of "workingmen":

Since the last meeting of the Workingmen's Convention at Lowell, Massachusetts, our members have been daily increasing, our meetings generally well attended, and the real zeal of the friends of equal rights and justice has kindled anew. Our number . . . is between four and five hundred, but this we consider a small part of the work which has been accomplished. The humble efforts of a few females united in the holy cause of human rights and human equalities, could not be expected to move the world in a day.

Nevertheless, there are unmistakable indications that Miss Bagley herself had succumbed in some degree to the persuasive arguments of the Brook Farm Associationists, who were con-

* The two earlier meetings were merely preparatory; this was the first after the formal adoption of a constitution at Lowell in March.

stantly stressing "the degrading littleness and insufficiency" of the ten-hour movement. She had been one of the committee to nominate officers and report business to the Boston Convention, and was thus partly responsible for its degenerating into an Associationist conference. William F. Young, the editor of the *Voice of Industry*, was so aware of the possibly paralyzing effects of Ryckman's philosophy on the youthful labor movement that in the issue of June 12, 1845, he urged that education toward Association proceed on one plane "while we are agitating the various speedy and partial ameliorations" on another. "Brothers," he pleaded, "there is no sound reason for disunion; our cause is one. . . ."

But Ryckman seemed singularly indifferent to unity within the working class, preferring "harmony" with the employing class. This position led him to take a stand opposed to strikes at the Workingmen's Mass Meeting at Woburn July 4, 1845. And again at the Fall River Convention of the New England Workingmen's Association in September, he offered a resolution betraying his complete lack of sympathy with any immediate measures to raise workers' standards:

> Whereas, We the workingmen of New England can see no practical means of improving their condition . . . Resolved, that we do hereby appeal to the wise and the good, the generous and the brave of all classes in behalf of this useful, suffering and numerous class of their fellow-creatures.

These amiable sentiments, so characteristic of the Utopians, failed to win the approval of the majority of the delegates. On two more explicit issues the Fall River convention voted contrary to the wishes of the Brook Farmers, rejecting political action for the ten-hour day, and approving the development of consumers' cooperatives. The Associationists, to be sure, favored cooperative production, as in their Fourierist colonies, but opposed cooperatives of consumers as a useless palliative of workers' economic hardships. Incorrigibly dogmatic, they refused to play when they were outvoted in the convention, and shaking their heads over their poor misguided fellow creatures, withdrew completely from the workingmen's movement.*

At the next convention of the New England Workingmen's Association, held at Lowell on October 29, 1845, thanks to the defection of yet another Utopian, George H. Evans, the leadership of the workingmen's movement reverted to the workingmen, where it might be said properly to belong. Evans would not attend the October meeting, but in lieu of a personal appearance sent a patronizing letter to the Lowell Female Labor Reform Association, chiding its members for their indifference to Land Reform and for their refusal to endorse political action, as he had urged. Like Ryckman, he felt that the working people were setting their sights too low:

> It must necessarily happen that among any body of working men or women, there must always be a large majority of those who from their youth have very little experience . . . and who, therefore, are apt, when they first discover this unnatural depression, to attribute it to superficial instead of radical errors.

Undismayed by these strictures, the Lowell convention speedily got down to business, which was principally to name the *Voice of Industry* as the official organ of the New England Workingmen's Association. This was of the greatest importance for the progress of the ten-hour movement, now centered in Lowell under the aegis of the Female Labor Reform group, for when the *Voice of Industry* shortly afterward moved to Lowell, it provided a badly needed medium. Inevitably this journal reached a wider audience in Lowell than when it was

* "The Associationists, in fact, staked out an ideal position. They could piously ignore or oppose all practical reform for its 'degrading littleness and insufficiency' without sacrificing for a moment the pleasant illusion that they were reformers. . . . They were, of course, not seriously interested in changing society. They were concerned with expressing their own fantasies and appeasing their own feelings of guilt. They secretly dreaded responsibility and preferred to luxuriate in gaudy visions of the future." Arthur Schlesinger, Jr., *The Age of Jackson*, p. 364.

published in Fitchburg, for Lowell was either closer or had easier access to the other textile towns where the ten-hour movement was making so much headway. The Female Labor Reform group could also publicize their fairs and meetings in the columns of the *Voice of Industry*, obtain attention in the press of the rest of the country by the then prevalent system of newspaper exchanges, and make use of the journal's presses to print their tracts and circulars.

The need for greater working-class solidarity had, in fact, been forcibly illustrated by a month-long strike of 4,000 Pittsburgh textile operatives for a ten-hour day in September, 1845. This well-organized strike was broken at last when the employers explained to the spokesmen of the operatives that they could not compete with other manufacturers who still maintained the twelve-hour day, the implication being that if their competitors adopted the ten-hour day, they would follow suit. Baffled and sore, the girls in Pittsburgh began corresponding with the Lowell Female Labor Reform Association, whose members they now entreated to stand by them. What support could the Lowell operatives give their sisters in the West? After long thought and several exchanges of letters a great decision was reached— operatives in Pittsburgh and in Lowell would celebrate the Fourth of July, 1846, with a "declaration of independence of the oppressive manufacturing power." This promised to be about as effectual as if they had all stamped their feet in unison, and no employer was deceived by it.

One wonders what might have happened if the Lowell girls had gone on strike simultaneously with the Pittsburgh mill-workers for a reduction of hours, instead of resorting to the feeble device of a "declaration of independence." But such action would have required far more organization, preparation, and understanding of trade union techniques than any of the girls, or, for that matter, most of the workingmen at that time possessed. Small local strikes, to prevent the further degeneration of standards, were however more successful around this period, particularly one at Chicopee in November, 1845. As reported in the *Voice of Industry* for November 21, quoting the *Cabot-ville Chronicle:*

. . . the young ladies employed in the Spinning Room of Mill No. 2, Dwight Corporation, made a very quiet and successful "strike" on Monday. The Spinning machinery was set in motion in the morning, but there was no girls to tend it. They had heard the rumor that their wages were to be cut down, upon which they determined to quit. They silently kept their resolve, and remained out until Tuesday afternoon, when they were requested to return to their employment, with an addition to their previous wages of fifty cents per week. The Ladies connected with the other mills ought certainly to present them with a banner, as a tribute of esteem.

Early in the spring of 1846, a small group of Lowell operatives registered a similar success. When the Massachusetts Mills announced that thenceforth weavers must tend four looms instead of three and accept one cent less per piece than before, the girls held a meeting and took a pledge that they would not take another loom except at the old piece-rate. Any girl who violated her pledge was to have her name published in the *Voice of Industry* "as a traitor, and receive the scorn and reproach of her associates." The reference to the *Voice of Industry* shows how important a place this journal had begun to occupy in the lives of the girls, for practically every job weaver at the Massachusetts Mills signed the pledge and kept it.

This was, nevertheless, the only strike ever initiated by members of the Lowell Female Labor Reform Association, and even this had a certain unpremeditated air that robbed it of its point. The Association could claim neither the responsibility for the walkout nor credit for any gains. In a new constitution adopted at the beginning of 1846 the group took a stand on this issue that might have reflected either the remnants of Ryckman's influence or timidity engendered by the failure of the Pittsburgh strike. One clause of this new constitution declared that the Association was opposed to "all hostile measures, strikes and turn-outs until all pacific measures prove abortive, and then it is the imperious duty of every one to assist and maintain that independence which our brave ancestors bequeathed and sealed with their blood." This did not mean that the group was content to remain passive, but that they placed more reliance on other expedients than on direct action: conventions of the New England Workingmen's Association, for example, and petitions to the Legislature.

There had been four workingmen's conventions in 1845; there were to be three in 1846, as well as various other congresses in which workingmen and women were represented. Indeed, they came so thick and fast that Huldah Stone once grumbled that she had nothing to report, since only a few months had passed since the last meeting. But it is possible that without frequent conventions of this sort interest might have flagged. The coming together of delegates from the various industrial towns enabled them to keep their enthusiasm at a high pitch.

At the first convention of 1846, held in Lynn in January, it became clear that with the withdrawal of the Associationists and the Land Reformers, the mill operatives from Lowell were taking the lead in the workingmen's movement. At this meeting there were more delegates from Lowell, and more women from Lowell than from any other place. The report of the Lowell Female Labor Reform Association to the convention, signed by Hannah Tarlton, vice president, and Mary Emerson, secretary *pro tem.*, revealed a spirit of undiminished optimism:

Since our last meeting in Lowell, particularly within the last six weeks, a deeper and more thrilling interest has been manifested in our "association" than at any time heretofore. . . . Another pleasing symptom . . . is a great increase of liberal feeling. They do not regard this measure [the reduction of the hours of labor] as an end, but only as one step towards the great end to be attained . . . "Onward," is their watchword, and "We'll try again" their motto.

But, once more, other problems than labor reform took up the time and energies of the delegates, the convention spending long hours discussing such matters as slavery in the South, and American foreign relations—important subjects, no doubt, but beside the point on this occasion. A resolution favoring the ten-hour day was passed, to be sure, an item of no great news value in itself, except that it was proposed to achieve this reform by calling still another convention, made up of both employers and employees, to obtain a reduction of hours by mutual agreement! At the March meeting of the New England Workingmen's Association in Manchester, this naive scheme received new impetus when a resolution was adopted calling for the reform of hours "by the mild influence of reasonable concession and mutual arrangement of the parties interested." The Industrial Congress sitting in Boston in June went even further and named a place and a day for representatives of employers and employees to get together on the ten-hour issue. Despite the split of the preceding year, this proposal still had a certain Utopian or more precisely Associationist flavor; it had, in fact, been outlined in the *New York Tribune* by Horace Greeley in September, 1845. Primarily a high-tariff advocate, mistrustful of labor and toadying shamelessly to Nathan Appleton and the other textile magnates, Greeley was a late-comer to the ranks of the ten-hour movement, which he championed somewhat reluctantly after his conversion to Brisbane Associationism.* With men of Greeley's type sponsoring the project, it is not surprising that it fell flat, for the employers showed their godlike indifference by simply failing to appear.

Meanwhile, the petitions for the Legislature were not being

* Greeley gave considerable space in the *Tribune* to the glowing pictures of life in Lowell such as the one published by the Rev. H. A. Miles, and another correspondent, C.D.S., who claimed that the operatives worked only ten hours a day. Forced to correct this false impression, he made the somewhat less than daring pronouncement that "the hours of labor in Factories ought to be eleven per day." Even after he had come around to the reformers' position, he approved it only theoretically, that is, on condition that labor abstain from strikes or any direct action to achieve its ends. His greatest opprobrium was reserved for those who assailed the corporations. "There is no limit to the combined stupidity and malice of the average Loco-Foco attacks on our Manufacturies," he cried in an editorial charging the operatives with responsibility for the low prices paid to the boarding-house keepers. See the *Tribune, passim,* September, 1845.

neglected. No little patience and cunning were required to obtain an impressive number of signatures, for it was forbidden to circulate petitions for the ten-hour day within the mills, although signatures to petitions against the annexation of Texas (as long as the corporation magnates supported that position) were solicited on factory property with the full approval of the agents. In spite of such difficulties the ten-hour group in Lowell sent a scroll 130 feet long, bearing 4,500 names, while petitions from the rest of the state contained 10,000 signatures. Even in these other petitions the prestige of the Lowell reform group asserted itself, for throughout the state the language they used to address the Legislature was adopted. Refusing to fall into the trap of asking for a law making ten hours a legal day's work, Sarah Bagley and her associates stuck to their guns, demanding legislation specifically "to prohibit all incorporated companies from employing one set of hands more than ten hours a day." *

But the Senate committee appointed to consider these prayers for relief again turned down the request on general principles, declaring that a ten-hour law applicable only to corporations would be unjust. They admitted that the Legislature had the power to define the number of hours that should constitute a day's labor, but stated the opinion that it "could not deprive the citizen of his freedom of contract." Here was one of the first official expressions of the convenient doctrine that the worker's freedom of contract was more sacred than his health, his happiness, or a living wage. Workers need not despair, however, the committee hastened to add:

Let the country be prosperous, let business be flourishing, and the competition consequent is the best guarantee the laboring man can have that he will be properly dealt by. When business is flourishing competition will be brisk, labor will be in demand, and those disposed to work will be sure to be well paid. But impose restrictions, you injure business, and the result will be, the laborer is sure to suffer.

* When New Hampshire in the following year passed a law making ten hours a legal day's work, the ease with which the corporations were able to circumvent the law proved the validity of this proposal.

Miss Bagley had not been present at the Manchester convention of the New England Workingmen's Association in March, 1846, although she was still president of the Lowell branch and her name was signed to the report of Lowell activities, which was read by Huldah Stone. Soon after her appearance at the legislative committee sessions the preceding year, she had left the mills, either because she was blacklisted, or, more likely, because of the press of business connected with the Labor Reform group, which required a large correspondence, a certain amount of travel, and frequent public appearances. But her post at the *Voice of Industry* could hardly have provided her with a living wage, for early in 1846 she became the first telegraph operator in Lowell.

Now in the spring of 1846, a new opportunity came to this high-spirited young woman, when William F. Young, editor of the *Voice of Industry*, fell ill and was obliged to quit work. For a while the publishing committee attempted to carry on, but in May the Female Labor Reform Association bought the type and presses, and Miss Bagley now assumed Young's post as chief editor, assisted by J. S. Fletcher and Joel Hatch. Versatile though she was, however, Miss Bagley was no great success as an editor, and after a month's trial she relinquished the post to John Allen. Nevertheless, the circulation, which had begun to decline after Young left, continued to fall off until his return in November, when the process had gone too far to be checked.

For Sarah Bagley, 1845 had been a great year, a year of miracles. Her leadership had been imaginative, resourceful, determined. But in 1846 her energies seem to have been somewhat dissipated, owing perhaps to poor health, or other disappointments. It was only to be expected that her acid comments on certain public figures should win her, and her cause, some powerful enemies. Of these William Schouler, defeated for office largely through her efforts, was an antagonist of no mean abilities. If he had had any basis for it, he would have blasted her reputation with the greatest relish, but on moral grounds Miss Bagley was unassailable. Her origins were respectable, her private life blameless; she was a stickler for observance of the Lord's Day, and deplored the proliferation of dram-shops in Lowell with the proper Sunday-school spirit.

Since there was no chink in Miss Bagley's armor, Schouler investigated her associates in order to track down someone more vulnerable. The scent led him to John Cluer, an English weaver who on coming to this country had allied himself with the ten-hour movement, gaining quite a reputation as a popular orator and opponent of the "vested interests." Cluer could give a three-hour speech without batting an eye, although it is not recorded whether his audiences were equally enduring. On several occasions he had appeared on the platform with Miss Bagley, notably at Manchester in November, 1845. With the tenacity of a Hearst editor on the trail of a particularly noisome scandal, Schouler now went to work on Cluer, unearthing evidence to prove that he was a liar, a drunkard, and a bigamist, and had moreover obtained money under false pretenses. The *Voice of Industry* attempted for a while to defend Cluer against these damaging charges, but forsook him in the end when he was accused of attacking the church.

This scandal must have been a source of grief to the president of the Lowell Female Labor Reform Association, although none of the available information would indicate that she felt more than a comradely interest in John Cluer. But like many present-day critics of reformism, Schouler had succeeded in casting doubt on a whole movement by smearing one of it adherents. Sarah Bagley, after her brief turn as editor of the *Voice of Industry*, gradually faded out of the picture. She was, to be sure, on the committee of arrangements for the Industrial Reform Celebration on July 4, 1846, when the "declaration of independence of the oppressive manufacturing power" was read. Her name was also listed as one of the delegates to an Associationist meeting held in Boston on September 21, but it is doubtful that she attended it. She was last heard from as a correspondent to the *Voice of Industry* from New Hampshire, where she was making a tour of the mill towns, but after September 25 her name disappeared from the masthead of the paper, and no further mention of her was made in

the reform movement. It was reported that Miss Bagley had suffered a breakdown.

This did not mean that the Lowell operatives were left leader-
less, however, for several other energetic young women, who had
been active in the ten-hour movement since its inception, now
came forward, among them Miss Mary Emerson, the new president of the Lowell Female Labor Reform Association, and Miss
Huldah J. Stone, its secretary. While not as brilliant or as ironical
as the inimitable Sarah, Huldah Stone was a sensible, steady
young woman, accustomed to bearing responsibility. During
most of the life of the *Voice of Industry* she had charge of its
Female Department. She had attended all the meetings of the
New England Workingmen's Association held thus far, participating in the discussions and serving on important committees.
At the Manchester Convention in March, 1846, she had been
chosen recording secretary, with a man as her assistant, and in the
absence of Sarah Bagley had read the somewhat overoptimistic
report of the Lowell Female Labor Reform Association: "Our
prospects were never more flattering—our faith in the final and
complete success of this humane and righteous enterprise never
more strong or well grounded than at the present time. . . ."

It was with this touching spirit of hope that Miss Stone attended the Nashua Convention of the New England Workingmen's Association, the last significant gathering of its kind, on
September 17, 1846. The Nashua meeting was not large, but it
was unusually businesslike and free of Utopian cant. With William F. Young in the chair, and Miss Stone a member of the business committee, the convention proceeded to adopt a new constitution and a new name. The new title, the Labor Reform League
of New England, was not only less unwieldy than the original,
but also conveyed the importance this by now dominantly
female organization attached to the idea of the reform of hours.
Three Lowell women, Miss Stone, Mrs. Quimby, and Miss Mary
Emerson, were elected to the board of directors of the league
under the revised constitution, with five men. Another item on
the agenda was the discussion of what was to be done about the

Voice of Industry, which was in financial straits because of its declining circulation. A committee consisting of four women from Lowell, Manchester, and Nashua was appointed to inquire into the problem and report to the convention, and a resolution was passed pledging the League to "assure its financial security."

This convention was enlivened by the presence of delegates from the more recently organized branches of the Female Labor Reform Association in Manchester and Nashua, who gave voice to a fresher viewpoint than the Lowell representatives. Miss Mehitabel Eastman, for instance, read an extremely realistic report on the activities and grievances of her group, with an account of how the male and female societies had been meeting together. In less than a year the membership in the women's organization had grown to over 300, but promising as this was, they did not deceive themselves about their "flattering prospects." It was not easy to get new members, she said. "We have frequent cause of regret that so many of our sisterhood are afraid of 'the old man' (as the overseer is called,) and men dare not move in our cause, from fear of being discharged." And yet conditions were constantly growing worse, she indicated, pointing to the evils of the premium system: "Money given to first and second hands to drive up us factory girls is making a bad matter worse. . . . The operatives who are members of this association do dread the sad effects of this premium system upon the minds and health of our fellow-operatives. It has our utter abhorrence." Her report then went on to tell of the important part taken by the Manchester branch in getting up a huge petition to the New Hampshire Legislature for a ten-hour day. It had been rejected, to be sure, but without dimming the zeal of the friends of the ten-hour reform. Apropos of this, the Manchester operatives wanted to see more of the *Voice of Industry* devoted to the ten-hour day, and less, presumably, to irrelevant matters.

The forthright tone of this report, unclouded by vague Utopian aspirations, encouraged the delegates to think along straight working-class lines. For the first time at one of these meetings of the Workingmen's Association, another serious grievance was taken up in a strongly worded resolution denouncing "the iniquitous conspiracy between agents and directors whereby they libel the character of virtuous girls, sending their names to the blacklist of other corporations and depriving them of their employment in other places."

But the highlight of the Nashua meeting was an object lesson in direct action that took place in Nashua during convention week. This was not, of course, on the agenda. It all began when the men in one of the large machine shops attached to the local textile mills walked off their jobs in protest against the long hours, seizing as the occasion for their turnout the annual fall "lighting up" of the workrooms. With the beginning of autumn, mill workers could look forward to six months during which they would be working by artificial light for several hours both morning and evening, and they were fed up with it. The action of the machinists was contagious, for on the Monday following, while the convention was still sitting, a group of girls in one of the mills also decided they would not work by candlelight. They filed down to the mill yard, where to their dismay they were imprisoned for several hours, as the overseers had locked the gates, refusing to open them before the evening bell.

While they were waiting to be let out, the word spread about the town, and a procession of nearly a thousand, including the convention delegates, marched through the streets, shouting that "they would be oppressed no longer," and cheering "loud and long in behalf of the ten-hour system." The marchers came to a halt outside the factory gates where the girls were being held, to offer them encouragement and give them a suitable reception when they should be released. Alarmed at last, the town authorities sent the constable to the scene to read the riot act, calling on the crowd to disperse. But no one paid any attention to him, the assemblage, as the *Voice of Industry* put it, drowning out his voice with a "universal Hurrah!"

With this street demonstration fresh in their minds, the delegates to the convention showed scant respect for several factory agents who turned up at their meetings to debate with the "radicals." When granted the floor, a Mr. Moulton, of one of the Nashua mills, began by defending "the beauty and intelligence" of the factory girls, but these remarks, which the operatives had come to recognize as the inevitable prelude to a complete whitewash of the corporations, were greeted with a prolonged titter. When Mr. Moulton, true to form, proceeded next to speak of "the healthful influence of factory life," he was laughed out of court.

In the end, however, the corporations had the last laugh, for this earnest convention had no sequel of any importance to the labor movement. The girls who had walked out in protest against "lighting up" lost their case, and very likely their jobs too. The machine-shop hands (men with votes) won a Pyrrhic victory; their hours were reduced, but their wages were cut proportionately. On the other hand, the corporations learned an important lesson: the next time there was a large demonstration in a mill town they would not be caught napping, with one wretched constable reading the riot act. In Manchester, a month later, they showed how they had profited by this experience when 2,000 mechanics and operatives tried to hold a meeting in protest against working on Sundays. The city hall, the churches, and all other public buildings were denied to the demonstrators, who finally assembled in a lumber yard to listen to speeches and pass resolutions. But neither was this to be allowed. Mr. Gillis, agent of one of the mills, had them expelled from the lumber yard, and when they carried their meeting out into the street, saw to it that it was broken up by the police. A torchlight procession of the mechanics in the following week ran into a barrage of rotten eggs, and was effectively broken up by men armed with bludgeons.

There were more strikes and more violence in the mill towns, but the Labor Reform League had no part in this, although it convened from time to time until 1848. The next meeting, held in Boston on January 17, 1847, heard resolutions on such questions as Negro slavery, free homesteads, and free trade, as well as the ten-hour day, but in an access of weakness voted on none of them, postponing action until their next meeting, to be held in Lowell on March 30. Huldah Stone indicated a new trend when she read the revised constitution of the Lowell Labor Reform League, which included provisions for mutual aid, a sick fund, and other benefits to be administered by the Sisters of Charity, in order to attract new members. In justification of this departure Miss Stone remarked: "We have long felt the necessity of having a constitution which should embody something much more definite. There seemed to be too much of theory and too little of the real practical in the old one."

Strangely enough, these new "practical" features proved much less alluring than the visionary theories of the earlier constitution. The membership was falling away in the whole organization. The *Voice of Industry* was hanging by a thread, although Young had returned to take charge, with Miss Mehitabel Eastman, the sprightly organizer from Manchester, as his assistant. By October, 1847, Young sold out to D. H. Jacques, who in a vain attempt to keep the paper going, moved it to Boston in the following year. But it did not survive the death of the Labor Reform League, which ceased to function after March, 1848.

For all practical purposes, the Labor Reform League was buried with appropriate funeral ceremonies at the significant Lowell convention of March, 1847. On this occasion the faithful Huldah Stone read a new petition she had written for presentation to the Legislature; and the resolutions laid over from the recent Boston convention concerning the ten-hour day and consumers' cooperatives were passed. But this was perfunctory by now, while a more alarming symptom was the shift in emphasis away from immediate trade union objectives toward free soil and anti-slavery agitation. One resolution passed by the majority of the delegates, for example, stated in part: "American slavery must be uprooted *before* the elevation sought by the laboring classes can be effected."

The most serious, and at the same time the most insidious, attack on the labor groups, however, came from one of their supposed friends, an Associationist, in a speech supporting the following strange resolution:

that the evils which oppress and burden the men and women of New England arise from a vicious social organization . . . and that we look for no change for the better until there is a fair and equitable distribution of the Profits of Labor . . . that for this we do not look to political action, but to the organization of Labor, and the Association of Laborers.

As a critic of the existing system, the anonymous author of this speech (later published as *The Condition of Labor*, and widely quoted) had many discerning things to say, and much that was calculated to appeal to his auditors. Capital and labor, he indicated, had opposite interests; labor was passive, while capital dictated the terms of their relationship. Labor's dependence upon capital was different only in degree, not in principle, from Southern slavery:

I do not say the two systems are identical; nor am I concerned now to point out their differences. I say their difference is not so great as is commonly supposed, nor so great as to justify the northern slaveholder in crying out very loudly against his Southern brother.

Emancipation of Southern slaves, he pointed out, would not help Northern workers any more than the absence of chattel slavery in Europe helped European labor.

But, having made these sage pronouncements, he then proceeded to demolish every plank of the reform platform, setting at naught the years of heartbreaking work and struggle of the New England labor movement. Shorter hours of labor, he conceded, were needed for the health and welfare of workers, but this did not go far enough, this did not change the immoral relationship between labor and capital by which some men grew rich through the toil of others. "It is not a mere shortening of the hours of labor that is to bring your redemption. The Southern slave frequently completes his task before the sun reaches the meridian. Is he therefore less a slave?"

Nor would the removal of tariff barriers bring relief to the oppressed. Nothing could be more monstrous than the tariff system, which fleeces labor twice:

> . . . your labor . . . bought at the price for which you may be compelled by necessity to sell it, and then you are compelled to purchase the articles which you consume . . . not . . . without paying the government or the manufacturer 25 or 50 percent on every dollar's worth you buy. . . . But the triumph of Free Trade alone will not suffice you.

Free land in the West offered no solutions to workers' problems either, explained this perceptive critic:

> One hundred and sixty acres of land even may be yours in Iowa or Wisconsin, if you will settle upon it, and yet this offer may be of no advantage to you. You may not have the ability to go there, or be able to make a settlement, when arrived. . . . You may not wish to exile yourself from your early and cherished home. . . . Besides, you are not cultivators; you are mechanics, clerks, laborers of every variety. . . . This is not a corrective of the evil; it is only a fleeing of it. And woe is left for them who cannot escape.

Better housing for workers, he granted, was needed, but like shorter hours was only a palliative. "Whatever is done in this way by capital for its employees must be received by them as a boon, as something which they are not entitled of right to demand, but which capital in its tender mercy will do for them." Instead of generosity, he called for justice, scoffing at the so-called philanthropy of the great capitalists. "The welkin rings with their benevolence, forsooth; they are installed as gods . . . flunky editors . . . take up the wondrous song, and they are handed down to posterity to be worshipped."

This was, indeed, social criticism of a high order, sane, thoughtful, clairvoyant, but for all that the author, like others of his dreamy kind, offered no solutions except in that dim, distant, and unforeseeable future which was the cherished objective of the Utopians. In the meantime, the reformers must content themselves with voluntary association. Only associations of laborers, using their own capital to produce, and obtain for themselves the profits of their labor, would correct the abuses he had described so precisely. The speaker forgot only one thing, that laborers, by his own analysis, possessed no capital with which to embark on such ventures.

This sad anticlimax must have had a very depressing effect on the working-class membership of the Labor Reform League, even though they voted down the author's proposition for voluntary association. The decision to support the anti-slavery and homestead movements completed the disillusionment of the mill operatives. Other groups, other organizations were better equipped, through long experience, to fight for such measures, but there was none to take up the cudgels for labor.* The Labor Reform League met three more times, but the attendance was small and no discussion of any importance was reported. At the last of these meetings, on March 22, 1848, the League adjourned *sine die.*

The ten-hour movement did not collapse when the labor movement of the forties declined. Petitions went out regularly to the legislatures and, in Massachusetts at least, were as regularly turned down, although after 1850 there were occasional minority committee reports favorable to the passage of the necessary legislation. The drive received a little impetus from the fact that in good old Tory England, where, as everyone admitted, factory conditions were below any possibility of comparison with our own infinitely higher standards, a ten-hour law was passed in 1847. Abbott Lawrence, a year or so earlier, had stated authoritatively that the members of Parliament would not pass

---

* With the exception of Wendell Phillips, the Abolitionists were antipathetic to workers' problems. Not without reason did William F. Young chide Garrison for his "aristocratic tendencies" and indifference to "wages slavery."

such a measure, but, disregarding his assurances, pass it they did. Perhaps inspired by this event the American corporations made a concession to the reformers shortly afterward by lopping fifteen minutes a day from the working time required! This came in the form that Harriet Farley had long been urging, as a "boon" —the lengthening of mealtimes. The operatives could now congratulate themselves that instead of working an average of twelve hours and 13 minutes a day, they were obliged to spend no more than eleven hours and 58 minutes at the mills. But there was a catch in this philanthropic gesture, for many complaints were heard that the time added to the dinner hour was more than compensated by the factory clocks' tendency to move sluggishly toward night.

In 1847 also, as mentioned earlier, the ten-hour forces rejoiced at the passage of a ten-hour law by the New Hampshire Legislature. This exultation proved to be a bit premature. It will be remembered that the Massachusetts legislative committees had turned down petitions for the ten-hour day with the argument that any such law ought to be of general application, not confined to corporations. While conceding that the legislative branch of the government had the power to establish the legal working day at ten hours, they maintained that they could not abridge the citizen's freedom of contract. Mindful of this, the New Hampshire legislators passed a law making ten hours a legal day's labor all over the state—in the absence of a contract. On the day that the law became operative, therefore, all the operatives in the New Hampshire textile mills were fired, and then re-hired only if they consented to sign a contract agreeing to the old hours. Any girl who refused to sign such a contract was blacklisted. True to their traditions of employing only peaceful pressure, the Manchester operatives held an indignant but orderly mass meeting to protest what they thought of as an evasion of the law. But when this same trick was played on the workers of Pennsylvania in the following year, mill hands in Allegheny, being less wedded to the genteel tradition, staged a riot, resulting in the conviction of six of the rioters to prison terms.

In Massachusetts, where the Boston magnates held a tight grip on the Legislature, not even this shadowy concession to working-class sentiment was granted. With the gradual dissolution of the Labor Reform League, active leadership of the ten-hour movement now passed into the hands of the politicians in the Democratic party, which in the North at least had always given the measure more or less tepid support. Not having the vote, the mill girls could take only a passive role in the campaign for reform of hours carried on by the Democrats in the decade preceding the Civil War. Some of these political leaders were men of high character, like William S. Robinson, husband of Harriet Hanson, one of the most attractive and intelligent of the Lowell mill girls, but others, like Ben Butler, simply used labor reform as a political device, a means of worming their way into office. Robinson, an able polemicist, who had formerly worked for the *Lowell Courier* under Schouler,* started his own newspaper, the *Lowell American,* in 1849, to carry on ten-hour propaganda, but by 1853 he was "starved out of Lowell" and devoted his talents primarily to the anti-slavery movement. As a member of the Legislature in 1850 he wrote the very able minority report of the committee that considered the ten-hour petition, citing the increasingly lamentable conditions of factory work, and predicting the emergence of a veritable proletariat, "unenlightened, of depressed moral tone," if these conditions were allowed to persist.

This was the first occasion on which a minority report on the ten-hour issue was issued by a Massachusetts legislative committee. But in spite of this hopeful sign, in spite of well-organized meetings throughout the state, and a steady stream of petitions pouring into the State House, the ten-hour movement in the

---

* One day in 1847, while Robinson was on the staff of the *Courier,* he accepted for publication "a piece of poetry" written by Harriet Hanson, who as a child of eleven had been one of the ringleaders of the strike of 1836. They met at one of the Improvement Circles, and were married in the following year. Although Harriet herself took no active part in the ten-hour movement of the middle forties, it is extremely likely that Robinson swung over to a more liberal position in this matter through her influence, for the *Courier* was no school for reformers.

hands of the politicians was not much more successful than when it was directed by the operatives in the Female Labor Reform Association. The mechanics and laborers in the mill towns, even though they had the vote, were not permitted to exercise freedom of choice at the ballot box. The corporations had one sure way of influencing the voters in the mill towns, as the *Lowell Advertiser*, a Democratic newspaper, indicated in its issue of December 16, 1842:

That the laborer gives the full and fair equivalent for the wages he receives, and that he is under no obligation to vote as his employer directs, Mr. Sam Lawrence declares, *after the election*, to be "one of the commonplaces of obvious justice, which no one will deny." But *before* the election, the opposite doctrine was used in his behalf to procure the votes of those in his and other Corporations' employment. *Then* the argument was used that laborers should vote for Whigs because Whigs employed them; and should not vote for Democrats because Democrats did *not* give them so much employment.

Ben Butler claimed that before the election of 1851 a notice was posted on the Hamilton Company gate saying: "Whoever, employed by this corporation, votes the Ben Butler ten-hour ticket on Monday night, will be discharged." This was, of course, before liberals succeeded in putting through a secret ballot law that would stick, the Whigs maintaining that such a device was an insult to "the manliness and independence of the laboring men."

But in 1852, in a sudden reversal of their old tactics, the corporations decided to use blandishments instead of threats to obtain votes. Just before the election of 1852, the hours of labor were reduced to eleven at Lowell, Lawrence, Biddeford, and Holyoke *in the machine shops only*. It was a critical year for the Whigs in Massachusetts, and the cleverness of such a concession was borne out by their gratifying success at the polls.

In 1853 another ticklish political situation arose when a new constitution for Massachusetts was to go before the people.

There had been no important changes in the Massachusetts constitution since 1780, and the new draft to be submitted to the electorate would have curbed the power of the Boston financial magnates in the state government. Many curious deals were made to prevent this dire contingency, among them Abbott Lawrence's friendly arrangement with Bishop Fitzpatrick to swing the Boston Irish vote against the new charter, and a strange truce between the growing party of Free-Soilers or "conscience Whigs" and the "cotton Whigs" * to the same end, because one clause in the proposed constitution "threatened the independence of the judiciary." But lest these alliances might fail to obtain the desired result, the textile magnates in command of the Massachusetts Whig party made one more grudging concession to popular feeling: in September, 1853, the hours of labor were reduced to eleven in all the mills owned by the Boston capitalists, the change coming in Lowell and in Lawrence on the same day. By granting the eleven-hour day the corporations threw a sop to the radicals, while proving to respectable liberals that the control of the mills, as well as of the Commonwealth, was in wise and humane hands. The new constitution was defeated by a wide margin.

But that was as far as the corporations would go in the reform of hours for another twenty years. It was not until 1874 that Massachusetts passed a ten-hour law for women and minors, but by then the charming, intelligent New England girls had long since ceased coming to the mills.

* "Cotton Whigs" as distinguished from "Conscience Whigs," made every possible concession to the pro-slavery forces in the hopes of some day winning a favorable tariff, and in the fear of disturbing business relations between North and South. Abbott Lawrence headed this group; Nathan Appleton and the other textile magnates naturally shared his views.

Chapter XIII

THE END OF THE IDYL

WHILE the ten-hour struggle was at its height in Lowell, the textile magnates in Boston held themselves aloof from any direct participation or comment, depending rather on their trained seals in the Legislature and in the press to defend them. This Olympian indifference cannot be attributed to their shrinking investments in Lowell, for although the stock ownership of the mills had begun to be widely disseminated by 1845, Nathan Appleton and Abbott Lawrence still dictated overall policy. Extensive though their other financial interests were, moreover, their control of the textile companies provided a base and leverage for manifold related operations.

But, if they abstained from speaking in their own defense, they were no less aware than Miss Bagley of the usefulness of well-placed propaganda and publicity, in which they were assisted not only by eager newspaper editors but also by several complaisant clergymen. In 1845 two gentlemen of the cloth, one an Englishman and the other an American, obliged by publishing books on the charms of the Lowell scene. The Rev. Mr. Scoresby, a visitor from abroad, dwelt on the gentility and elegance of the operatives, while the Rev. Henry A. Miles, a Lowell resident, stressed the magnanimity of the corporations and the "moral police" system whereby the girls kept themselves free of the merest taint of vice. Both books were widely, and, needless to say, favorably reviewed, Horace Greeley waxing lyrical over Mr. Miles' glowing account:

Such is the condition of the Laboring Class in the principal Manufacturing town in America. . . . Let those who would overthrow this state of things go to work to build up something better. . . . Until they have some notion of this sort, ought they not to cease their incessant warfare on American Manufactures?

Obviously this admonition applied to the girls also. But the demand of the labor reform group for a reduction in hours happened to coincide with the biggest boom the textile industry had yet experienced, and some people were naive enough to ask why this prosperity could not be shared with the workers who contributed to it. A query of this sort could not be answered properly by a mere clergyman, or even by the sycophantic editor of the *Tribune*. To refute the base charge that the corporations were making too much money, therefore, the Boston magnates chose one of their own, Thomas G. Cary, son-in-law of the formidable Thomas Handasyd Perkins, and treasurer of the Hamilton Company at Lowell. In a pamphlet called *Profits on the Manufactures at Lowell*, published in 1845, Cary repudiated the idea that great fortunes were made in the city of looms and spindles. Not one of the rich men connected with the Lowell factories, he said, had made his fortune there.

They are merchants who have grown rich in foreign trade, or eminent lawyers or physicians, who have invested a part of their property there, and who have invested other portions of it in insurance stocks, real estate, etc., where in many cases it has yielded them a much larger income than any manufacturing stocks.

Thus to the charge that the operatives were working too long hours, the corporations replied that their contentment could be read in the girls' bright faces; to the charge that stockholders were growing fat on the low wages paid to their help, the reply was that they made their money elsewhere. But the feelings of

the Boston Associates were also hurt by attacks on the fundamental organization and structure of the textile industry in the
corporation towns, on the paternalism which they considered so
humane. It therefore devolved on still another corporation
apologist to redefine the whole arrangement, in an article called
"The Lowell System of Manufacturing," published in the *New
Bedford Mercury* late in 1847. Nothing could express more
clearly the attitude taken by the great textile magnates toward
their "charges" than the analysis of this obscure author:

> The manufacturing interest of New England is a new world. In
> Lowell especially . . . it is a perfect *imperium in imperio*. It has been
> said, that an absolute despotism, justly administered . . . would be a
> perfect government. But the policy of Lowell adds a trait . . . for,
> at the same time that it is an absolute despotism, it is a most perfect
> democracy. Any of its subjects can depart from it at pleasure without
> the least restraint.

With the failure of the ten-hour movement as led by the operatives in the middle forties, those girls who had an alternative
did in fact depart from the absolute despotism, the perfect
democracy that was Lowell. When the absolute despotism from
its Boston citadel vouchsafed the mercy of the eleven-hour day
to its subjects, few of the more militant operatives were left to
enjoy this gratifying indulgence. In 1845 ninety percent of the
mill girls in Lowell were of native American stock, farm girls
from the New England states, and of the remainder only seven
percent were Irish. By 1850 one half of the operatives were Irish,
recent arrivals in this country, while the Yankee girls who were
left seemed trapped, either because they could not afford to
return home, or because they did not possess the skills to take
advantage of other opportunities elsewhere.

Several factors had a share in this sudden displacement. A
slump in industry in 1848, partly caused by heedless overexpan-
sion without corresponding increase in purchasing power,
brought about widespread unemployment and a general reduc-

tion in wages that were reflected promptly in textiles. The depression was also felt severely by the farmers of New England, causing large numbers of them to pull up stakes and move to the richer agricultural lands in the West. This westward migration had been going on for over fifty years, but it was accelerated by poor crops and low prices in 1848. Moreover, the progress of the Industrial Revolution itself, exemplified by the expansion of cotton manufacture, tended to deprive the New England farmers of their self-sufficiency, which in earlier years had made it possible to weather depressions. Because of this shift in population the original sources of mill labor were drying up just as the rewards and working conditions were ceasing to be attractive.

At the same time richer opportunities elsewhere were drawing the more intelligent and enterprising girls out of the mills.* Their factory experience had given them a taste of independence, without any loss of respectability, which gave them the courage to venture into other fields just opening up for women. Some now went West to teach school; others by continuing their education for a period qualified themselves to teach in the East, where as a result of Horace Mann's tireless propaganda the pay for teachers was beginning to compare favorably with that earned by factory workers. Lucy Larcom did both. In 1846 she quit Lowell and went to Illinois with her sister Emmeline, who had just been married. After a year as a country schoolteacher, having decided that she herself needed more formal education, Lucy left her one-room prairie schoolhouse to enter the Monticello Female Seminary at Alton, Illinois, where she earned her way by teaching some of the simpler subjects. After her gradua-

---

* The discovery of gold in California in 1848 was *not* one of these opportunities. According to Carter Goodrich and Sol Davidson ("The Wage-Earner in the Western Movement," *Political Science Quarterly*, Vol. 51), many citizens of Lowell joined the gold rush, but only one employee of the mills, a man who as it happened was lynched at the mines. The money needed for such an expedition was beyond anything mill operatives could command, not to speak of the risks and dangers of getting there. For the same reason a group of young women from Lowell who traveled out to the state of Washington in 1864 could hardly have been operatives in the mills, since the factories had been shut since the beginning of the Civil War, and the cost of passage to the Northwest was over $300.

tion in 1852 she returned to Massachusetts to teach, first in Beverly, and then at the Wheaton Seminary at Norton. Lucy never married, unlike most of the young women who went West to teach. (Westerners were in the habit of complaining that instead of being content to teach other people's children, the schoolmarms very soon got to teaching their own.) But her verses soon began to attract favorable attention from men of letters, Whittier and Longfellow being among her admirers. After leaving her position at the Wheaton Seminary, she was for many years editor of *Our Young Folks,* a popular magazine for children published in Boston, and found time besides to issue one volume of poems after another.

Of those who returned to their native villages to teach, Sarah Shedd, of Washington, New Hampshire, was typical. She had begun teaching at the age of fifteen, but worked in the mills during the winter so that she could help her family, and take advantage of the educational opportunities at Lowell. As a teacher in later life, although a woman of great reserve, she was much loved, her most distinguished pupil being Carroll D. Wright, the first United States Commissioner of Labor. It was no accident that Wright was one of the first men in the country to compile labor statistics and make careful studies of factory problems. At her death Miss Shedd, mindful of her own early passion for reading, left $2,500 to her native town for the establishment of a free public library.

Naturally, more is known of the later career of the contributors to the *Offering* than of the other operatives who made Lowell famous, since they had formed friendships that were kept up over the years by correspondence. But with such great homogeneity of background and experience among the girls, it is likely that these cases were typical rather than exceptional. Besides teaching, they found or made openings for themselves in offices, in journalism, in missionary work, and in small business ventures. Sarah Bagley's position in the Lowell telegraph office has already been commented on, and, although it was an entirely new field, many of the other operatives were quick-witted enough to do the same type of work. After the *Offering* folded up, Harriott Curtis was employed for a year by the *Vox Populi*, a Lowell newspaper of somewhat liberal leanings, as head of the miscellaneous department, a situation she was obliged to renounce in order to act as sick-nurse to a succession of aged relatives. Margaret Foley returned to her art studies after a period at the Merrimack Corporation, and won some favorable notice as a cameo cutter in Boston. Among the distinguished people who sat to her for their portraits were Longfellow, Sumner, and Julia Ward Howe. The last years of her life were spent in Italy, whence she sent some examples of monumental sculpture to the Centennial Exposition at Philadelphia.

Meanwhile Lydia S. Hall, another contributor to the *Offering*, left Lowell in 1848 to become a missionary to the Choctaw Indians. Other interests, however, soon claimed her, for she was next heard from as the proprietor of an inn in Kansas, where her strict rules against drinking and swearing gave her almost a legendary renown. After the Civil War, although married by then to a Mr. Graffam, she took a job in the Treasury Department at Washington, where it is said she once served as acting United States Treasurer in the absence of her chief. Another one of the literary girls, Eliza Jane Cate, took up writing seriously after she left the mills, and published eight volumes, as well as articles for magazines like *Peterson's* and *Sartain's*, earning a reputation as the "Maria Edgeworth of New England."

Something is known also of two other Lowell girls who were not in the *Offering* group. Clementine Averill, author of the ringing answer to Senator Clemens' charge that Southern slaves were better off than Northern mill operatives,* founded a Co-operative Industrial Home in Florida after the Civil War, facing rough pioneer conditions there alone, and with great courage. Of Miss Mehitabel Eastman, who was co-publisher of the *Voice of Industry* for a while, it is related that after its demise she remained in Boston as an officer in one of the protective unions, or consumers' cooperatives.

* *Weekly Tribune*, March 6, 1850.

But while the later activities of some few of the better-known girls can be traced, most of them faded into obscurity with marriage. Indeed, the marriage prospects of Lowell operatives were somewhat above the average, their virtue and industry being so renowned that young men were said to make pilgrimages to the mills to pick themselves a spouse. But even after marriage several mill girls achieved a modest distinction. For example, Harriet Hanson Robinson, though the mother of two children, and overshadowed by her distinguished husband, gave much of her time to the anti-slavery movement, and later became widely known as a woman suffragist, a lecturer, and a clubwoman. Her memoirs of life in the Lowell mills, *Loom and Spindle*, along with Lucy Larcom's *New England Girlhood*, furnish us with the only first-hand accounts of that period, written from the point of view of the operative.

Of the lesser-known girls, Lura Currier, who married a Mr. Whitney of Haverhill, New Hampshire, also established a free public library in the town where she lived. Another went with her husband as a missionary to India; still another, married to a sea captain, sailed around the world with him, and there were rumors for a time that another Lowell operative had married General Herrera, the President of Mexico! Though this last was quickly corrected when it was revealed that the Lowell girl in question had married a bookkeeper named Hanschild, who had settled in Durango, Lucy Larcom gave the story another fling when she wrote:

> *There's a girl*
> *I used to know, who went to Mexico*
> *When cotton-mills were built there, and is now*
> *Wife of some ruling officer, and at home*
> *In halls of the Montezumas.*

It is important to remember that all the women spoken of here, except Miss Averill, had left the mills before 1850. After that date no other Lowell girl, or girl from any of the New

England mills, made a name for herself. There can be no doubt, therefore, that the exodus of the more intelligent and spirited operatives was due to the failure of the ten-hour movement, a portent of the utmost gravity, for if they could not win this concession, universally admitted to be desirable, it followed that any other attempt to obtain improvements in wages and working conditions would receive short shrift at the hands of their employers. This was no less true of those among them who were too timid to take an active part in the work of the Labor Reform Association. In its heyday this group had only 600 members, but many more girls came within the circle of its influence, for 4,500 signed the petition of 1846. Writing long after the event, with some confusion in her mind about the issues of the middle forties, and a genteel reluctance to be associated with labor agitators, Lucy Larcom expressed the attitude of large numbers of operatives who withdrew from the mills at this period. Alluding to the "tyranny" of the employers, she quotes an operative as saying:

> *If they grind*
> *And cheat as brethren should not, let us go*
> *Back to the music of the spinning-wheel,*
> *And clothe ourselves at hand-looms of our own*
> *As did our grandmothers. . . .*
>   *If indeed there is*
> *Injustice,—if the rule of selfishness*
> *Must be, invariably, mill-owners' law,*
> *As the dissatisfied say,—if evermore*
> *The laborer's hire tends downward, then we all*
> *Must elsewhere turn; for nobody should toil*
> *Just to add wealth to men already rich.*
> *Only a drudge will toil on, with no hope*
> *Widening from well-paid labor.**

---

* Lucy Larcom, *An Idyll of Work*, Boston, 1875. Forgetting that there were no strikes of any importance at the period she was referring to, Miss Larcom frowned on such measures as "unwomanly." It is interesting to note that John Greenleaf Whittier, whose close friend and collaborator she became, did not

It goes without saying that Lucy Larcom did not go back to the spinning wheel and loom to clothe herself.

The retreat of the Yankee girls from the mills grew to the proportions of a rout when new and drastic wage-cuts were announced for 1848. Even Harriet Farley, who in 1847 had launched the *New England Offering*, a magazine *for*, if admittedly not *by* the workers, now professed to be alarmed by the possible consequences of this economy drive.* In an article called "The Rights and Duties of Mill Girls," that appeared in the *New England Offering* of July, 1849, she assured the operatives that the depression would end shortly and wages would be restored:

> To say nothing of the patriotism, the humanity of Abbott Lawrence, the Lowells, and others of our most influential capitalists, their self-interest must lead them to the adoption of such measures as will induce the better portion of our New England girls, the vigorous, the moral and the intelligent, to resort to the mills as their place for gain.

But poor Miss Farley had less authority than ever to speak for the Boston magnates, who asked for no interpretation either of their humanity or self-interest by her, while her counsels of patience carried no weight at all with the operatives. The departure of the New England girls from the mills was manifested first in a sharp reduction in the length of time they spent at the factories. In 1845, the average sojourn of the operatives in the mill towns was four years; in 1848, the average time at the Merrimack Company was only nine months, and this in the most con-

---

share her abhorrence of strikes. On the contrary, Whittier took time off from his anti-slavery activities to aid strikers at the Salisbury Company in Amesbury in 1852, by drawing up the resolutions for a protest meeting and heading a committee that appealed for the ten-hour day.

* As usual Miss Farley was torn between her sympathy for the sufferings of the operatives and her reverence for the textile magnates. She and her family were still pensioners of old Amos Lawrence, indebted to him for small if irregular sums of money, just enough to keep her in line without compromising her "independence," as she thought. Around 1848 she gave up her literary career when she married an inventor named Donlevy and went to live in New York.

sistently prosperous of all the textile factories. In earlier years
the girls had returned to their rural homes to spread the word of
high wages, adequate living conditions, and a stimulating social
life among their neighbors, but after the middle forties they had
nothing to report but the grueling pace, the crowded quarters,
the steady decline in wages, and the thwarting of all their desires
for improvement.

All through the forties the employment agents, "slavers" or
"speculators," as they were called, had been obliged to go farther
and farther north to find mill hands, until finally they reached
the edge of English settlement in Canada. These girls of English
descent were with very few exceptions literate, or had at least
the rudiments of an education, which, as the factory managers
realized, made them very desirable as operatives, since they were
quick to learn and acquire a high degree of efficiency. The textile magnates would have been willing to do anything to maintain their labor force at that high standard except grant any of
their demands.

But by 1848 a solution of the problem presented itself naturally. Because of the potato famine of 1845 and 1846, Irish
immigration to the United States rose to 160,000 during the
forties, five-sixths of these arrivals settling in the cities of the
Eastern seaboard. Ever since the first building operations had
begun in Lowell, there had been a large Irish contingent in the
town, and it was a matter of course that these older residents
should invite their distressed relatives and friends to join them
there.

Thus, just as the New England girls began leaving the mills
in ever larger numbers, this unexpected labor supply flowed in to
take their places. The change was not made by design of the
textile magnates, as when in later years they moved their mills
to the South to be able to draw on a cheap, unorganized labor
supply. In unguarded moments the Boston nabobs even referred
to the Irish immigrants with contempt; for example, at the semi-
centennial of Lowell in 1873, John Amory Lowell, speaking
regretfully of the good old days, said: "At *that time*, we were

not overrun with Irish." The illiterate Irish girls, coming from
an ancient rural society, had some difficulty in adjusting themselves to American mechanical ways. It took longer to teach
them how to tend the looms and spindles, to make them understand what was required of them. In 1848 a reduction in wages
at the Boston Manufacturing Company at Waltham led to a
walkout of the New England operatives, their places being taken
immediately by a group of Irish girls. The output per worker,
which had been increasing steadily up to that time, thereupon
fell off so sharply that the company switched production to a
coarser type of material than it had manufactured in many years.

And yet the new type of operative had several advantages
over the old, from the point of view of the corporation magnates.
Despite the obsequiousness of the Harriet Farleys, the mill owners
had been alienated by the attack on their prerogatives by such
radicals as Sarah Bagley, a viper they had nourished in their
bosoms. The new Irish hands were docile, since they had no
tidy farm homes to return to, and accepted the low wages established during the depression of 1848 without protest. They
had known more dreadful misery in the "old country." Without
any experience of better working conditions, and without any
formidable body of public opinion behind them, they had no
standards the corporations were obliged to respect.

The advent of the Irish also hastened the decline of the boarding-house system, since most of the newcomers settled in the
mill towns with relatives and friends, increasing the congestion
and spreading the slum area. This also suited the book of the
mill owners, because it relieved them of the responsibility of
providing decent housing for their new employees. Even the
New England girls had begun to resent the obligation to live in
company boarding houses, some because they disliked the proximity to the noise and dirt of the mills, others because they felt
that the boarding-house keepers were used by the agents to spy
on all their comings and goings.

It was inevitable that some of the native operatives should feel
resentment against the incursion of this new type of mill hand.

In the early days there were so few Irish girls in the mills that they rose quickly to the standards of the New Englanders, with whom they lived side by side in the boarding houses on terms of equality and friendship. Harriet Hanson Robinson wrote, for example, that the children of the Irish immigrant laborers were "as good as anybody," being assimilated more easily, no doubt, because of American schooling. But the troubles of the mid-forties, coupled with the great waves of immigration, made even the more advanced New England girls a bit edgy. The *Voice of Industry* pointed out that, although the tariff shut out foreign goods that might compete with American manufacturers, there was no law to prevent foreign workers from coming to this country to compete with American labor.

Of course, this new idyl of subservient operatives was not destined to last forever. Even the poorest immigrant, after a few years in an American factory, acquired standards and was capable of comparing present with past conditions on the basis of his own experience. The fifties were to see strikes by the Irish workers in towns like Chicopee that were not half so ladylike as the earlier turnouts, for the new labor force had nothing to lose. But the textile mills were fortunate enough to find fresh sources of labor in new waves of immigration: Dutch, Greeks, and French Canadians down to our own times. By the time of the Civil War, the Yankee farm girls had ceased to be a factor in the situation; after the Civil War, they were a rarity.

To explain the deterioration of standards in Lowell and the other mill centers in New England, some commentators have persuaded themselves that a change in the personnel of management was to blame. According to this theory, a second generation of officers and stockholders, related to or descended from the original entrepreneurs, but with less understanding of labor's needs, coldbloodedly put pressure on wages and working conditions which their more humane predecessors shrank from. But the facts do not sustain this thesis. Except for Francis Cabot Lowell, the original investors in cotton manufacturing in northern New England were a long-lived set of men, who retained their autocratic control of the industry as long as they had breath in their bodies. Various functions were delegated by them to others from the beginning, but the final decisions on matters of policy in their farflung textile empire rested with them. Nathan Appleton and Abbott Lawrence were the acknowledged leaders of the Boston magnates with large holdings in textile mills, the court of last authority in the business and financial world, and both of these men were alive and active in the affairs of Lowell and the other textile cities throughout the period here dealt with.

This control they succeeded in maintaining whether their holdings were for the moment large or small, even after the stock began to be widely dispersed. Abbott Lawrence in 1843 might have reduced his stock interest in the various mills to a mere $110,000, but that did not prevent him from blocking the revolt of a dissatisfied stockholders' group, headed by Henry Lee and others. Fifteen years later, James C. Ayer, an outsider who had bought his way into various Lowell corporations, led another rebellion of stockholders when the Middlesex Mills, the Bay State Mills of Lawrence, and the great commission house of James K. Mills failed during the crash of 1857. Curiously enough, Ayer's charges against the managing directors of the textile companies were the same as Lee's: nepotism, high salaries, extravagant purchases of raw material to help close connections, etc. When Ayer went before a Massachusetts legislative committee to plead for laws protecting the stockholders against the directors, who seemed to have lifetime tenure, Nathan Appleton wailed that the Legislature was "discriminating against corporations." Seconded by John Amory Lowell, who had somehow managed to hold on to his many directorships over the years, Appleton tried to obstruct reforms by advising the directors of the Merrimack Corporation to "continue to exercise their discretion in the management of their affairs, without reference to the cavils of others."

Some of Ayer's most serious charges were made against Samuel Lawrence, another member of the old guard, who, he said, was responsible for the failure of the Middlesex Mills in Lowell and the Bay State Mills in Lawrence. Ayer told the legislative committee that at one time the Middlesex books had been falsified by $103,000, and that $89,000 had been spent by the corporation presumably to bribe members of Congress. Sam Lawrence had also forfeited bonds of $25,000 each to the Middlesex Mills and Lawrence Stone & Company, but had never been obliged to make good on his bonds because his friends took over the companies and never pressed him for payment.

The truth of the matter is that the older investors had milked the corporations, in a gentlemanly manner, of course, by taking almost all the operating profits in the form of dividends, and by declaring huge stock dividends when they were about to embark on new ventures, regardless of the long-run requirements of the business. Another incidental method of milking the corporations was by placing younger relatives in high-salaried jobs in the mills. Such appointments were supposedly given on the basis of "character," but since that word in the mind of the Boston magnates was synonymous with membership in the inner circle, the appointees sometimes made costly mistakes through ignorance or incompetence. The son of Thomas G. Cary, treasurer of the Hamilton Company, for example, caused that company a loss of $50,000 through having bad cotton palmed off on him. Examples like this caused the irate Ayer to refer to "fatuous imbecility glutting itself with fabulous remuneration." The Boston magnates had so many brothers, sons, sons-in-law, nephews, and cousins who had to be "placed" in a situation befitting their rank in society, with emoluments corresponding, that during the fifties they became as heavy a charge on the textile industry, as the courtiers of Louis XVI on the economy of France. But this new strain on the profits of the textile mills merely confirmed the earlier trends toward speed-up and piece-rate reductions for the operatives. Half of the New England girls already had left the mills between 1848 and 1850, it must be remembered, as a result of policies dictated by Nathan Appleton, Abbott Lawrence, and their associates, not by their scions.

The labor agitation of the forties died down in the next decade not only because the movement lost its leadership, but even more because the slavery issue was beginning to assume greater importance in the minds of men and women all over the country. Workers in the North, including the New England operatives in the textile mills, grew increasingly sensitive to the injustice of the South's peculiar institution, even to the point of postponing their own struggles for improved conditions in order to limit the greater evil. The Lowell girls signed anti-slavery petitions, joined anti-slavery societies and contributed money to the anti-slavery cause, in many cases more willingly than they had helped the ten-hour movement.

But in this humanitarian enterprise they met as much resistance from the Boston magnates as in their struggle for labor reform. Aside from their powerful economic and financial ties with the Southern slave-owners, aside from their desire to placate the South on all other grounds in order to obtain the tariff, the New England capitalists were extremely susceptible to the reasoning of John Calhoun, who pointed out in his *Disquisition on Government*

that the assaults which are now directed against the institutions of the Southern States may be very easily directed against those which uphold their own [the Northern capitalists'] property and security. A very slight modification of the arguments used against the institutions [of the South] would make them equally effectual against the institutions of the North, including banking, in which so vast an amount of its property and capital is invested.

Calhoun therefore proposed an alliance between "gentlemen" of both the North and the South, whereby the Southerners would help fight labor agitation in return for Northern help in fighting anti-slavery agitation.

To men like Nathan Appleton such arguments were irresistible. Writing to the Reverend I. N. Danforth on August 9, 1847, he expressed his views of the slavery issue in the most detached terms:

African slavery . . . is a curse which has been entailed upon us. I consider it a tremendous social evil. But we of New England are free from it and ought to be able to look at it calmly and coolly. . . . As to the existence of slavery in the slave states, I see no reason why we of the free states should make ourselves very unhappy about it. Why not leave it to the parties immediately concerned? It is a matter sufficiently troublesome without our interference. . . . As a political question the abolition of slavery in the slave states has difficulties apparently insurmountable at present. As a question of property it involves an amount of about a thousand millions of dollars. Was such an amount of property ever voluntarily relinquished or annihilated? Would it be possible to make the owners indemnification on any principle of law or equity?

Appleton was right in that no such amount of property was ever voluntarily relinquished. Up to the moment when the great fratricidal war began he continued to assure his Southern friends that sober men in free states were no less determined to perpetuate slavery forever than the slave-owners themselves. In line with this attitude, Appleton, Abbott Lawrence, and the other financiers and manufacturers of Boston approved the entrance of Texas into the Union as a slave state, condoned the war with Mexico, sustained the Compromise of 1850, with its rigorous Fugitive Slave Bill, and swallowed the Kansas-Nebraska Act. They egged on the mob that nearly lynched Garrison; they deplored the freeing of the slaves in the British West Indies. They ostracized Charles Sumner after he declared in a speech at Worcester in 1848 that the nomination of Taylor had been brought about by "an unholy union or rather conspiracy between the cotton planters and flesh-mongers of Louisiana and Mississippi, and the cotton spinners and traffickers of New England— the lords of the lash and the lords of the loom." By order of Nathan Appleton all but a few houses around Boston were closed to Sumner, Richard Henry Dana, Jr., and Charles Francis Adams, the leaders of the Free-Soil Party in Massachusetts. On the other hand, the youths of Southern families studying at Harvard were made most welcome in the homes of the magnates, Southerners

in general, according to Henry Adams, being courted more assiduously than any other visitors to the Hub except titled foreigners. Drawing rooms barred to Summer always stood open to
Southern fire-eaters, men who were to head the Confederacy a
few years afterward. In fact, William Appleton played host to
Robert Toombs of Georgia shortly before that flower of Southern chivalry saw Sumner trapped and beaten almost to death by
Preston Brooks of South Carolina, Toombs standing by with a
revolver to see that no one came to Sumner's aid. This incident
shows how closely related were the sentiments of the Northern
capitalists and the Southern slave-owners, for had not Nathan
Appleton written to Sumner, before their rupture: "I believe in
the law of *force* . . . and that human nature . . . can be governed by no other. I should be very unwilling to rely on simple
abstract justice—without force to back it."

As the storm gathered, several of the younger textile magnates
began to waver in their allegiance to the status quo, the god of
their fathers. Amos Abbott Lawrence, the son of old Amos and
the nephew of Abbott, was stirred enough by the attack on Sumner to offer the Senator his home in which to recuperate. But
poor Amos Abbott could never make up his mind which side he
favored. He was impulsive enough to give John Brown of Osawatomie money to buy rifles for the fight in Kansas, and contributed
$310 to the fund to purchase the farm in New York State for
Brown's wife and family; but the clamor after the Harper's Ferry
raid frightened him nearly out of his wits. In a crawling letter to
Jefferson Davis, then sitting in the Senate, he denounced Brown's
criminal fanaticism, and called on Davis' old friendship for his
father to save him from being implicated in Brown's foray.

There must have been many other moments of embarrassment
during these years for the hard-headed older New England mag-
nificoes, the most awkward perhaps when the citizens of Charleston published a card of thanks in a Boston newspaper, stating that
they were beholden to the "gentlemen of Boston" for returning
a fugitive slave. The episode was given an even more bitter flavor
when it was learned that the slave had been publicly whipped in

the streets of Charleston on being turned over to his master. But Nathan Appleton was staunch to the end. As late as 1860 he published a letter to W. C. Rives of Virginia, blaming all the "unrest" on William Lloyd Garrison and the Abolitionists, repudiating the actions of John Brown in the strongest terms, and ending with the reflection that, after all, the North and South had nothing to quarrel about. After this false prophecy it was fitting that he should die in 1861, just as the great conflagration he had done so little to prevent burst forth.

The Lawrence brothers, though younger than Nathan Appleton, passed away before he did, Amos succumbing after twenty years of invalidism in 1852, and Abbott surviving only until 1855. During his lifetime Amos had disbursed $639,000 in charities, but still left a fortune estimated at over a million at his death. Abbott, a more active operator, accumulated over two millions, of which he left $50,000 (in addition to his original bequest) for the Lawrence Scientific School at Harvard, and $50,000 for model lodging houses in Boston. The most enduring monument to Abbott Lawrence was not to be found in his benefactions, however, but in the industrial city of Lawrence, which was developed principally through his initiative.

Lawrence the city, which it was hoped would duplicate the history of Lowell, was founded under similar circumstances, following the discovery of an excellent water-power site eleven miles farther down the Merrimack River. The first step was the quiet purchase of all the surrounding farm land by intermediaries. When these negotiations were finally completed after two years, the Essex Company, a million-dollar corporation, was chartered in 1845 to develop the area for the manufacture of textiles. As mentioned earlier, the largest investors in the new project were also important figures in the earlier venture, men thoroughly acquainted with the risks and the rewards in the business of making cloth. How could they go wrong?

And yet an observer would have perceived an essential difference between the new development and its prototype. The introduction of manufactures in Lowell had been in a sense experimental: a test of how a factory community would be received by a dominantly agricultural society. Since manufacturing was looked down upon by some people, and was feared and hated by others, it behooved the entrepreneurs at Lowell to be on their best behavior. It was for this reason, and not because of their natural benevolence, that Lowell was designed as a place where factory workers could live according to fairly high standards of human dignity.

But, by the middle forties, when the plans for the city of Lawrence were conceived, such considerations had long ceased to have any weight. The Lowell experiment had proved successful from the financial point of view, and as the profits piled up the magnates felt no need to justify their venture on civic grounds. Indeed, the pursuit of profits now extenuated every step in the degradation of the operatives and in the disfigurement of the town. Moreover, between 1823 and 1845 the Boston Associates had reaped as much if not more gain from financial manipulation and the various side-lines of the industry as from the mere production of cloth, which at the end of the period had become a kind of abstraction—as the commodities turned out by a new industrial plant might be regarded in Wall Street today.

The men who dreamed up the city of Lawrence therefore started out without any sense of responsibility to society in general or to the men and women who were to live and work there. And since they "knew how to make money," as Abbott Lawrence used to say, and guided themselves by the old formula, they were nonplussed when things went wrong from the very beginning. Part of the trouble must have been due to the man appointed to direct all the operations. Lawrence's vast financial and political interests prevented him from taking personal charge, even if he had been equipped to do so. Looking about for someone of the required "character" and social position to act as his deputy, he picked on Charles S. Storrow, and offered him the post of treasurer and general agent of the Essex Company. He also invited Storrow to subscribe to stock in the corporation, assuring him that he need put up only half of the money, as the company would carry the rest on an interest account. Storrow, gratified by this mark of confidence, but a modest man withal, confessed that he knew nothing about the business, to which Lawrence replied that such considerations were beside the point; he could hire assistants who did.

Whatever Storrow's social qualifications, he was no Kirk Boott. He could neither superintend the work properly himself nor choose the best men to do the work for him. The construction work on the canals and mills was on such a large scale that from the first there was a shortage of housing for the laborers. Carpenters, bricklayers, and ditchdiggers walked three miles morning and night, to and from the job, for months on end, since no dwellings could be found nearer, and it was said that no one complained of his lodging if only he had a roof over his head. Real estate values within the town as it grew rose to fantastic heights and collapsed over and over again. The streets were made of loose material, poorly graded, uncomfortable for vehicles in good weather and fairly dangerous in bad. More like a raw boom town of the West than a respectable New England community, Lawrence in its early years was noted for what Harriet Farley described as "fomenters and *nuclei* of crime and iniquity": its hoodlums, its street fights, its gambling dens and saloons, its filth and squalor.

Meanwhile, special corporation charters had been granted in 1846 to the Atlantic Cotton Mills and the Bay State Woollen Mills, and construction went forward briskly. But there was no attempt to plan the town on the basis of any relationship between the various elements of the population, as Kirk Boott had done at Lowell, the designers of Lawrence concentrating all their interest instead on the mills, which were to be as up-to-date as any in the country. To be modern in this sense the Lawrence mills had to be of vast size, and profiting by the experience at Lowell, where the open spaces between the mills at that very time were being filled up, the architects of the Atlantic and Bay State Mills drew plans to make the two factories extend in a solid wall against the river for a distance of half a mile. In the shadow of this long ridge, blocking the light and air, "model" boarding houses were erected for the benefit of New England operatives, if any could be induced to come to work in Lawrence under the same conditions that had led them to leave Lowell.

With huge investments at stake, the work progressed feverishly. Endless wagon trains carting building materials lumbered into town, gangs of bricklayers and carpenters swarmed about the rising factories and boarding houses, ditchdigging crews toiled at the canals and dams to supply the power. There was, indeed, too much haste in the whole effort, for on October 12, 1847, a coffer dam that had been built to shut off water from the unfinished part of the permanent dam for the Bay State Mills gave way, and fifteen men were killed. It was a sad omen.

This unfortunate incident delayed the finishing of the dam for almost a year, while stockholders fretted, especially as 1848 was a bad year in textiles. Happily there was enough recovery in 1849 for several of the older corporations to come through with thumping big dividend payments, and spirits revived. Meanwhile Abbott Lawrence's political activities had borne fruit in the shape of an appointment as Minister to England, when his personal candidate, Zachary Taylor, was elected to the presidency.

On his return from England in 1852 Lawrence found affairs in the new settlement in a deplorable state, the stocks of the Essex selling far below their subscription cost, and various parts of the plant as originally conceived still incomplete. William H. Prescott, Lawrence's son-in-law, tells what followed:

Great advances were required to be made for the completion of works in which Mr. Lawrence was largely interested. It was difficult to obtain such advances in the depressed state of the stocks. With his usual spirit, Mr. Lawrence came forward to the rescue, and not only bore his own share of the subscription [assessment on the original stockholders] but took stock to the amount of $350,000 more; though, in doing so, he sacrificed half of that amount, the stock having fallen 50 per cent in the market.

Work on the canals and mills was therefore resumed, but greater haste and greater economy in construction than provisions for safety required would be demanded, in view of the mounting costs that were to be faced. In 1853 building was begun on the great Pacific Woollen Mills, capitalized at two million dollars, and in the same year ground was broken for a new cotton factory chartered as the Pemberton Mills. The Pemberton Mills were described by contemporaries as the finest example of a factory building in the town.

But, in spite of the injection of fresh capital, the Lawrence venture did not prosper, nor was Abbott Lawrence able to straighten out the disorder before his death in 1855. The Pacific Mills went through a long period of "difficulties and embarrassments," and during the panic of 1857 the Pemberton and the Bay State Mills went under. In a general reorganization after the panic, the Pemberton Mills, which had cost $800,000 to build, were put up at auction and sold in 1859 for $325,000, while the Bay State company was revamped as the Washington Mills. The Pacific Mills were relieved of their difficulties only by the advent of the Civil War.

Before the guns at Fort Sumter began to speak, however, a fearful, a monstrous calamity befell the ill-starred city of Lawrence. Under new ownership, the Pemberton Mills resumed production after two years of idleness, and operatives who had long been unemployed trooped happily back to work. On January 10, 1860, at 4:45 in the afternoon, there were over 900 persons in the factory, most of them women, when with a noise like that of a heavy tree falling in the midst of a thick forest, the huge building collapsed. Within half a minute it was completely demolished. Startled by the strange uproar, and even more by the sudden silence that followed immediately after, men and women rushed to the spot from all over the town, and without losing a moment began to extricate the victims and search for relatives and friends. The rescue work was hampered at first by a dense cloud of dust that rose like smoke from the wreckage. And then at eleven o'clock that night, before all who were caught beneath the timbers and masonry could escape, fire broke out. The rescue crews redoubled their efforts and fought their way blindly, with bursting hearts, toward where they could hear cries for help, until they were at last driven back by the flames. At least fourteen were still alive in the ruins when the rescuers gave up. The final check list showed 88 killed, 116 severely injured, and 159 slightly injured. But many went mad, and all lost their jobs.

Naturally, there was an inquest. Enough evidence was produced to prove that the disaster had been caused by the use of cast-iron pillars too weak to bear the weight of the floors, the roof, the machinery, and the shafting. It was revealed, too, that when these pillars had been submitted for inspection to the engineer in charge of constructing the mill, one of them had broken before his eyes. To replace them would have been costly, and would have caused further delays in completing the building. In this the jury found no evidence of criminal intent, but, to satisfy public indignation voted to censure Captain Charles H. Bigelow, the chief engineer.

The inquest went no further in attempting to assess the blame. Abbott Lawrence and many of the other original directors were dead and buried by then. And what would it have availed the dead or mangled victims or their wretched families to lay the responsibility at the door of those eminent personages, who had certainly never wished them any harm? Was it the fault of the Lawrences and the Appletons and their associates that the new philosophy of business enterprise set the safety, the health, and the welfare of human beings at nought in the scale against the right of property and the rewards that must flow from them? The chapter that had opened with so much hope had closed with a cruel and stupid tragedy. Long years of unremitting labor struggle were to pass before mill workers won back the essential social services that had been theirs as a right when the experiment was first launched. And perhaps even today they lack certain less palpable satisfactions, a personal dignity, a joy and pride in their work that Lowell offered to the artless New England farm girls in its idyllic days.

Bibliographical Note

THERE is a fairly large literature on the city of Lowell, but a smaller body of work to draw upon for the lives of the mill girls and the textile magnates. In view of these circumstances it was necessary to fall back on newspapers of the time and on the unpublished correspondence of contemporaries to fill out the picture. *The Lowell Offering*, Vols. 1–5 (1840–45) and the *New England Offering* (1848–49), which were written and published by factory operatives, furnished information not otherwise available. The private papers of the Boston worthies on deposit at the Massachusetts Historical Society provided source material for the study of the textile magnates.

Among the secondary source books, the most useful have been the following, listed in order of publication: Edith Abbott's *Women in Industry* (New York, 1913), the earliest work to give serious attention to the mill girls' background and aspirations; Norman Ware's *The Industrial Worker, 1840–1860* (Boston, 1924), an elaborately documented exposition of their struggle to protect their standards; Caroline F. Ware's *Early New England Cotton Manufacture* (Boston, 1931), the most authoritative study that has appeared thus far, concerned principally with the development of the industry, but with rich material on working and living conditions in Lowell; Vera Shlakman's *Chicopee, the Economic History of a Factory Town* (Smith College Studies in History, Vol. XX, October 1934–July 1935), a brilliant account of the development of a town similar to Lowell; and John Coolidge's *Mill and Mansion* (New York, 1942), an illuminating treatise on Lowell's growth and decline as seen through its architecture at various periods.

Bibliography

UNPUBLISHED MATERIAL

Nathan Appleton Papers, Massachusetts Historical Society, Boston
Bagnall Papers, Manuscript in the Baker Library, Harvard School of
   Business Administration
Amos Lawrence Papers, Massachusetts Historical Society
A. A. Lawrence Papers, Massachusetts Historical Society

NEWSPAPERS

Lowell Advertiser, 1842–1845
Lowell Courier, 1836–1845
Lowell Journal, 1845
Lowell Mercury, 1830–1833
Middlesex Standard, Lowell, 1844
Vox Populi, Lowell, 1845–1852
Voice of Industry, Lowell and Boston, 1845–1848
New York Tribune, 1844–1845
The Man, New York, 1834

BOOKS AND PAMPHLETS, MAGAZINE ARTICLES

Abbott, Edith, *Women in Industry*, New York, 1910
Adams, Charles Francis, *Richard Henry Dana, Jr.*, Boston and New
   York, 1891
Adams, Henry, *The Education of Henry Adams*, Boston and New
   York, 1918
Addison, Daniel Dulany, *Lucy Larcom, Life, Letters and Diary*,
   Boston, 1895
American State Papers, Vol. VI, Finance; 12th Congress, 2nd Session

Amory, Cleveland, *The Proper Bostonians*, New York, 1947

Andrews, John B., and Bliss, W. D. P., *Report on Condition of Woman and Child Wage-Earners in the U.S.*, Vol. X. *History of Women in Trade Unions*. 61st Congress, 2nd Session. Senate Document #645

Appleton, Nathan, *Correspondence between Nathan Appleton and John A. Lowell in relation to the Early History of Lowell.* Boston, 1848

———, *An Examination of the Banking System of Massachusetts,* Boston, 1831

———, *Introduction of the Power Loom and Origin of Lowell,* Lowell, 1858

———, *Labor, its relations in Europe and the United States Compared*, Boston, 1844

———, *Letter to Rives on Slavery and the Union*, Boston, 1860

———, *Memoir of Abbott Lawrence*, Massachusetts Historical Society Collections, Series 4, No. 4

———, *Remarks on Currency and Banking*, Boston, 1841

———, *The Doctrines of Original Sin and the Trinity*, Boston, 1859

———, *What is a Revenue Standard? and a Review of Walker's Report on the Tariff*, Boston, 1846

Appleton, William, ed., *Massachusetts Railroads, 1842–1855*, Boston, 1856

Ayer, James Cook, *Some of the Usages and Abuses in the Management of Our Manufacturing Corporations*, Lowell, 1863

Baird, Robert H., *The American Cotton Spinner*, Philadelphia, 1887

Batchelder, Samuel, *Introduction and Early Progress of the Cotton Manufacture in the United States*, Boston, 1863

Beecher, Catherine E., *The Evils Suffered by American Women and Children*, New York, 1846

Bishop, J. L., *A History of American Manufactures*, Philadelphia, 1864. 2 vols.

Bradford, Samuel D., *Letters of S. D. Bradford to Abbott Lawrence, in reply to those addressed by Mr. Lawrence to William C. Rives.* (Published in the *Boston Post*, February 17, 18 and 19, 1846.) Boston, 1846

Brooks, Van Wyck, *The Flowering of New England*, New York, 1936

Brownson, Orestes, "The Laboring Classes," *Boston Quarterly Review*, July, 1840

Burgy, J. H., *The New England Cotton Textile Industry*, Baltimore, 1932

Butler, Benjamin F., *Butler's Book*, Boston, 1892

Calhoun, John C., *Correspondence*. In the Annual Report of the American Historical Association, 1899. Vol. II

Cary, Thomas Greaves, *Profits on Manufactures at Lowell*, Boston, 1845

Chasles, Philarète, *Anglo-American Literature and Manners*, New York, 1852

Chevalier, Michel, *Society, Manners and Politics in the United States*, Boston, 1839

Clark, Victor S., *History of Manufactures in the United States*, New York, 1929. 3 volumes.

Coburn, Frederick W., "Art and Literature in Lowell," *Americana*, October, 1919

——, *History of Lowell and its People*, New York, 1920

Cochran, Thomas, and Miller, William, *The Age of Enterprise*, New York, 1942

Cole, Arthur C., *The Irrepressible Conflict, 1850–1865*, New York, 1934

Cole, Arthur H., *The American Wool Manufacture*, Cambridge, 1926

Cole, Arthur H., and Smith, Walter B., *Fluctuations in American Business*, Cambridge, 1935

Cole, G. D. H., *Life of Robert Owen*, London, 1930

Combe, George, *Notes on the United States of America*, Philadelphia, 1841

Commager, Henry Steele, *Theodore Parker*, Boston, 1936

Commons, John R. and associates, editors, *A Documentary History of American Industrial Society*, Cleveland, 1910. 10 volumes.

Condition of Labor, The. Boston, 1847

Coolidge, T. Jefferson, *Autobiography*. Boston, 1923

Copeland, Melvin T., *The Cotton Manufacturing Industry of the United States*, Cambridge, 1912

Cowley, Charles, *Handbook of Business in Lowell*, Lowell, 1856

——, *Illustrated History of Lowell*, Boston, 1868

——, *Reminiscences of James C. Ayer*, Lowell, 1879

Crawford, M. D. C., *The Heritage of Cotton*, New York, 1924

Crockett, Davy, *An Account of Col. Crockett's Tour to the North and Down East*, Philadelphia, 1835

Cummings, Ariel Ivers, *The Factory Girl, or Gardez la Coeur*, Lowell, 1847

Currier, T. F., "Whittier and the Amesbury-Salisbury Strike," *New England Quarterly*, Volume 8, March, 1935

Curti, Merle, *The Social Ideas of American Educators*, New York, 1935

Darling, Arthur B., *Political Changes in Massachusetts, 1824–1848*, New Haven, 1925

Davis, John P., *Corporations, a Study of the Origin and Development of Great Business Corporations*, New York, 1905

Davis, William T., *Professional and Industrial History of Suffolk County, Mass.*, Boston, 1894

De Tocqueville, Alexis, *Democracy in America*, New York, 1899. 2 volumes.

Drake, Samuel A., *History of Middlesex County, Mass.*, Boston, 1880

Edson, Theodore, *Address delivered at the opening of the Colburn Grammar School*, December 13, 1848. Lowell, 1849

Emerson, Ralph Waldo, *Nature: Addresses and Lectures*. Boston, 1903

Engle, Flora A. P., "The Story of the Mercer Expeditions," *Washington Historical Quarterly*, October, 1915

Fish, Carl Russell, *The Rise of the Common Man*, New York, 1939

Forbes, A., and J. W. Greene, *The Rich Men of Massachusetts*, Boston, 1851

Fuess, Claude, *Daniel Webster*, Boston, 1930. 2 volumes.

Goodrich, Carter, and Sol Davidson, "The Wage-Earner in the Western Movement," *Political Science Quarterly*, Volume 51

Green, Constance M., *Holyoke, Massachusetts*, New Haven, 1939

Hall, Basil, *Travels in North America in the Years 1827 and 1828*, Philadelphia, 1829

Handlin, Oscar, *Boston's Immigrants, 1790–1865*, Cambridge, 1941

Handlin, Oscar and Mary F., *Commonwealth: Massachusetts, 1774–1861*, New York, 1948

Hawthorne, Nathaniel, *Mosses from an Old Manse*, New York, 1892

Hayes, J. F. C., *History of the City of Lawrence*, Lawrence, 1868

Hayes, John R., *American Textile Machinery*, Cambridge, 1879

Henry, Alice, *The Trade Union Woman*, New York, 1915

Hill, Hamilton A., *Memoir of Abbott Lawrence*, Boston, 1884

Historical Sketch of the First Baptist Church, Lowell [1926]

Hofstadter, Richard, *The American Political Tradition*, New York, 1948

Homans, George C., "The Puritans and the Clothing Industry in England," *New England Quarterly*, Volume 13

Howe, Julia Ward, *Reminiscences*, Boston, 1899

Howe, Mark A. DeWolfe, *Boston, the Place and the People*, New York, 1903

Jackson, Patrick Tracy, *Report on the Production and Manufacture of Cotton;* Friends of Domestic Industry, Boston, 1832

Johnston, James F. W., *Notes on North America*, Boston, 1851. 2 volumes.

Keir, Malcolm, *Manufacturing Industries in America*, New York, 1920

Kenngott, George F., *The Record of a City: a Social Survey of Lowell, Mass.* New York, 1912

Larcom, Lucy, *Poems*, Boston, 1881

————, *An Idyll of Work*, Boston, 1875

————, *A New England Girlhood*, Boston, 1890

Lawrence, Abbott, *Letters to William C. Rives of Virginia* [on the tariff], Boston, 1846

————, *Letter of the Hon. Abbott Lawrence, to a committee of the citizens of Boston, on the Subject of the Currency, etc.*, Boston, 1837

————, *Remarks of Mr. Lawrence of Boston, on the duty of Congress to continue . . . the protection of American labor;* Boston, 1842

Lawrence, William, *Life of Amos A. Lawrence*, Boston, 1888

Lawrence, William R., *Extracts from the Diary and Correspondence of Amos Lawrence*, Boston, 1859

Livermore, Shaw, "Unlimited Liability in Early Corporations," *Journal of Political Economy*, Vol. 43, 1935

Lothrop, Samuel K., *Memoir of Samuel Appleton*, in Massachusetts Historical Society Collections, Vol. 3, 4th Series

————, *Memoir of William Lawrence*, privately printed, Boston, 1856

Lowell, Massachusetts: *Handbook of Lowell*, 1848

——, *Handbook for the Visitor to Lowell*, 1851, 2nd edition

——, *Contributions of the Old Residents Historical Association*, 1879–1904. Lowell, 6 volumes

——, *Exercises at the 75th Anniversary of the Incorporation of the Town*, Lowell, 1901

——, *Proceedings in the City of Lowell. At the semi-centennial celebration of the incorporation of the town of Lowell, March 1, 1876*. Lowell, 1876

Luther, Seth, *An Address to the Workingmen of New England*, Boston, 1832

Manchester, N. H., *Semi-Centennial of Manchester, New Hampshire*, Manchester, 1897

Martin, J. G., *Seventy-three Years' History of the Boston Stock Market*, Boston, 1871

Martineau, Harriet, *Society in America*, New York, 1837

Massachusetts: Bureau of Statistics of Labor, *11th Annual Report*, January 1880. Public Document No. 15

——, *16th Annual Report*, 1885

——, *House Documents*, No. 50, 1845; No. 153, 1850

McGrane, Reginald C., *The Panic of 1837*, Chicago, 1924

McMaster, John Bach, *History of the United States*, New York, 1931–38, Vol. 6

Meserve, H. G., *Lowell, An Industrial Dream Come True*, Boston, 1923

Miles, Henry A., *Lowell as It Was and as It Is*, Lowell, 1845

Mims, Helen Sullivan, "Early American Democratic Theory and Orestes Brownson," *Science and Society*, Vol. III, No. 2

Montgomery, James, *A Practical Detail of the Cotton Manufacture of the United States*, Glasgow, 1840

Morison, Samuel Eliot, *The Life and Letters of Harrison Gray Otis*, Boston, 1913, 2 vols.

——, *The Maritime History of Massachusetts, 1783–1860*, Boston, 1921

Morpeth, Lord, *Extracts from the Diary of his journey to the United States in 1841–42*, Manuscript in the Harvard College Library

Murray, Charles A., *Travels in North America in 1834, 1835, 1836*, London, 1841

Nelson, C. A., *Waltham Past and Present; and its Industries*, Cambridge, Mass., 1879

Nevins, Allan, *John D. Rockefeller*, New York, 1940

Nute, Grace Lie, *American Foreign Commerce*, Ph. D. thesis in Radcliffe College Library

O'Dwyer, George, *The Irish Catholic Genesis of Lowell*, Lowell, 1920

Palfrey, John G., *Papers on the Slave Power*, Boston [1846]

Parker, Theodore, *Works*, Centenary Edition, Boston, 1910, Volume 10

Parrington, Vernon L., *Main Currents in American Thought*, New York, 1927–1930, Volume 2

Persons, Charles E., *Early History of Factory Legislation in Massachusetts*. In *Labor Laws and Their Enforcement*, edited by Susan M. Kingsbury, New York, 1911

Pierce, Edward L., *Memoir and Letters of Charles Sumner*, Boston, 1894. Volume 3

Porter, Kenneth Wiggin, ed., *The Jacksons and the Lees*, Cambridge, Mass., 1937

Prescott, William H., *Memoir of the Honorable Abbott Lawrence, prepared for the National Portrait Gallery*. Printed for private distribution [Boston] 1856

Robinson, Harriet H., *Early Factory Labor in New England*, Boston, 1889

———, *Loom and Spindle*, New York, 1898

Sanborn, F. B., *Recollections of Seventy Years*, Boston, 1909

Schlesinger, Arthur M., Jr., *The Age of Jackson*, Boston, 1946

Scoresby, W., *American Factories and Their Female Operatives*, London, 1845

Sheppard, John H., *Sketch of the Honorable Nathan Appleton*, New England Historical and Genealogical Register, Vol. 16, 1862

Smith, Albert, *History of the Town of Peterborough*, New Hampshire, Boston, 1876

Smith, Thomas R., *The Cotton Textile Industry of Fall River, Massachusetts*, New York, 1944

Stanwood, Edward, *American Tariff Controversies*, Boston, 1903

Stearns, Bertha Monica, "New England Magazines for Ladies, 1830–60," *New England Quarterly*, October, 1930

———, "Factory Magazines in New England," *Journal of Economic and Business History*, Volume II

Taft, Lorado, *History of American Sculpture*, New York, 1924

Taussig, Frank W., *Tariff History of the United States*, New York, 1892

Trollope, Anthony, *North America*, New York, 1862

Usher, James M., *Paris Universal Exposition 1867*, Boston, 1868

Van Tyne, C. H., ed., *The Letters of Daniel Webster*, New York, 1902

Villard, Oswald G., *John Brown*, Boston, 1910

Walton, Perry, *The Story of Textiles*, New York, 1937

Webster, Fletcher, ed., *The Private Correspondence of Daniel Webster*, Boston, 1857

Whittier, John G., *The City of a Day*. In the prose works of J. G. Whittier, Boston, 1892. 3 volumes

Winsor, Justin, *The Memorial History of Boston*, Boston, 1881–83

Winthrop, Robert C., *Memoir of the Hon. Nathan Appleton*, Boston, 1861

Zahler, Helene S., *Eastern Workingmen and National Land Policy*, New York, 1941

Index